Norman H. Clark

MILL TOWN

A Social History of Everett, Washington,
from Its Earliest Beginnings on the Shores
of Puget Sound to the Tragic and Infamous
Event Known as the Everett Massacre

Seattle and London

UNIVERSITY OF WASHINGTON PRESS

Copyright © 1970 by the University of Washington Press
Second printing, 1971
Third printing, 1972
Washington Paperback edition, 1972
Second printing, 1975
Third printing, 1978
Fourth printing, 1982
Library of Congress Catalog Card Number 75-117726
ISBN 0-295-95079-X (cloth)
ISBN 0-295-95241-5 (paper)
Printed in the United States of America

For ROBERT E. BURKE

Contents

vi   CONTENTS ✿

Illustrations

vii

Mill Town

I

Prologue: A Banquet Hall Deserted

‖‖

FROM the high snowfields of the Cascade Mountains, the Skykomish River falls away to the west, gathering in each glistening mile the crystal waters from tumbling creeks and streams. The river rolls white through rock canyons, then darkens under forests of cedar, fir, hemlock, and fern. It washes through drifts of broken granite and drops for silent moments into pools that flow more pure than an ideal and more deep than a dream. It drops away again and again, pausing, then twisting and rushing on toward the lowland. In the foothills at its confluence with the Snoqualmie, the river becomes the Snohomish. Then slow and wide, it moves with the depth of a thousand years to cut through the hills and spill over a broad estuary, to swing north around a peninsula of high ground, west again to Port Gardner Bay, to Puget Sound, and to the North Pacific Ocean.

The Indian names belong to those who first knew these rivers as the quiet avenues which salmon haunted in their relentless circles of life and death. The English names are from the charts of George Vancouver, the British captain whose guns aboard the sloop *Discovery* first spoke across the sound. On an afternoon in the spring of his thirty-fifth year, 1792, Vancouver walked the beach below the bluffs that rim the high ground. Standing there in an infinite wilderness, he looked west to the dark islands, west to the fabled Strait of Juan de Fuca, west to the mystic Orient. He rejoiced that the English, who had so recently lost thirteen colonies, had come at last to these shores which he claimed for their melancholy king. It pleased the captain then to record that "the serenity of the climate, the innumerable pleasing landscapes, and the abundant fertility that unassisted nature puts forth, require only to be enriched by the industry of man . . . to render it the most lovely country that can be imagined." In a mood of warm satisfaction, he ordered the issue of a generous round of grog and raised his country's flag while his men shouted and fired cannons.

The echo boomed across the waters, disappearing finally into the soft blue light. In a brief moment the *Discovery* was gone, and the forest again stood silent. For a generation after Vancouver's triumph, the only sound of his language near Port Gardner Bay came with the annual brigade of Hudson's Bay Company fur traders who turned their boats toward Vancouver's Island and British Columbia. Even into the 1840s, while English and American diplomats negotiated their differences and determined their boundaries, no white men thought to disturb the Indians of the Snohomish. And when the great rush for California gold inspired a few Americans to explore northward into the Puget Sound country and to settle around the sawmills that became Seattle, Olympia, and Port Townsend, only occasionally did an adventurer draw his boat into the English anchorage of 1792.

It was a century after Vancouver's cannon shot that Americans brought their full energies to what they called the Oregon Country or the Pacific Northwest. Having grasped again the dream of westward expansion that they had so terribly distorted by civil war, they were eager to possess this last of their continental frontiers. When in the 1880s the Northern Pacific Railroad linked its rails from Lake Superior to the Columbia River and then to Puget Sound, every corner of the land began to stir and clatter with steel, men, and dollars.

Nearly one hundred thousand people came into Washington Territory during the first two years of this sustained frenzy. Some found their futures and their fortunes east of the mountain passes in the golden land between the Cascades and the Rockies where the topsoil was three feet deep. Others stood among trees fifty feet in circumference and estimated that on the shores of Puget Sound alone there was timber worth millions. Still others whispered secretly about the gold, silver, iron, coal, and copper they had seen mined along the rivers. Washington achieved statehood in 1889, the year when the Northern Pacific's receipts rose to two hundred thousand dollars a month. In the cross-currents of lumber, wheat, land, mills, and investment, thousands of capitalists were roaming upsound from the depot in Tacoma to seize the fabulous opportunities they believed awaited them on every beach and in every cove. They came from a thousand banks and offices in New York and Boston, in St. Louis and St. Paul. They rushed from boat landing to railhead and back again, bringing their friends and families, buying land, planning towns, and calling for the machines that would industrialize their exploitation of an almost untouched wilderness.

In 1892 at Port Gardner Bay, there were groups of excited men all along the beaches and the bluffs. They talked and shouted, hammered and blasted, crossed back and forth from ships to boats to fires, mud, tools, tents, and lean-to saloons. They were building cedar shacks among the primitive stands of trees still so thick and so tall that the matted ground turned under pick and shovel had never dried in the light of the sun. As Vancouver had done, these men looked west toward the mythical kingdoms. But they raised their glasses high to two kings of their own industrialized nation whose names were John Davison Rockefeller and James Jerome Hill.

The word in 1892 was that Jim Hill, the Empire Builder, was ready to unlock the treasures of this country by bringing the main line of his Great Northern Railroad—second of the northern transcontinentals—over the Cascade Mountains, down the river valley of the Skykomish, and to the sea at Everett, the city to be erected on the peninsula above Port Gardner Bay. The signs were that Hill, even then a legend of shrewdness and practical wisdom, could, like a conquering emperor, see the horizons of fortune and power. There was more than enough space and bounty for two railroads, and when he chose to do so he could transform the northern beaches into a smoky focus of noise, wood, brick, and steel. He could make the place called Everett into a prestigious address on a new avenue of finance, speculation, and industry. Hill knew, as did the men of Everett, that John D. Rockefeller had shown an interest in such projections and energies. This fact alone was enough to support a sober belief among speculators that the very hand of Providence was behind every announcement of the Great Northern Railroad and the Everett Land Company.

In February, 1892, they waited through a long and dreary winter. They had perhaps eight hundred houses on the fringes of what they called their city, but hundreds of men and women were sleeping in tents and even cruder shelters. A few slept in coffins which others had carried to the peninsula on the rumor that at Everett one could sell anything. During every hour of daylight men labored to erect a huge shipyard and, beside it, a factory for the manufacture of steel barges. Others worked far into the night on the construction of a nail factory, a smelter, and a paper mill. Still others pounded spikes to steady the rail line they had hastily laid to connect their city with Tacoma and Seattle. Five hundred men were clearing land in an area defined as the city. Yet these people had no church, no graveyard, no jail. And no one could buy or rent any of the cleared land, for the men who with providential wisdom had laid out the city were withholding its substance for an indefinite and highly speculative season.

Those who came north to buy lots waited without favor. They paid forty dollars a month for shacks they could have built for a few hundred dollars. They borrowed cash at 12 percent. Their city was, on the face of it, a mud-drenched community of idiots. Yet they stayed through the dark days of sodden misery. As they paced the margins of a promised land, the faithful knew that the future was not in the red mud and wet blankets but in their dreams of the moment when Jim Hill and John Rockefeller would in unmistakable words say that the promises of Everett were good and true.

Port Gardner had a newspaper, and its weekly circulation of rumors brought more hundreds of men. The editor boasted of more subscribers east of the Mississippi than he had in the state of Washington. "Capitalists," he reported, arrived daily "on every boat and railroad car," and they found beds at Nelson's Saloon for twenty-five cents a night. They met a proprietor who pulled corks with his teeth and served whisky, sugar, and bitters at twenty-five cents a glass. "A poetic beverage," the editor noted, for no man could "put more than one under his shirt before breakfast and navigate on dry land." Every toast was the occasion for hyperbole which even sober men could believe. Any whisper in the night could surround the offices of the Everett Land Company with wild crowds, exchanging rumors in the lantern light.

Gardner Colby, treasurer of the land company, could state that "the time is not far distant when Everett will be to the Pacific Coast what Boston and Lowell are to the East." With this conviction he had already given the name Lowell to the south-and-river side of the peninsula. He had no doubt, he said, that where forests had stood silent for centuries, he himself would soon stand to "hear the whirl of the looms and factory wheels and see the smoke of the iron and smelting furnaces on all sides." Colby and the other high-collared men from New York formed a phalanx around Henry Hewitt, Jr., president of the land company, who, it was said by other wishful geographers, had won the confidence of John D. Rockefeller. Hewitt used the company, they said, to deploy Rockefeller's money at the foundation of a greater Pittsburgh at Everett, for he had learned that the Cascade Mountains held iron enough to supply the world.

Under such circumstances, the word was that James Hill simply could not afford to bypass Everett—as some cynics had sneered that he would—by leaving the river valley in the foothills and cutting directly south to Seattle. This word was reinforced each day by more rumors from Nelson's Saloon. One story was that the Lombard Trust Company had an agent somewhere in the forest examining investment opportunities for British millionaires. Another was that the Everett Development Company, supposed to be a cover for Rockefeller's intelligence division, had discovered coal, oil, and gas in vast quantities only eight miles east of the river delta. Men huddled to hear that Rockefeller would shortly announce his retirement from the Standard Oil Company in order to give his full attention to his new mining and industrial interests in the Cascades and in Everett. Others listened eagerly to reports that an eastern syndicate planned to build fifteen whorehouses. A complementary story was that Rockefeller, more than usually concerned about the moral environment in which he had invested, had thoughtfully ordered his Baptist Gospel Car up the tracks with clergymen and Bibles to aid the Everett Missionary Society. Men most recently from St. Paul said that Jim Hill was bringing Frederick Weyerhaeuser, who would make Everett the timber capital of the world. Others recalled that when the timber was gone—Jim Hill had said so—the soil beneath it would prove to be the most fertile on the continent. Men with money had heard that Colby, Hewitt, Hill, Rockefeller, and Weyerhaeuser all believed that a smart man would put everything he had in Everett.

Many, of course, *had* put everything—from a distance if necessary, on the site if they could. By March there were some two thousand men around the bay, and they had come from all parts of the United States and Canada. Some were so new to the region that they believed the rainy season would be over in January. Their optimistic rumors carried so far that one ancient and nostalgic miner from the Rockies who had heard that Everett was a mining town came looking for a gulch bristling with pistols and heated with the excitement of gold. The place was phony, he said: phony excitement, New York money, New York methods. There was nothing in Everett a "red-blooded crook" could steal honestly, and none of the other crooks had "the courage of their convictions."

It was true that men in Everett did not rob and shoot; they schemed and screamed at each other. Anxieties ranged so high and so far off key that the spirit of Christmas, 1891, had degenerated into a marathon of drunken brawling that lasted a whole week. At Nelson's Saloon, with the *News* editor in almost constant attendance, gentlemen capitalists were "rolling and fighting on the floor six deep." If they kicked in the sawdust, it was because the promises of Everett were too far above the mud, the rain, the kerosene smoke, the damp cold. Everett would continue as a city of tense confusion until Jim Hill came personally to join dream and reality. When it was at last certain that Jim Hill had in fact come west and was in Seattle, that Hewitt and the Rockefeller men had gone hence to escort the hero north to Port Gardner Bay, men drank whisky and danced in the streets. This was the first, and the most predictable, rite in the ceremonial validation of their new estate as partners with giants in the exploitation of the frontier.[1]

When Hill's private car arrived late in February, 1892, a

wild-eyed crowd had already been cautioned that Hill was an abrupt and unsentimental industrialist who scorned popularity and public acclaim. This was fair warning. As he stepped from his rail-car mansion, he had nothing for the crowd. There were obviously more important things that demanded his immediate attention, and a man who deals with Rockefeller has no time for public pleasantries. Men could ponder the brusque remarks reported to them from Seattle, where Hill told interviewers that he had "no interest in a square foot of land in the state of Washington," and "not one cent invested in Everett." The Great Northern, he said curtly, was not a "real estate road." Such candor moved the *News* to proclaim that "Mr. Hill is not only the greatest railroad builder the world has ever produced. He is also one of the greatest men intellectually."

That night the few hundred men whose demeanor Henry Hewitt found most pleasing gathered in the Bayview Hotel to honor Hill with a ceremony so elaborate as to defy the elements of wilderness around them. There were courses of fish and fowl and beef to be floated in a fine champagne and a Château la Rose, 1878; then café au kirsch and cigars. The men of Everett would gladly have reached for any luxury or any symbol of it to impress the Empire Builder and cause him to acknowledge without equivocation that Everett would be rich beyond the dreams of Monte Cristo—which was, in fact, what men were calling the mining area of the Cascades then being developed with Rockefeller money and alleged to be stuffed with gold.

Looking alternately hard and gracious, Henry Hewitt joined the small talk that began with the fish and wine. Then suddenly even he was overcome with anxiety, and to the dismay of those at the head table he stood and introduced Hill before the gentlemen had been served their beef and claret. As capitalists drew nervously on their champagne, Hewitt told them that Jim Hill was "the only man who had ever undertaken to build a railroad from St. Paul to the Pacific

Coast without asking for an acre of land." Gentlemen applauded, and Hill smiled. Jim Hill, the speaker continued, "had never taken a dollar from the people through whose land his railroad will be run." Hewitt struggled on amid greater applause until it was at last necessary for Hill to stand and look sternly into the faces that surrounded him.

Though he was a stout man of only medium height, Hill seemed at this moment to dominate the room. He began slowly. He was not an accomplished speaker, and he left no hint that he wanted to be one. He was a carefully guarded dealer in concrete ideas expressed concretely, a manipulator of quantitative skills far beyond the appreciation of his audience. Hill could without notes talk for hours about degrees of grade and about the differentials of long hauls and short hauls. Audiences of men conditioned to respond warmly when a speaker gloried in the conventional deductions about thrift and diligence, or about local pride and national grandeur, were bewildered by his weird algebra of preferential rating and costs per ton-mile. And he bewildered still more the audiences that had come to hear him say they were wise in following his lead and, like he, would—God willing—become men of wealth and social substance.

But what James J. Hill wanted this evening was, first of all, to eat his dinner. He may have concluded earlier that Henry Hewitt was a fool. His opening humor was ambiguous—about how everyone in the Puget Sound country seemed to have founded a townsite since he arrived; in his week here, he said, he had "found only four stumps without a name." When the laughter dropped, he added more grimly that there were too many people around here "trying to get something for nothing." Gentlemen drew even more heavily on their champagne while Hill worked that observation into a small sermon. Then he jumped abruptly toward the thoughts central to the evening.

"Lumber, gentlemen, is your greatest resource today. . . . What you want, gentlemen, is a cheap railroad connection.

. . . You will find that we will treat you well. . . . You have no reason to fear any city south of you. . . . We could be persuaded not to haul our tonnage any farther than absolutely necessary to reach Puget Sound." These words opened finally an unchoked roar of approval.

Then a qualification: "I might need a whole school section in Everett. . . ." Gentlemen thought about this while Hill continued to say that if the acquisition of such land were no difficulty, he was "ambitious enough to put a line of fast ships from our western terminal to run to Japan." This brought long cheers. But then instead of naming that terminal with a quotable clarity, Hill went on toward no particular point about the hard facts of the railroad business—his favorite, well-worn observations about low grades and mean low rates, mileage, tonnage, the warp and woof of the Great Northern and the career being celebrated. To Jim Hill, reality and beauty and intelligence were percentages of mean low grades and consolidated feeder lines. He painted a precise and monotonous picture, but suddenly impatient to get on with his dinner, he concluded with a sweeping platitude about the great American people and sat down. Gentlemen toasted Hill with unrestrained enthusiasm and for an hour brooded over their claret.

With the cafe au kirsh, Henry Hewitt rose again to press matters, if he could, toward the issue at hand. Getting down to reality, he said, every property owner should "give Mr. Hill the right-of-way through his land," and he added with deep conviction that "any man who bids against Mr. Hill when the school section goes upon the market should be boycotted." Hill looked pleased. Hewitt presented the honorable John Foster, who punctuated his brief remarks by saying that as a state legislator he had "always been opposed to anti-railroad legislation." Hill seemed interested. Next an Everett attorney made a flowery plea for the future, for the churches and the schools, for "intellectual, spiritual, and aesthetic progress." Hill clapped vigorously.[2]

To move the evening toward a penultimate blending of

mood and expectation, Hewitt introduced Emory C. Ferguson, who stood proudly as the pioneer symbol of the frontier past. Anyone with only shallow roots in the region knew him as Old Ferg, and at sixty he seemed as old as the trees. He could talk vividly about sluicing gold in California, in the Fraser country, and on the upper Columbia before anyone had ever thought of railroads. He could tell how, when he was twenty-seven years old, he had stood utterly alone by his log cabin on the Snohomish River and realized that he was master of his destiny and his Presbyterian soul. On the Fourth of July that year—and this was a favorite story—he had thrown a party, but no one came but he himself, not even an Indian. Still, as he told it in later years, he had opened a keg of powder and primed an ancient firing piece, and just as his grandfather would have done, he had given three cheers for George Washington and Lafayette before blasting a mighty salute down the river. He had whooped and shouted and blasted again, igniting, he felt, a moment of genuine elation in a forest of impenetrable gloom.

For Old Ferg, the more shaded tributaries of the past extended back into the squalid years of Indian trading, squaw brothels, and Indian saloons along the river delta. He had been there when men felled the giant cedars into tide water, trimmed them, and waited for San Francisco schooners to buy them on the spot. He had felled trees in the river and towed them by row boat to the steam-driven saws of the Pope and Talbot Company at Port Gamble across the sound. These were years when the petty timber pirates around the river joked about Old Ferg being "king of the County."

The jest had straight historical lines. Ferg's fortune, such as it was, rested in part on the circumstances of 1860 in Washington Territory and his being a Lincoln man in a county where the other dozen or so Indian traders called themselves Jacksonians. A new Republican governor allowed Ferg to reorganize the county boundaries in such a way as to cut out these Democrats and then to take all the spoils. At his squatter's claim on the river about ten miles inland—where, he imagined, a proposed military road would bring him riches— he built the Blue Eagle Saloon. He was, in the words of a friend, ready "to serve drink or food, in his capacity of bartender, to hand out mail, as postmaster, to disperse justice [as probate judge and Justice of the Peace], to transact business for the county [as county commissioner and county auditor], or to discuss affairs of the territory as a legislator." He was also commissioned, in this clearing which had neither public business nor children, to handle the affairs of the county notary and county superintendent of schools.

Though the Civil War never reached Snohomish County and the army never built the military road, Ferg did, in a minor way, begin to prosper. This was true especially after the government surveys of 1867 made the filing of homestead claims possible. In a striking coincidence of this date and his sudden economic well-being, there is the unmistakable suggestion that Ferg was herding homestead entrymen for the Pope and Talbot Company, which was eager to acquire all the timbered land it could get for its Port Gamble mill. This was a service that Ferg was admirably equipped to provide. He could easily gather witnesses around the bar (and before a notary public and the county auditor) to sign the necessary affidavits, pay the taxes on the land to the county commissioner, file the title at the county seat (his home), transfer the title to Pope and Talbot's Puget Mill Company, and, finally, pay the entrymen their customary one hundred dollars. In his capacity as the "Father of Snohomish," he might encourage the former homesteaders—refugees, for the most part, from the Rocky Mountain mining camps—to buy cheap lots from Ferg's townsite where they could build a shack near the saloon and live the good life taking logs from the public lands along the rivers and selling them to the Pope and Talbot Mill.

As Ferg grew older, he married and became something of a landmark and an institution. As a symbol of the western frontiersman in 1892, he projected at least in part a caricature of that image: he had gone broke three times seeking gold; he had entered the Indian trade just as the furs and the Indians were disappearing; he had even gone to jail once—a mirthful sentence of two hours—for selling whisky to the Indians. Inspired one year to build a road from the Snohomish River to the Columbia, he had with incredible hardships blazed a trail through a pass across the mountains, but it was not the one Jim Hill would use. He had founded a town for a road that was never built. He had perhaps been a procurer for Pope and Talbot. He had once competed with that company by starting a mill of his own, but almost immediately the United States timber agent had brought a halt to the traditional theft of timber from government land, and that left no timber for sale because Pope and Talbot had all the homesteads. It didn't matter anyway: the market went to hell and wages fell alarmingly; Ferg's fellow townsmen rioted and drove his Chinese millworkers out of the county. He sold the mill and invested in a small rail line to Seattle, only to be overwhelmed by Jim Hill. Though selling his own land did keep him prosperous, he was never adequately perceptive of the shrewd deal or the ruthless man. Only months before this banquet, he had sold a piece of land for $4,000 to Henry Hewitt, who quickly sold it to his brother-in-law, who in turn sold it for $128,000 to Hewitt's Everett Land Company, which sold it during the fever of 1892 for $500,000.

Yet there he stood that night, the grinning nexus of a grubby past and a shining future, the frontiersman in a high collar drinking French champagne with the men from New York who made machines. He had waited thirty years to cash in a squatter's claim, and he could see at this fateful moment that the hand on the bank door was Jim Hill's. To fulfill this moment, to blend in the candlelight the images of the frontiersman and the industrialist, he spoke again as a king. His message was classically simple and direct, the poetic essence of the mood that had carried the evening: in his county, he said,

Mr. Hill could have anything he wanted. James J. Hill looked pleased.[3]

There were more toasts. To make it clear that the cere-monies had not reached their apex, Henry Hewitt spoke again and suggested with a keen delicacy that gentlemen would still like to hear Mr. Hill say that Everett was his western terminal. James Hill accepted the floor again and addressed further remarks to the railroad business. The editor of one paper thought sure that Hill said Everett had it, but another editor reported that Hill intimated only that he had not yet decided. Others understood him to have suggested that he and Providence had not built an empire on benevolence alone, and that he would surely await the disposition of that square mile of land known as "the school section."

At one hour after midnight, gentlemen gave three cheers for Jim Hill and Henry Hewitt, then strode boldly into the mud and darkness. If they carried doubts about the inscrutable Mr. Hill or the zealous Mr. Hewitt, such doubts were never recorded, and they would, in any event, have blurred in the raging optimism. The gentlemen of Everett were convinced that forces of progress more powerful than any two individ-uals were in irresistible motion.

As the hall darkened behind them and grew cold, the smoke of burned candles lifted upward, and the smell of wet cedar returned. It was a night rich in echoes, images, and symbols: the frontiersman and the industrialist; the ceremonial offering of virtue itself to win the favor of a stiff-necked god; the words spoken in wisdom; the verbiage uttered in folly. It was a night for sadness, for in a few short months the Panic of 1893 would sweep across the United States and rush like a fierce nightmare down Jim Hill's main line. In Everett the collapse would put a bald face on that night's greed and pan-dering. It would scatter capitalists like fat mice, reduce the survivors to humble barter, and speak in the voice of Job to the most proud of that generation.

But the strongest would endure. Jim Hill would come again to raise his glass in more sober toasts and take his measure of more sober men. "Lumber, gentlemen," he had said, "lumber. . . ." That word would ultimately integrate the loose ends of his driving vision, but the men to build his city had not been among the deluded capitalists of Port Gardner Bay.

Though the Empire Builder did not often reveal or betray a confidence, rumors of his manufacturing interests were the most nearly true. As Hill read the mandate of his northwest empire, he would entrust the barony of Everett to those friends whose substance he need not question, to Frederick Weyerhaeuser and David Clough of Minnesota, and to even brighter minds of a younger generation—the Weyerhaeuser sons, Clough's son-in-law, the protégés of Hill himself and of John D. Rockefeller. These were men who, like Hill, could see a mill town drawn in the hard steel of saws and rails, a unity of smokestacks lining the river bank and circling the high ground, a unity of machines feeding on a wilderness. And like Hill, they would understand that machines also shaped a human condition.

The chapters which follow explore a metaphor implicit in Hill's conception: the human spirit would not forever sustain the iron heart and would not without rancor respond to the iron hand. They seek the community experience which defined the character of Hill's barons and conditioned the anguish of their wage slaves. They follow the historical record through an elliptic poetry which rises from two basic ironies: the first is that the opportunities of 1892 could so quickly turn toward farce and tragedy, that so fanciful a beginning could come so quickly to such a sorry end; the second and more elusive is that in twenty-four years the "forces of progress" Jim Hill set in motion across a region could turn upon themselves to induce economic paralysis and to rend the flesh at the Everett Massacre, a moment curiously close to the hour of Hill's own death in 1916, when the community founded on his vision tore itself apart.

II

The Wreck of Misspent Fortunes

HENRY Hewitt, Jr., was born in England in 1840, but he grew up in rural Wisconsin, where his father became a minor timber capitalist in the shadow of the Weyerhaeuser interests. Within twenty years, the elder Hewitt had made the family respectably rich. Henry, Jr., studied business for a season at a Lawrence College in Appleton, but his real education took place in his father's office as he learned how to put money into land and timber. By 1862 he had served a successful apprenticeship and was already involved in several manipulations which promised impressive returns. By paying a substitute to serve for him during the Civil War, he was able to give these prospects his full devotion.

The war years were rewarding for Hewitt, and they equipped him with experience and capital to take advantage of the acceleration in the timber business during the following decade. While the new saws and a new technology of the 1870s increased the productivity of work crews by perhaps 500 percent, the railroads were there to haul the wood to national and international markets and to bring in the thousands of farmers who were hungry for the slashed acreages. High taxes and high rates of interest passed land from hand to hand as fast as speculators could turn a profit, and Henry Hewitt turned more than most. He was among those who survived the Panic of 1873 with holdings still worth a million dollars.

It was clear to Hewitt in the early 1880s that the methods of business and the margins of profit to which he had grown accustomed would soon be impossible in Wisconsin. Across the broad reaches of the upper Mississippi Valley, timber men and farmers had stripped the forests. As the bonanza years faded, Hewitt's thoughts and conversations began to shift toward the Pacific Northwest, where, he had heard, the Douglas fir would make the fortunes of the next generation. This tree, the lumber manufacturers were saying, could serve American industry as well as pine. It covered thousands of square miles and grew to 250 feet as straight as a ship's mast from a ten-foot diameter. And, most importantly, the Northern Pacific Railroad was pushing triumphantly into this last frontier and inviting men of vision and courage to follow with their wits and their money.

Hewitt responded in 1888, when he left for Puget Sound with four hundred thousand dollars and his sharp eye for land and trees. His first investments were in acreages from the Northern Pacific land grants and in a Tacoma lumber company, both of which were reasonably secure. Then he began a careful survey of the region with a view to more daring opportunities. When his eye caught an article in a small newspaper published at the village of Snohomish, he took a boat upsound.

Looking up the Snohomish River, to the east and to the north, over the hills and to the peaks of the Cascades, he convinced himself that this lush world of water and wood held a hundred fortunes that Weyerhaeuser alone could not open. And he could not believe that the Northern Pacific held the only key. Other railroad men would see the same riches, and they could follow this very river down the mountains and to the inland sea. With such thoughts, Hewitt rented a boat and sounded Port Gardner Bay. He found deep water, and, in his excitement, he could suddenly see New York. His mind's eye evoked a metropolis with both salt water and river moorages, a railhead, and factories feeding on resources beyond calculation. Knowing little about New York and even less about river deltas, he could imagine the high ground above the beach crowded with buildings and the river teeming with a thousand ships below. In a few days he began quietly to buy land for the city he was to name.

Hewitt would, of course, need help. He was not a man to share his vision with any casual speculator, and he did not. He waited, and with time and good fortune he soon met Charles L. Colby from New York. Colby was, like Hewitt, middle-aged, though he was better educated than Hewitt and more sophisticated, more carefully restrained by a rigid upper-class reserve. He also had more money and more connections to sources of significant wealth. He too had come to Puget Sound to explore the region for his own investments, but he was then a man of national reputation in financial circles: president of the American Steel Barge Company, executive board member of the Northern Pacific, broker, banker, investor. Colby had good reason to believe that the Northern Pacific, at the proper moment, would move up from Tacoma toward the Canadian border. He shared with Henry Hewitt the faith that the proper congruence of insight, chance, and capital would make the next generation of Carnegies and Rockefellers. Both knew the importance of being first to perceive the dimensions of opportunity, and they soon developed a warm rapport.

Deeply impressed by Hewitt's ideas, Colby returned to New York in 1890 to share the plan with an intimate group of friends and relatives that included other directors of the Northern Pacific, the most prominent of whom was Colgate Hoyt. With Hewitt, Colby, and Hoyt leading, this group incorporated the Everett Land Company. In these deliberations, Hewitt made himself indispensable. Though he had the least capital, his Port Gardner holdings gave him strategic strength, and he was cheerfully willing to risk it all. The others soon relied upon his energy, optimism, and confidence, as well as upon his knowledge of land and timber. With these satisfactions, he adjusted easily to the proprieties of the eastern elite, and the partners named him president. Hewitt himself had already suggested a name for their enterprise. At a dinner party in the home of Charles Colby, his eye caught the host's son, Everett, who wanted more dessert. "That's it!" Hewitt chuckled. "We should name our city Everett. This boy wants only the best, and so do we." [1]

Returning to Port Gardner Bay, Hewitt worked quickly to buy more land. To his dismay, he discovered that in his absence much of what he wanted had been taken by Wyatt J. Rucker, recently from Ohio, who also had money and expansive ideas about railroads and timber. Hewitt learned that Rucker, with his brother and a group of Tacoma investors, had been buying homestead titles and had already discussed platting a city. Given these circumstances, Hewitt had no choice but to take the Ruckers into his confidence. He was able to buy a good share of their titles, but the Ruckers retained holdings which, as development continued, would appreciate fabulously: as part of the deal, the Everett Land Company was obligated to build a city with a heavy industrial base. Hewitt promised sawmills, a shipyard, docks, a railroad.

Meanwhile in New York, Colby and Hoyt produced commitments for a paper mill and a nail factory. Colby also convinced Charles W. Wetmore, a New York capitalist interested in steel and cargo vessels, to build his whaleback ships at Everett. These were to be long, low steel craft designed to ride under the waves with decks constantly awash. They had been con-

Everett before Jim Hill (Photo courtesy of *Everett Herald*)

Logging near the Snohomish River, 1890's (Photo courtesy of Everett Community College Library)

Snohomish River Front: Everett Land Company promotion photograph, 1893 (Photo courtesy of Everett Community College Library)

Henry Hewitt's city, 1892 (Photo courtesy of Everett Community College Library)

ceived in the unconventional imagination of Angus McDougall, an inventor and close friend of Charles Colby, who assured investors that these ships would be virtually storm-proof, would drive out the competition for oceanic transportation, and would become the ships of the new century. In this same optimism, Colby took money for a rail line from Everett to Snohomish which was planned as a sort of pre-emption that the land company could later offer to James Hill.

While one achievement followed another, news came from Hewitt that an engineer he had sent into the Cascades just east of Everett had uncovered evidence of great mineral wealth—lead, silver, iron, and gold. Their city would be the new Pittsburgh. This report electrified the New York group, who then rushed millions into the stock of a mining company, a railroad to the mines, and a huge smelter. Even to men as somber as Colby and Hoyt, prospects of this magnitude were truly staggering. After long deliberations, they decided to expose their plans to the most awesome of all investors, John D. Rockefeller himself.

Rockefeller was no stranger to them. Both Colby and Hoyt were communicants at the Baptist Church on Fifth Avenue, where they greeted him each Sunday. Their access to Rockefeller at this particular time was even easier than they could have hoped, for Rockefeller, having for decades worked beyond the capacity of most men, had in 1891 overreached his own. He could not decide how to use his income of ten million dollars a year; he could not, in fact, even keep track of where it went. Then fifty-two years old, he was on the edge of nervous collapse. At that very moment he needed his friends, and the more Hoyt and Colby talked, the more Rockefeller saw in them a partial relief from his burdens.

Hoyt and Colby offered Rockefeller apparent security for at least some of his millions. They seemed to him hard-working men, intelligent and educated; they worshiped right, they knew money and land, and they would, he assumed, use his money at least as carefully as they did their own. Thus Rockefeller was persuaded to give them his trust and a share of his fortune. Later, in a clear mind, he would call these investments "unfortunate." He had understood the commitments to be for "mines, steel mills, a nail factory, railroads, smelting properties," though at the time he was not really sure. He had understood that he was a partner sheltered by the larger commitments of others. But as Hoyt, Colby, and Hewitt rearranged their affairs, Rockefeller's money became the major resource for their operations.

As nothing else could have done, Rockefeller's entry turned the Everett flash fire into a speculative explosion. Eastern Baptists were eager to buy land or stock. Capitalists from every part of the country swarmed around the promise of the Rockefeller name. Rockefeller, they knew, could never be wrong, and whatever he touched would surely turn to gold. Possibly even Hewitt, Colby, Hoyt, and the other directors of the Everett Land Company themselves believed that Rockefeller's confidence could not be misplaced, that it had ordained them princes whose decisions now by definition could not go awry.

Certainly Henry Hewitt suffered no restraint. At the heart of his conception of Everett was a plan to make a city that James Hill could not possibly ignore, and with Rockefeller's money he knew he could do this. He bought more thousands of acres of land. He summoned the construction crews that began work on the shipyards, the nail factory, the paper mill, a street railroad, hotels, mines, the smelter. More crews came to build roads, docks, store buildings, homes, and banks. It seemed that at Hewitt's pace a wet forest would in a matter of months become a city of timber and steel, banks and smoke and men.

During the winter of 1892–93, no rain or mud could slow Hewitt's drive. Work gangs crossed back and forth over the high ground while other more cleanly dressed gangs filled hotels to incorporate, to buy, to sell, to build. After a lengthy dispute with the state, Hewitt won the waterfront for the

Everett Land Company. This victory marked the time to incorporate the city, and in this operation he carefully excluded the waterfront industrial sites from the city limits and city taxes. He ordered more roads and streets. At an inspired moment, he presented a plan to dredge a river harbor that would indeed make Everett resemble New York. It was an extraordinarily imaginative scheme to clear the main channel for deep navigation far up the delta and to build a gigantic gate that would hold water in the river at low tide and open only when the tide flooded. As his mind raced ahead, his workers in the shipyards were hammering steel plates for the whaleback *City of Everett*, which was to carry the nails, gold, silver, paper, and timber to the waiting world. On a happy day in 1892 the nail factory produced its first spike—a rod of Monte Cristo silver. By then the smelter was already processing the first carload of colored ores.

When Henry Hewitt left his rooms each morning, lesser speculators clawed for a place in line at the doors of the Everett Land Company. His fragment of a city was a bedlam of impatient greed. During the days and nights, crowds overflowing from the disorderly saloons made progress down the sidewalks almost impossible. Prostitutes swore in public and sang dirty songs as they pulled men at random from the streets. The obstreperous brawling of drunken women on Sunday mornings offended some eastern sensitivities, just as did the manure and garbage and seepage from shallow toilets that formed in piles and pools. But men could say it had been the same at the beginning in San Francisco or Denver or Butte or Spokane: grand ideas did not wait on small details.

All the while, Henry Hewitt was thinking most about Jim Hill and the Great Northern. The Empire Builder's remarks at February's banquet had left a tortuous ambiguity which only the Empire Builder himself could dispel, and Hewitt worked steadily toward that climax. He let it be known that Frederick Weyerhaeuser had said that Everett would be a "great city." It is likely that Hewitt spread the rumors, with or without evidence, that oil, gas, and coal had also been discovered just east of the city, and that British investors were eager to take any crumbs that Rockefeller might let fall from the bountiful table. It seems certain that Hewitt arranged the election of a conservative Democratic mayor to suit Hill's politics.

Hewitt could and did use Jim Hill's name to bring about accomplishments which would impress even the Empire Builder. He held out the threat that Jim Hill would bypass Everett and starve friend and foe alike if the Everett Land Company were denied its purposes. Such a threat, coupled with Hewitt's power to withhold land or to release it for sale, silenced the few county Populists who snorted at corporations, railroads, or the Democratic party. It disciplined a mob of petty speculators and Rockefeller parasites who spoke against country bond issues and taxes or argued against incorporation laws that excluded the waterfront. Organizing and pushing, threatening and persuading, Hewitt was soon called "the father of Everett," and he was seriously suggested for the United States Senate.

In January, 1893, Hewitt's skills faced a major test when the section of school land went at public auction. By the American tradition set in 1787, Section 16 of each township was reserved to provide revenue so that—in the words of Thomas Jefferson—"schools and the means of education shall forever be encouraged." In Everett this land included extensive waterfront acreage and the proposed terminal grounds for the Great Northern. Hewitt's triumph was that there were no competitive bids after Jim Hill's agent called his price. Hill took about two hundred acres at seventy-six dollars an acre, while other parts of the section went to the Everett Land Company at more than four hundred dollars an acre. Capitalists had indeed given Hill everything he wanted. Within a week, Hill's brother-in-law, James D. Farrell, drove the spike that tied Everett into the Great Northern empire.[2]

After the celebrations, the Everett Land Company fulfilled

a long-delayed promise to put cheap residential lots up for
sale. They were on twenty-five foot frontages and sold for
$200 at 10 percent down if the buyer would agree to build a
house costing at least $250. At a time when money still went
easily at 12 percent and existing houses rented for forty dollars a month, these sales were a blessing to the four thousand
wage earners who had waited in the mud and squalor. They
went to work vigorously, fixing Everett in Henry Hewitt's
rigid and enduring pattern of common urban blight—small
houses almost touching one another, thrown up with the
cheapest lumber and the least imagination. But they could
be homes. The construction workers and the factory hands
were joined by their families who came from Seattle, Tacoma,
and Portland, from Minnesota, Wisconsin, or the Dakotas.
A third of them were foreign born. Many came directly from
Canada, Norway, Sweden, and England.

In other parts of the new town, businessmen with complete
faith in the insights of Rockefeller and his sidesmen bought
lots costing a thousand dollars. They were men like John J.
Clark, who, when he had heard about Everett in 1892, had sold
his Bazar of Bargains in Racine, Wisconsin. He invested one
hundred thousand dollars in land and in a large brick building
for five stores on one of Hewitt's new streets. He rented these
stores to men like H. J. Bebeau, who had made what he
called a "handsome fortune" in farming, merchandising, and
developing towns in Michigan. Or A. A. Brodeck, who came
up from Tacoma to sell shoes, overalls, hats, gloves, and under-
wear. B. E. Aldrich arrived in 1891 and opened his "working
man's grocery" with money he had made in St. Paul. O. N.
Nelson, the saloonkeeper, was from Tacoma. Walter Swal-
well, born and educated in Quebec, came in 1892 to sell school
and office supplies and to speculate in real estate. Joe Irving,
born in England, had learned business in Montreal, then moved
to Everett in 1891 as a clerk in the land company's Bayview
Hotel. By 1893 he was managing the new hotel, the Monte
Cristo, and selling lumber on the side.

The Monte Cristo immediately became the social center for a somewhat more imposing circle of men from the East who took the same pride in the titles "capitalist" and "speculator" that their fathers and grandfathers had found in the title "gentleman." New York bankers and technicians, St. Paul railroad men, they had all followed Rockefeller's money or Jim Hill's instincts toward the new West. Among them was William C. Butler, manager of the smelter, who had come from New York, where his brother, Nicholas Murray Butler, was then a professor at Columbia. Butler organized the Everett Tennis Club and the St. Nicholas Club, where the initiation fee was a hundred dollars. He and his wife were popular guests at the yachting parties that brought splendor to Port Gardner Bay. To bring in the Christmas season of 1892, Mrs. Butler and other ladies, all of them in green silk and diamonds, formed a receiving line in the hotel ballroom to welcome Everett's elite to an evening of musical entertainment, dancing, and champagne. From among their own number the ladies themselves produced a quartet that played "Dame Cuckoo," "The Farmer and the Pigeons," and "Down in the Dewey Dell."

When ladies in diamonds and men in black ties could dance in Everett, shut out from the noise of ores and nails, whores, ships, and lumber, Henry Hewitt felt that his city had passed through the period of crisis. It was time for Jim Hill to come again, and he could come appropriately on the first through train from Lake Superior, which was scheduled to arrive in Everett in June, 1893. Accordingly, the Monte Cristo group secured a plate of solid silver, encased in velvet, and inscribed with an invitation to James Jerome Hill to honor again the "city of smokestacks," as Hewitt was now pleased to call his soggy peninsula. He advanced preparations for a ceremony that might well have surpassed any glorification which the Empire Builder had before enjoyed.

But Hewitt would never have his ceremony, and Everett would soon forget its plate of solid silver. It had been clear

for some time to the more perceptive pessimists that Hill was
taking the Great Northern through Everett and on to Seattle.
Some thought that he either feared or distrusted Rockefeller.
Others said that he saw in Seattle a more spacious harbor for
his Oriental lines, a more promising economy, and a more
stable society for his "terminus," however he defined it.

In any event, both cities would have their railroad, but in
1893 even this would not matter. Men who read the newspapers had early that year felt suspicions which were turning
to gloom and fear. Money was scarce, and all across the
country construction had halted. The price of lumber was
falling sharply. Wage cuts in Everett and Seattle had already
blown the breath of panic. "Business conditions," Hill wired,
would not permit his coming west that year. During the week
that Jim Hill was to have celebrated investments and profits
there, the Bank of Everett closed its doors.

The Panic of 1893, which was a panic of lost confidence,
crumbled cities like Everett for which confidence was the
only adhesive in the foundation of community life. What the
lords of finance had given, they could as easily take away,
and as they withdrew their promises the very fiber of Everett
began to shake and then to shatter. Three of the five banks
went down, taking with them modest savings accounts, city
and county funds, and large blocks of eastern investment capital. By August, the Northern Pacific was bankrupt and the
Great Northern had stopped all its construction. Neither
bought lumber in Everett, where lumber was the only hard
reality in an economy of soft promises. With some mad logic,
the completion of railroads to the Pacific Northwest became
a cause of regional economic collapse.

By August, too, the Everett Land Company was in deep
trouble. Hewitt, Colby, and Hoyt saw their wealthy friends
beat an abrupt and discourteous retreat from any possible
risk, taking with them the raiment of the Everett dream.
Hewitt, as president of the company, faced the full fever of
panic. The Rucker contracts obligated him to build a city,

but he was suddenly denied his money and his friends. Dozens of investors in New York, Everett, Tacoma, and St. Paul—who now saw themselves as creditors—waited with increasingly critical apprehension.

Hewitt's own preference, quite naturally, was to relax and wait out the return of better days. But he was not heard. In New York, the distressed partners issued bonds against the company for one and one-half million dollars at 8 percent, hoping to use the money in such a way as to convince Rucker and the investors that their enterprise still had promise. Hewitt said again that he was preparing to dredge the harbor and get on with his work of building a New York on Puget Sound. His optimism was given high credence when people learned that Rockefeller himself had graciously taken most of the bonds as a sign to the financial world that his associates still claimed his esteem. The litany went up again that Rockefeller never lost money and that his stake in Everett was a providential guarantee of ultimate success.

But in 1893 even Rockefeller's faith could not conceal the real desperation of the Everett Land Company. Two months after the bond issue, Hewitt offered to sell to the city government, at a loss, the company's water works, electric works, and street railway. The money, he said, would finally assure the river harbor with its tide gate and miles of fresh-water moorage. Though many businessmen endorsed the idea of the city's owning these utilities, the voters defeated the proposition in the spring of 1894. There is a sad and enduring significance in this particular crisis, for Hewitt had given the city an opportunity to accept the principle of municipal ownership without philosophical agony—a chance it would not have again.

For the "father of Everett," this rejection brought personal ruin. In the East, Hewitt was being threatened with law suits and bankruptcy proceedings, and accused of incompetence and malfeasance in the use of company funds. His personal interests in the company, his land, and his other holdings were all, in fact, in jeopardy. As he contemplated the meaning of depression, he received an ominous summons to appear again in New York, where Rockefeller, in better health, had at last determined to look carefully into the management of the Everett Land Company.

Rockefeller did so with rising indignation. His first decision was that he could no longer trust any of his affairs to Henry Hewitt; his second, that he would not impetuously precipitate any further panic by destroying the company itself. While Hewitt looked on helplessly, Rockefeller assumed all of Hewitt's personal debts and quietly took all of Hewitt's stock in the company. He allowed Hewitt to hold a few parcels of land and a handful of money—fourteen thousand dollars in cash, figured, perhaps, as enough to keep him in style for a year. This solved one problem. Rockefeller sent Hewitt on his way and called for Charles Colby, whom he named president of the company in Hewitt's place.

When this news reached Everett, capitalists learned that Mr. Rockefeller was not pleased with foolish optimism. The situation in Everett, Colby announced, was "not reassuring." Mr. Rockefeller, he said further, was interested only in "business propositions," of which there were none in Everett, Washington. When the newspapers raised a piteous cry for the many citizens who had invested everything they had in what they thought were Rockefeller propositions, Colby replied stiffly that neither the Everett Land Company nor Mr. Rockefeller had forced these men to leave their homes and come to Puget Sound. What they were to do now, he added, was no concern of Mr. Rockefeller's; only they themselves could decide.

At Port Gardner Bay, these words seemed too cruel to believe. The newspapers pumped hope after desperate hope into the deflated dream. Nothing, they said, could be permanently wrong. Rockefeller could not have taken a personal interest in the land company unless he was sure of its soundness. Colby "would never have consented to go to the head

of any enterprise that did not promise certain success." Colby
—or Rockefeller—had, in fact, completed the concentrator
at the Monte Cristo mines, the railroad to the mines, and the
smelter. They must then have faith, and this faith would be
Everett's salvation.

Even so, some men were known to have muttered in public—and it had reached the newspapers in print—that the city
was "conceived in fraud and brought forth in iniquity." The
land company, they were saying, had robbed innocent men.
The Monte Cristo mines had been salted with Mexican ores.
Everett, the underground whispered, was a "swindling townsite boom" where "owls and bats revel in the wreck of mis-
spent fortunes."

Such sentiments were in fact remarkably parallel to those
of John D. Rockefeller, who learned by November, 1894,
that the land company could not pay the 8 percent on
its bonds, most of which he himself still held. Though he had
never seen Everett and had no intention of doing so, it was
clear to him that everything there—the nail factory, the
paper mill, the shipyards and barge works—was sinking. Now
fully alert and genuinely interested, he forced the resignations
of Colby and Hoyt, both of whom, he was convinced, had
misused him. Determined to end a host of petty annoyances,
Rockefeller instructed Frederick T. Gates, his confidential
secretary and trusted assistant, to extract him from the Everett
mess.

Gates appeared in Everett for the first time in November,
1894. Only a few knew his purpose or his reputation for
flawless efficiency. He had no reservations about wiping out
the interests of eastern Baptists, no matter how pious or loyal
they may have been. With his keen sensitivity to brilliant
minds, he brought together as his personal advisors William
C. Butler, the young engineer who managed the smelter,
Francis Brownell, the land company attorney, and J. B.
Crooker, one of the Minneapolis investors. From their recommendations and from his own analysis, he proceeded to

liquidate Rockefeller's sorry principality in the empire of Puget Sound.

Frederick T. Gates took Rockefeller's money out of the hotel, the city lands, the street railway, the nail factory, and the paper mill, accepting major losses with each withdrawal. Thus cut away from their eastern resources, most of these enterprises sank in a few months, or at most a few years. Turning to the more heavily capitalized mines and their subsidiary industries, Gates learned the dismal truth that the mines of Monte Cristo were, for his purposes, more phony than any pessimist had dared to believe. His own investigation showed that Hewitt's report of commercial ore deposits had been either fraudulent or flagrantly inadequate. Without hesitation, Gates dumped the mining properties. He then abandoned the Everett–Monte Cristo Railroad that had been built from the mines to the smelter with a generous draft of Rockefeller's funds. This last move alone represented a loss to Rockefeller of over two million dollars.

With a minimum of publicity, Gates sold the smelter to the Guggenheim interests, who bought it to eliminate a threat of competition to their own concerns and then literally, brick by brick, destroyed it. Whatever money Gates realized from all these sales he reinvested through the Everett Timber and Investment Company, a satellite company he decided to retain, increasing its holdings by thousands of acres. When he had finished in Everett, he sold this last of the "Rockefeller propositions" for maybe five times its investment, proving that the optimists had been right all along: Rockefeller did not lose money. In this dazzling series of financial exercises, conducted over a period of three years and during the worst depression the country had ever known, Gates covered losses on the one hand with gains on the other and cleared for Rockefeller several more millions of dollars.[3]

In so doing, Gates had left the people of Everett just where Charles Colby, soon dead from a heart attack, had said they should be—entirely on their own. Literally thousands fled through the only safety valve available—cheap rail tickets that would return them to the family farm in the Dakotas or homestead in Indiana or city house in St. Paul, wherever parents or relatives would take them. The exodus was steady rather than precipitous, for there were always a few lingering hopes that depended upon tomorrow. In 1894 and 1895, maybe nine hundred men found sporadic work in common labor, maybe eight hundred more in manufacturing. In the last hours of the death watch, some of the mill-owners maintained their machines in the hope that their most recent order was not really their last. Before the smelter was destroyed, it turned out a few bars of bullion and ran through several shipments of ore from Idaho. The nail factory operated for a while on a shipment of iron rods from Antwerp.

For those who did find occasional employment, wages after 1893 fell about 60 percent. A family could rent a house for ten dollars a month, though one man shot his landlord for trying to collect that amount. When the schools opened in 1895, there were funds for only three months' operation. Because their parents could not buy them books, many children simply did not report to school. Teachers took their chances on tax money coming in after three months, but they lost. By 1896, the sheriff had sold twenty-five hundred platted lots and twenty-seven thousand acres because of tax delinquencies.

Downtown, prices fell about 40 percent. In 1896, one dollar would buy ten pounds of bacon or four gallons of canned fruit at Metzger's Grocery. But many businesses closed forever; others moved to Seattle, which was almost as bad, and still others ran on friendship and credit for as long as the goods lasted. Many saloonkeepers closed rather than pay the annual license fee.

This loss almost ruined the city government, which spent sixty thousand dollars in 1895 while it took in half that amount. The city council let the streets go without lights.

It released most policemen, retaining enough, however, to identify vagrants, who made up the chain gang used for labor on city projects. The council also passed laws against gambling and prostitution, then regularly fined cardmen and whores to take in one thousand dollars a month, which at least sustained the city's identity, if not its integrity. Without a past, Everett had no experience to guide its present or future. Men grasped for patterns of order they remembered from St. Paul or St. Louis or Spokane, but all patterns seemed grotesquely irrelevant to the reality of idle factories and empty stores.

When the minister of the First Baptist Church gathered raw material for a sermon during the summer of 1894, he found, he said, seven hundred men without work. Dependent upon these men he counted nine hundred women and children. He urged them to trust in God and Rockefeller, the mines and the smelter, and meanwhile, he said, they should till the soil just as their forefathers had always done. This myth of the soil—periodically resanctified by Jim Hill's speeches—held that the ground under such magnificent timber could surely produce equally magnificent wheat and potatoes. In fact the soil was acidic, sandy, and lean in minerals, good for fir and cedar but terrible for food crops. Without fertilizers, which few people could obtain, it might yield at best a few grubby vegetables when cultivated with prayer and desperation.

It was more practical to eat as the Indians had always eaten: the salmon came in primeval abundance, and any rocky shore held a variety of clams. Living from the sea and the beach, families could still somehow feed a cow and a few chickens and bring together beans and bread. Men and boys split wood cut from the lands of forgotten speculators and bartered for milk, flour, and pork. Though a few individuals did sleep in stables and eat from restaurant garbage, most people found that they could endure from week to week.

For the little cash that circulated in Everett, there was a

fearful competition. A Merchants' Protective Association organized to publish the names of persons who spent their
money in Seattle, and the Everett *Times* urged that such
people be run out of town. H. J. Bebeau, former capitalist
from the Dakotas, formed the Everett Exchange and Cooperative Association to organize the bartering of goods and
services. The association failed because Bebeau could not sell
a thousand shares at five dollars each. For those who were
fortunate enough to find work, five dollars might be a week's
wages counted out in pennies. During the Christmas season,
Metzger's Grocery sold bread for one cent a loaf.

There can be no quantitative measure of the moral impact
of the panic on Everett. One can only suppose that for the
men and women who lined up at Metzger's, the city represented a sadness that they alone could weigh. The sky had
fallen, and each person would define his personal disaster
by what he believed the sky had promised him. For example, there was Isaac Cathcart, an illiterate and ambitious
Irish immigrant who had been a logger, then saloonkeeper,
then merchant. He had ridden the accelerating boom to the
ownership of a hotel and one hundred thousand dollars in
land, stock, and timber. In 1895, creditors took it all, and
Cathcart sank into sullen obscurity. His wife, who did the
writing, told a lawyer in Seattle that she cooked for sixteen
men and a despondent husband, that her children could not
attend school, and that she was utterly exhausted of hope
and energy, and despairing for money. She wanted to know
if her suicide would allow her children to collect her life
insurance.

During these years the newspapers told of men who suffered from "strange hallucinations" and of others who hanged
themselves or simply disappeared without notice to relatives
or friends. In the woods near the Cathcart homestead, Eldridge Morse sat and stared at nothing. An early friend of
Old Ferg, he had come to Snohomish as a young, vigorous
lawyer and publisher. He stayed to raise a family and become

a community leader. Before Everett, he had been the man with the library, the county's philosopher, a correspondent and informant for the historian H. H. Bancroft, and, unhappily, an investor. His wife died during the panic, and thereafter he supported five young children by growing vegetables. Within a few months he fell into an emotional stupor and never became intellectually active again.

There were reports that John Keefe, a storekeeper, had not been seen for weeks; friends sold his merchandise for seven hundred dollars. Professor Davenport, the music teacher, left town under "unmentionable charges." A thirteen-year-old boy, working in a shingle mill, fell into a saw and lost his arm at the shoulder. He was taken not to a hospital but to his home. Men, women, and children died in their beds in tiny houses on twenty-five-foot lots from loss of blood, shock, "inflammation," pneumonia, fever, or tuberculosis.

But the climate, unlike that of the real New York or Pittsburgh, was mild, and nature offered a liberal bounty: a man could chop wood, eat fish, and somehow get by. In the leisure that adversity forced upon him, one editor reflected in counter-nostalgia that the boom times had actually diminished the roots of humanity, while bad times released a flow of human warmth. In the days of rabid speculation, he wrote, men yelled in crazy voices and fought with their fists over silly rumors. Greed made them "wild and artificial." But in the duller days, he said, men "discovered life itself"; poverty eroded their pretenses, and they found a sense of community in a common destiny. The churches and the fraternal lodges "worked for survival and brotherhood rather than for exclusion." Talk in the homes and on the streets was about life rather than about money. It is remarkable that he would meditate publicly on such thoughts during the worst of bad times. Many others may have shared his feeling that the times did cut through arrogance and hypocrisy.

In the absence of pretense, even impoverished businessmen were capable of a certain plain humor. When Metzger sponsored a "Hard Times Ball," his invitations were on brown paper, his door prize a sack of potatoes. He presented a lively program, with musical notes in striking contrast to the Monte Cristo elegance: "Labelle—The Nail Works Don't Run. Schottish—The Paper Mill Won't Run. Waltz—The Ore That Never Came. Medley—Change in 60 Days."

Beyond the soulful jokes, men and women could find some security in the harmonies that tradition could illuminate in contemporary travail. They could, like Old Ferg had done in the misty past, at least make the most of the Fourth of July. The holiday in 1896 was rich in the ceremonial sharing of past and present. After two long speeches and a reading of the Declaration of Independence, there were shingle-weaving contests, ball games, foot races, a greased pig, a brass band, and an industrial parade. At night, a bicycle processional by torch light brought a moment of awe and splendor to a dull progression of dull days.[4]

During the 1890s in Everett, the depression could at times veil the smoke and the steel, and remind survivors that this was still the century of Thomas Jefferson. Beyond the silent factories, muddy streets led through trees that thickened step after step into a rich and dark wilderness. Children who had never known industrial affluence could play ball in the streets and swim a river in the summer sun. They could know Indians personally and repeat the names of every resident in the city jail. They could hunt in the woods, fish in the lakes and rivers, sell bottles and firewood, and roam freely through a community that was suspended for a moment between urban industrialism and the fragile purities of a doomed frontier.

This dualistic character is apparent during these years at almost any level of community thought· or experience that historical evidence can reveal. The newspapers show, for example, that at the Monte Cristo Hotel, members of the Ladies'

Book Club in 1894 gave serious attention to Mrs. Joseph Irving's reading of "Thanatopsis." They were likewise pleased to hear a paper by Mrs. Joseph Colby titled "The Religion of the Indians," which Mrs. Colby based upon her own intuition and her study of the poems of William Cullen Bryant and Henry Wadsworth Longfellow. What passed for serious thought among at least some of the ladies and maybe their husbands was heavily laden with the frontier mystique—that belief or faith in the romantic, mysterious qualities of the wilderness which were supposed to refresh and strengthen the spirit as well as to refine the moral perceptions of those who approached Nature's essence. It is significant that this mystique—at the same time but at the other end of the Great Northern line—was being given eminent respectability by Frederick Jackson Turner, who was advising a new generation of American historians to discover how their countrymen had been made a wonderfully individualistic, practical, and optimistic people by their instinctive embrace of the frontier.

A less romantic observer might have seen in Everett certain values or moral imperatives that are more difficult to celebrate—anti-Turner values, even, which one can with equal facility associate with the frontier experience. Racism was one. It is reasonably sure that Mrs. Colby had never known a Northwest Indian and that no one of her acquaintance had ever taken the slightest interest in the people of the Tulalip Reservation just three miles across the river delta. If the closed moral circuit exposed in the newspapers can be taken as a collective state of mind, this mind saw the Tulalip Indians as simply "drunken Siwashes," a sort of subhuman species at once totally immoral and totally improvident, forever inferior for the fact that they were incapable of being purified by the wilderness from which they came. One could hope that they all would shortly disappear. Furthermore, there was an equally vicious racism in the pride many people in Everett found in the fact that not since the 1885–86

Chinese riots in Tacoma and Seattle had Orientals been allowed to reside in the county. One could be slightly more
tolerant of the maybe two dozen Negroes in the city if they
stayed quietly and almost invisibly employed in hotels and
saloons. Finally, there was in anti-Catholicism a narrow blade
of racism being sharpened in 1893 by the furtive satisfactions
many of the most prominent citizens were taking in the
secret handshakes and passwords of the American Protective
Association.

A second value—and one more dramatically reinforced by
the frontier—was the interpersonal violence in Everett which
erupted so casually in daily life. Everett was essentially an
armed society in which almost every home had its arsenal
and almost every man his hand gun. Many could still recall
the Civil War, but younger men had within easier memory
killed Indians, beaten Orientals, or responded with a gun to
some verbal or physical threat to their security. Shootings
occurred in Everett almost every month and caused no enduring concern, for underlying the act was the assumption
that there shall be times when a decent individual has no
honorable recourse but to go home for his pistol. Decency
or honor may demand that a man shoot—an Indian, a Negro,
a Chinese, a vagrant harvest hand or logger. And only if the
dead were gentlemen or capitalists would the killer face a
judge or court. Even so, when the editor of the Everett
News, James Connella, was charged with murder for shooting and killing another Republican at the climax of a local
political meeting, a local jury would not find him guilty.

Thus Mrs. Colby's assumptions about Indians and their
religion were no more romantic than the assumptions generally held in Everett about race or honor, violence or individuality. The romantic mind was, unhappily, the deductive
mind, glowing with unchallenged generalizations, vaguely
hostile to any desire for compiling evidence that might alter
a view of race, humanity, decency, or justice.

To their growing sorrow, the people of Everett had accepted similarly massive and unchallenged assumptions about industrial capitalism, railroads, corporations, Rockefeller, Monte Cristo, and world trade. It was healthy, one assumed, for the economic system to have its ups and downs. Railroads were a glory of the system. Rockefeller had infallible wisdom. With such convictions, Jacob Hunsaker had come to Everett in 1892 and put the entire cash accumulation of his thrifty life into real estate. He ran his lots up to one thousand dollars each, then saw them drop to twenty-five dollars with no buyers. When he lost his new home and rented a small house for ten dollars a month, his only son had to quit school and work in a lumber mill for a dollar a day. But the mill too was soon defunct. Yet when Hunsaker became mayor in the bleak hour of 1894, he could say sincerely that "Our city is built upon the heads of corporations, by them conceived and rocked in the cradle of their nursery . . . their interest and that of the humblest citizen cannot but be identical." [5]

The bitterness he was trying to suppress could not be put down. The rector of the Episcopal Church, standing on ground donated to his parish by the Everett Land Company, was soon speaking out against the evils of "heartless monopolies" and "heartless capitalists." In 1894, an angry group of men had formed a local chapter of the Farmers' Alliance and Industrial Union, and they immediately excluded from their membership all "bankers, lawyers, and saloonkeepers." John W. Frame, editor of the *Democrat*, faced the gloom around him and took a more comprehensive inventory of villainy, beginning with the "infernal nature of the traitorous banking class." Looking beyond the rascals, he told his readers that "the industrial classes of our country are waking up to the fact that there is something wrong, but many do not understand the operations of our false industrial system." He thought he understood, for he had studied law and taught

school and read the speeches of Eugene Debs. The most last-
ing impact of the collapse of Everett on the minds of its
citizens—and the grim legacy that shadowed the bloody Everett Massacre two decades hence—was the bitter radicalism
for which Frame became the most articulate spokesman.

III

A Radical Response

IKE almost everyone, John W. Frame had been around
the bay only a few years. Born in rural Illinois, he had
attended a "mercantile" school for a year or so, then was a
postmaster and real estate clerk. Later on, he had been a
teacher and a principal in elementary schools, then a newspaper editor. In 1889 at the age of thirty-five he graduated
in law from the University of Iowa. He apparently never
opened a law office, for immediately after taking his degree
he left Iowa for Old Ferg's Snohomish, where he became
managing editor for the Snohomish *Sun*. From this position
he leaped quickly into politics, which was probably always
his goal. As a Democrat, he went to the state legislature in
1891, where he demanded attention by charging that the
forces behind Watson C. Squire had offered three thousand
dollars for Frame's vote for United States Senator. But Wash-

ington was not yet a good state for reformers, and Frame did not get his scandal. Defeated that year, Frame settled back to his editing and to watching Everett emerge only a few miles down the river.

His *Snohomish County Democrat* began to appear weekly in Everett in 1895. Like many western newspapers, the *Democrat* offered its readers a blunt but adequate instrument for verbal aggression, one particularly effective during this time of rising hostilities. Frame saw himself as a Democrat of the most virile Jacksonian persuasion. He was never reluctant to present himself as the conscience of common decency and the common man. He stood bitterly opposed to "hard times, high taxes, and boodleism." He took a Jacksonian pride in irreverence and invective, and a high delight in striking directly at the substance and the style of the community's aristocracy. Show him a woman, he said, who is crying for an ordinance against keeping cows in the city, "and we will show you one who drives a bob-tailed horse, wears bloomers, and takes subscriptions for Armenians while poor people under her nose are starving to death."

This was but a mild beginning. When William C. Butler opened the doors of the Everett Commercial Club, Frame described its membership as that class of men who do not pay their bills, who desert their wives, yet always wear clean shirts and new shoes. The opening night, he wrote, was "the most notorious drunken carousal that ever occurred in Everett . . . should our wife ever become an attendant at the Commercial Club rooms on a ladies' night, we would apply for a divorce the next morning."

John Frame's view of Jacksonian morality was that he should stand straight for God, party, and the common man, and that he should forever battle against prostitution, special privilege, Republicans, and the "wine-woman-nigger saloon" society. He supported the Good Citizens' League and opposed "all those things which tend to degrade humanity and impoverish our citizens." Most of these things, he was convinced, originated with the upper classes. If prostitutes were to be driven from the town, as the Good Citizens' League urged, then Frame would send along with them those "respectable" ladies who spent their nights playing "cross-legged whist" with "amorous bank clerks." If the clergy would support him, they were welcome to do so, he wrote, but he warned that "unless the preachers of Everett cease their preaching for John D. Rockefeller's sake and do a little more for Christ's sake, the kingdom of Heaven will never be established on this sand pit."

His view of Everett and all he saw there was in every way refracted through an obsession with the moral purity of the common man, and he usually drew a viciously straight line from what he regarded as moral squalor to an equal depth of political debauchery. Republican candidates, he observed, reminded him of illustrations in "a Lost Manhood advertisement." When the two ministers of the gospel who had earlier helped him close the Gold Leaf brothel both announced for William McKinley in 1896, Frame found it remarkable that such a change could have overtaken two men in so short a time. When a Republican judge dismissed charges of embezzlement against a banker, Frame wrote that the banker had "slept with his honor that night. Lord, how close those two fellows must have slept." And shortly thereafter when another banker did go to jail, Frame counted "one vote less for McKinley." More and more fascinated by events in the superior court, Frame saw another Everett man convicted of raping his own young daughter. When the man was freed by the court on a legal technicality, Frame editorialized outrageously that "Republicans can check up one more Republican vote."

When the Republican *Herald* choked on these blasts, Frame conceded that its editor was not "an absolute, unmistakable fool, but having the requisite inborn talent for folly, there is no pinnacle of dullness to which he may not soar." When an anonymous letter-writer told Frame that "your dirty Soul is So mean and Small that you cannot tell the truth," Frame gleefully printed his letter. It must have been clear to most readers that his editorial soul did have a malicious and even sadistic twist. He gloried in rape stories, printing apparently all that he could find anywhere. Then he would demand that if rapists were tortured and burned in Texas, those who rape cities in Washington should be similarly burned. And before burning, they should have their hands cut off for signing fraudulent warrants, their tongues cut out for violating their oaths of office. Nor did he hesitate to print stories of adultery and divorce, naming the principals and detailing the circumstances. He wrote of venereal disease among teenagers, of child brides, of insanity and suicide—all, as he saw it, the daily offal of a rotten system. In a rather obvious way, he was writing the pornography of social protest. Or in a more generous word, Frame was a frontier Puritan, damning and punishing, insisting that people open their eyes and look straight at the reality of evil as he saw it and call it by its right name.

Another rival called the *Democrat* the most ably edited but also the "most anarchist sheet in the state." This charge was based in part upon Frame's obvious sympathy for those who said they had to steal in order to eat. When an Everett woman killed herself because, she had written, her husband could not feed his family, Frame wrote that she had been murdered by those who made it impossible for them to earn a living. If this was anarchism, he added, "make the most of it." When a millowner imported "leprous Chinese" to work his lumber in Tacoma, Frame said the capitalist was destroying the only thing white workingmen had—their labor. He noted that white workers could also destroy with fire what the capitalist had in lumber and mills.

In all of this verbal violence, Frame's hatreds were predictable—bankers, industrialists, Republicans, Chinese. And he was no isolated crank. A visceral unrest in the United States had already found voices in Ben Tillman, Henry Demarest Lloyd, John Peter Altgeld, Ignatius Donnelly, and Eugene Debs. Out of a broad American experience, wage earners and small entrepreneurs brought to Everett their anxieties about the corporate control of their lives. In the decade before 1896, monopolistic pricing, urban slums, immigration, the Pullman strike, Coxey's Army, and that fallen symbol of purity, the silver dollar, had turned millions besides John Frame away from politeness and restraint. In every election after 1890, the Populists gained votes from Americans who felt an urgency in their desire to lash out against their known or unknown oppressors. In the state of Washington, there were more Populists voting in 1894 than there were Democrats. The Populists' cause had issued largely from the depths of agrarian grievances in the wheat counties, but the cities also had their real griefs.

On New Year's Day, 1896, Frame resolved never to vote Democratic again. Cleveland, he said, had destroyed prosperity and "bonded the country to the Rothschild syndicate" of gold and corruption. He invited his readers to follow him into the People's party where he saw the Jacksonian heritage alive and vital. Frame took the leadership of the county organization, then became its delegate to the state convention in the year that the Fusion ticket of Populists and reform Democrats won the state.

That year Everett was still a superstructure of industry sitting uneasily on a corner of a region that was not so much agricultural as frontier. In the countryside beyond the city there were fewer farmers than squatters on "stump farms," lone loggers, shingle splitters, and Indians. As county chairman, Frame had said that his new party was made up of "ranchers"—surely a depression euphemism—and "loggers, shingle weavers, laboring men." But his constituency was primarily in and of a broken city. On another occasion, he described his readers as "laboring people and shop keepers," and this was an accurate description. The candidates he supported for city offices were men like James Leonard, a carpenter; Bryan Majors, a "civil engineer"; James Lafreniere, "tonsorial artist"; Thomas Napier, mechanic; Frank Call, insurance salesman; and Joe Waldron, a hotel keeper.

In speaking to and for such people, Frame was articulating his own distinctly urban response to the painful failures of the American economic system after 1893. He was, first and last, a polemicist, not a theorist. In a single issue he could discover that "land is the source of all wealth"—an insight neither unique nor very perceptive in 1896—then rush on to attack the "criminal levels of municipal indebtedness" or to bark viciously at the Commercial Club, businessmen, and the "smokestack gang." In scores of such editorials one can trace the barbed perimeters of what populism meant in Everett.

Contrary to his clichés about land and wealth, Frame was no romantic agrarian. At the center of his anger was a conviction that industrialization had been the most significant step in human history because of its potential for relieving drudgery and enhancing the quality of human life. From his position on a frontier where natural resources had only recently become available for industrial exploitation, he saw the railroads as the "greatest invention of human intelligence." But he knew the bite on the common man of preferential rating and monopolies, and he said that the capitalist class was using the railroads "to plunder, not to ennoble."

Yet he was not in any consistent way a Marxist. When in 1896 the price of nails in Everett rose from $.85 to $2.80 a hundred pounds, and wages in the nail factory rose not at all, Frame called this simply "robbery." When he read about progress and poverty in New York City, where, he learned, a machine had replaced three hundred workers in a cigarette factory, he said that a tariff would not help the wage earners, but owning the machine certainly would. At times he called for "public control" of all land and major industry; at other times he wanted "public ownership" of all property "used for the benefit of the public." He was no philosopher of the

frontier proletariat. To him, theory was always less significant than rhetoric, and results more important than either.

Free silver, for example, was to Frame only a device—
greenbacks would have done as well—to get money into the
hands of people who would buy groceries. He saw the gold
standard as "the gold rule against the liberties of the people,"
which meant, more concretely, "high taxes, starvation, corruption." Other devices he urged were the Australian ballot,
which he said would protect Everett's railroad workers from
the Republicans, and the initiative and referendum, which,
by allowing the people themselves to vote on all legislation,
would achieve what he called "public control."

This was the sum of Frame's radical critique. It was less a
systematic body of thought than a point of view, generated
out of local circumstances and grievances. It placed justice
and opportunity higher than order or tradition. His ideas
were somewhat more radical than the Omaha Platform of the
People's party, and they were similarly to the left of the
state Populist platform—more urban than rural, more industrial than agrarian. He never showed interest in the postal
savings banks, in soldiers' pensions, or in the breaking of
land monopolies called for by the national Populists at
Omaha. He never commented on the farmers' demands for
non-interest-bearing warrants receivable for taxes, laws against
railroad passes, tax exemptions for personal property, lower
salaries for state officials, or women's suffrage. He never commented, in fact, on the Washington State Grange. In a sense
he had stripped the Populist platforms of their more rural
concerns and taken their radical core for his appeal to the
labor and shopkeeper vote in Everett.

This may be why Frame never wrote an editorial about
John R. Rogers, the Populist who became the governor of
Washington in 1897. There was, at first glance, much in the
man for Frame to admire. Rogers was also an editor and
publisher, a pamphleteer and novelist, a liberal reformer who
was unquestionably the most intellectual Populist on Frame's

horizon. Rogers' liberalism, however, was more purely Jeffersonian. He saw agriculture as a morally superior way of life, and he thought that agrarians were morally superior people. To hold land was to Rogers an inalienable right, and he wanted those who worked the land to dominate American society. Rogers wanted the Restoration. His was the sincere faith of a man who read Jefferson and Emerson and wanted his sons to be farmers, but it came out in 1896 like a trumpet of doom that assembled a legion of tax-cursing, bank-bitten, anti-urban fanatics who expected Rogers to restore the simple life that Jim Hill had spoiled. Rogers gathered around him the more wild and blank-eyed of the state anti-industrial prophets, behind whom stood the stern ranks of prohibitionists and Catholic haters.

These followers turned Frame cold. He saw nothing sacred in private property or even in agriculture, and he questioned the relevance of the agrarians' faith in individuality, in self-reliance, and in "moral and spiritual" reform. He detested the anti-Catholic paranoia that was even then becoming endemic. There were indeed many aspects of the Rogers candidacy that Frame, as an urban radical, might have torn apart. But he had cursed the Democrats and hoped to live with the Populists of his state. In 1896 he ignored John Rogers, jeered at capitalism, and praised Debs.[1]

One of the most significant distinctions between Everett's populism and the protest that thrived in rural areas was Frame's relentless attack on the American Protective Association. His stand against the anti-Catholic movement could not have been easy for an urban politician who knew that anti-Catholicism was exceptionally strong in the states from which most Washington voters had so recently come—Minnesota, Wisconsin, and Illinois. These new residents could hear Southern European languages around the mills and on the streets; if properly instructed, they could fear that an ancient fatalism and all that they could imagine about parochial schools and convents were a threat to new-world purity and American self-reliance. They could hear these languages in their new neighborhoods and fear that the Catholic Church, as rumor had it, was actually plotting to fill the western states with men who would vote according to instructions from Rome. This fear and hatred had a particularly strong appeal to Northern European immigrants eager to demonstrate their Americanism, and many Norwegians, Swedes, and Danes in the state too easily accepted fear and suspicion as a basis for political consciousness in their new homes.

In the summer of 1893, the APA movement had been sufficiently cultivated by depression and agitators to bloom in Seattle, where one-sixth of the population was Italian. Other cities seemed to welcome the APA organizers. By 1896, the state APA had enrolled one of every four voters. What the APA intended, of course, was to keep Catholics out of public life, and it tried to control schools, hospitals, elective offices, and patronage. In Seattle, Spokane, and Tacoma, members of the APA dominated the school boards. Spokane had an APA mayor who was determined that no city jobs should go to Catholics. In 1894, members of the APA held a majority in the state legislature, and they elected John Wilson, from the APA "roll of honor," to the United States Senate.

APA leadership in the state of Washington was a remarkable mixture of fanatics, businessmen, professional men, and politicians who used the APA for their own self-interest. They moved naturally toward the Republican party, which was the obvious source of power. In 1896, they were strong in the areas most susceptible to populism, and the delicate balances of three-party politics gave the APA politicians an unexpected weight. At the Republican and the Populist conventions in 1896, APA discipline was everywhere a matter of concern. The Populist-Democratic Fusion ticket became particularly vulnerable to APA infiltration when the association made a direct appeal to reform-minded rural delegates by endorsing the political program of the Washington State Grange: woman's suffrage, prohibition, and direct legislation.

When Frame first settled in Everett, the APA had already applied pressures to have the federal government close a Catholic school which had for years served the Indian families at Tulalip. The APA controlled the city school board and was making the most of the confusion in county and municipal politics. Among the Democrats whom Frame found in city politics, old Bourbons like Henry Hewitt still dominated, but the wage earners were rebelling against them. The Republicans too were split between the "silk stocking" corporation crowd and the small businessmen—arguing taxes, free silver, reform, patronage, and municipal contracts. "Apaism," as Frame called it, easily infected every dispute or debate. Frame was infuriated by the political behavior of many recent immigrants from Norway, Sweden, Germany, and England—some of them unable to speak English—who had swallowed "Apaism" and were incanting "America for Americans" against the local Catholics, most of whom were native-born.

Frame immediately used his editorials to condemn "government by resolutions adopted in secret meeting . . . municipal policies adopted, county affairs conducted, courts controlled by grip and password." He tried to expose the unpublicized precinct meetings which excluded those who had shown no sympathy for the APA. Business and professional men, he wrote, were joining the APA in fear of losing business or in hope of gaining it. "Religious bigotry and plutocracy," he said, always go hand in hand. He scorned the Commercial Club, where, he said, businessmen spent their time "drinking whiskey and licking Catholics." In city and county politics, he wrote, the APA was a "Republican annex." He despaired for justice in a county where many citizens were Catholic and where the judge and the prosecutor were both "high APA muck-a-muck."

During the campaign for city offices in 1895—before he had converted to populism—Frame had attacked the APA control of the Populist ticket and rejoiced to see that ticket defeated by six votes. Six Populists, he said, who had been "patriotic enough" to cross over to the "citizens' ticket" of reforming Democrats and Republicans, had saved the day. Then in 1896, as a new party leader, he wrote into the Everett Populist platform a strong resolution condemning the American Protective Association, but he could not carry this through the county or state conventions. His failure may explain why he himself was not nominated for any state office that year. Deeply alarmed by the extent of "Apaism" among the Populists, Frame approached the Fusionists with considerable distrust. He frankly suspected their presidential candidate, William Jennings Bryan, of being anti-Catholic, and he feared that even the concept of Fusion had come from scheming APA leaders who hoped to use the Populists as a front. If Populists allowed themselves to be so used, he wrote, they would become prostitutes for the Democrats who wanted "marriage on the European plan"—respectability and convenience for a brief season.[2]

A city radical surrounded by Bryanites, Frame attended the Fusion convention in obvious discomfort. With no grace at all, he muttered that Bryan might be a better Populist than he was a Democrat and that Tom Watson, the raging southern radical whom the Populists had chosen as their vice-presidential candidate, was "the coming Andrew Jackson." But he seemed mostly to ignore the national ticket and to rake carefully instead across the local field, with a special focus on the APA. He pointed out, for example, how the Populist candidates for county clerk, county coroner, and state legislative representative were all APA members and former Republicans who had sneaked over on the free-silver line to escape McKinley, that "damned old man from Ohio."

It was remarkable to Frame how the cause of coining silver at a ratio of sixteen to one could be sublimated into a transcendental equation in which silver became the good, the pure, and the sublimely American. With some glee he saw that many silver Republicans believed that "free silver" would not simply end the depression, it would cleanse the American soul. While Frame resented the pollution of reform sentiment that occurred when these tortured individuals crossed over, their agony did give him moments of real satisfaction. When the county McKinley Club sought a chairman, the members turned inevitably to the pioneer prestige of Emory C. Ferguson, the county's first Republican. Old Ferg took the honor graciously, but in his acceptance speech before a full audience of state and county dignitaries, he identified himself as a "16 to 1 Republican." After some embarrassment, the club found another leader.

For Frame there were many such delicious moments. Shortly before the election, William C. Butler, who was also a state Republican official, went to some effort to pay his smelter employees their weekly wages in silver coin so that they might learn the horrors of a soft economy. Frame watched carefully, then reported that what the workers had learned from Butler was that when they could work, they could pay their bills, and silver was as good as gold. He delighted to report that the silver issue had caused the editor of the Republican *Times* to lose even his rhetorical stability. When Butler addressed an Everett audience one evening before the election, someone in the back of the hall lifted a rebel yell which gave the *Times* a fitful vision of bloody treason. "In 1861," said the *Times*, "the rebel yell meant . . . dismemberment of the union. In 1896, it means Tillmanism, Altgeldism, Bryanism, political and moral suicide, Socialism,

Frontier and industry, 1892 (Photos courtesy of Everett Community College Library)

Law and order, *circa* 1903 (Photo courtesy of *Everett Herald*)

Hewitt Avenue, 1908 (Photo courtesy of Everett Community College Library)

Communism, dishonor, disgrace, shame . . . the death of the republic."

In October, the nail factory began production again after a long pause, then closed abruptly just before election day. Mark Hanna's orders, said Frame. On the night before the polls opened, torchlight parades passed each other in the streets without incident. The next day Everett voters, as did the state's majority, chose Fusion. The county total for Fusion was 2,792, against 1,816 for Republicans, but in the city the majority was only 42 votes.

Frame publicly rejoiced in the state and local victories, but he saw little hope for the country under President William McKinley. Some of his friends, he announced, were going to Mexico to avoid "McKinley confidence." In December, when the local Fusion fell apart and allowed a Republican victory in the city elections, Frame showed little concern. He noted a quiet Christmas. He lingered a while into the new year, scraping a living from a dying newspaper. But when the first word of Klondike gold sparkled over those dreary days, he was off for Alaska and a new life.[3]

Frame's dedication to populism left him few enduring satisfactions. The thin majority of forty-two wage earners and shopkeepers who had seen his truth was no triumphant measure of his skill, and the election of APA members of the Fusion ticket to county and state offices in 1896 was indeed a measure of his failure. Fusion had clearly not integrated the different perspectives of city radicals and agrarian restorers. John Frame, like many others across the country, felt that meaningful change had been compromised by bigotry and Bourbonism. But the sorry showing for urban reform in Everett may have occurred because the real radicals had left on empty box cars before the election. The moderates who stayed chopped their wood and ate their fish, wait-

ing not for revolution but for the return of better days.
They distrusted the silver symbol and heard in Bryan a dusty
wind blowing through the wheat fields, not the clear voice
of industrial or urban necessity. Or, quite simply, they knew
that their futures, as the Republicans were saying, depended
upon the confidence of those whom the Populists were attacking—corporations and investors. If Rockefeller or even Jim
Hill wanted McKinley, why kick at them to vote with Frame?

John W. Frame had tried to make populism the Jacksonian
movement of his day—a call to strike at corruption and
privilege, to restore to the republic an iron sense of right and
wrong, to equate again freedom with opportunity. Yet beneath the sentiment there was a current of radicalism that
had little to do with the older verities of Jacksonian America.
In an industrial age, Frame was increasingly impatient with
the institutions of private property, the profit motive, and
all their sacred vestments. He was increasingly drawn to a
violent language that suggested violent passions, increasingly
willing to make final judgements or to accept the final conflict: rich against poor, property rights against human rights,
capitalist against wage slave. He did not openly urge men to
steal, shoot, and burn, but this seems to have been his strong
inclination. He wanted to crush evil with a club, to persecute
wickedness with a sword; he could be utterly without com-
passion. This was a fearful legacy for the next generation of
radicals in Everett and for those—radical and reactionary
alike—whose equally fierce righteousness converged twenty
years later in the Everett Massacre.

As Frame left the city, F. T. Gates was proving to Rockefeller that the industrial base of Everett rested upon myth
and foolishness if not fraud or deception: the nail factory
had no iron, the smelter had no ores, the shipyard had no
market, the fresh water harbor, emptied daily by the tides, had
no river channel that ships could negotiate. In 1897, Gates
dropped the Everett Land Company into receivership and the
angry clutches of its creditors. Two years later, on the steps of

the county courthouse built by the company, an auctioneer released the frail assets that remained for $15,000 in cash and $750,000 in the company's own bonds, then quite worthless. In these figures and in the quiet fall of a gavel, Henry Hewitt's dream was finally buried.

But those who watched from the courthouse steps—the wage earners and shopkeepers who remembered both Hewitt and Frame—knew that the gavel sounded a new hope. McKinley had indeed brought confidence, just as the Klondike had brought gold, and a war had brought the pulse of a new century. The man who delivered the bonds was, curiously, Wyatt J. Rucker, who nine years before had imposed upon Henry Hewitt the conditions which had that day brought his ruin. On that day Wyatt J. Rucker was representing James J. Hill.

In the next few months, Hill quickly swept up the wreckage. He organized the Everett Improvement Company, which would be the symbol of the new era. There was much to be improved, but to Hill it was a reasonable business proposition. With Rockefeller and the others gone, Hill opened his ambitious plans for a "city of smokestacks" at Port Gardner Bay.

IV

The Sawdust Baronage

||||||||||||||||||||||||||||||||||||||||||||||||||||||||||||||||||||||||||||||||||||||||

NO LESS than Rockefeller, Jim Hill demanded style and performance. His man in Everett was John T. McChesney, who after 1899 managed the interests of the Everett Improvement Company. Then forty-two years old, McChesney had come from upper-class Virginia and held a master's degree from Washington and Lee University. He had behind him impressive administrative achievements as a banker, as a town developer, as mayor of Aberdeen, South Dakota, and as an investor in lands and industry. He commanded respect from Minneapolis to New York, where he had been known for years as a personal friend of the Empire Builder.

McChesney came to Everett with his family and served as a sort of viceroy over the landholdings, the water and electrical systems, the streetcars, the docks, the theaters, and the American National Bank that Hill wanted salvaged from

the Hewitt and Rockefeller remnants. Though these enterprises yielded handsome returns, they were all subordinate
to Hill's master plan for the Northwest empire—and McChesney's mandate in the province of Everett—to build cities
that would work the timber from the vast land grants of the
Northern Pacific and feed freight to the Great Northern
Railroad.

Among McChesney's first obligations, then, was to accommodate a new oligarchy. Foremost of the new entrepreneurial
elite was Frederick Weyerhaeuser, whose enormous resources
and brilliant organizational techniques had made him the most
powerful timber industrialist in the nation even before the
Great Northern reached west. While living in St. Paul,
Weyerhaeuser had spent many a long winter evening together
with his neighbor, James J. Hill, discussing the decline of
the timber industry in the Mississippi Valley and the almost
incalculable promise of the Puget Sound country. When
Weyerhaeuser finally concluded that he should move geo-
graphically as well as conceptually into the twentieth century,
his relocation marked a major transition in a major industry.

Weyerhaeuser organized the Sound Lumber Company in
1899. In 1900 he negotiated with Hill one of the largest land
transactions—and most fantastic bargains—in American history: nine hundred thousand acres of timber from the Northern Pacific land grants at six dollars an acre, a price estimated
then as about ten cents a thousand feet for the wood. To
exploit his forests, Weyerhaeuser organized the Weyerhaeuser
Timber Company and ordered the company's first major
construction in Everett. The new mill had no equal. It was
the largest lumber mill in the world, and it expanded steadily,
increasing production from twenty-eight million feet in 1902
to seventy million in 1912. This mill alone could have supported a growing city.[1]

But the Weyerhaeuser move was only the beginning. By
1900 Hill had also convinced David M. Clough, a former
governor of Minnesota, to relocate on Puget Sound. Clough

was then fifty-four years old and had already made and lost a fortune in Minnesota timber. Widely regarded as one of the toughest and shrewdest of the timber capitalists, Clough could work with the energy of a man thirty years his junior. He had the confidence of a statesman of the Weyerhaeuser generation, and he knew, as Hill knew, that money from Minnesota would follow his reputation.

Clough was borne to Everett in Hill's private car and received there in imperial elegance by McChesney. He liked what he saw. He soon organized the Clark-Nickerson Lumber Company, in which two of his former associates were major investors, and built for it a new mill which, as a model of its kind, attracted national attention. Then he brought forth the Clough-Hartley Company and the Clough-Whitney Company to cut both lumber and shingles. The Clough-Hartley Mill dominated the waterfront on bayside and was soon the greatest producer of red cedar shingles in the world. Around these major mills, Clough formed a galaxy of milling and logging outfits, some solid, some ephemeral, all of them in constant change. Clough was driven by a commanding view of himself as a strong man among men and by intense personal and family loyalties. He made his own lieutenants, and he became the patriarch of the new aristocracy.

The first to follow Clough was his son-in-law, Roland H. Hartley, a Canadian by birth who had worked his way up to power in the Clough family enterprises in Minnesota. In Everett he took assignments willingly from the older man, and invested heavily in Clark-Nickerson, Clough-Hartley, and several of the satellites, especially the logging companies.

After Roland Hartley there were nephews, cousins, brothers, and friends. David Clough's extended family came to include five male Cloughs and six male Hartleys, nearly all of them working for the grandfather and for each other in an intricately related aggregate of ambitions. The Hartley-Lovejoy Logging Company, for example, logged land owned by Clark-Nickerson and sold to the Clark-Nickerson Mill. The

Everett Logging Company and the Irving-Hartley Logging Company bought timber rights from—and sold logs to—Clough-Hartley, Clark-Nickerson, and the Hartley Shingle Company. Though baronial in its patterns, this extended family was loose enough to include a few others who clearly shared the family values and energies. It accepted, for example, Fred Baker, who had come from Detroit to operate the Ferry-Baker Mill on the waterfront next to Clough-Hartley, and Baker's son-in-law W. G. Hulburt, who built next to Ferry-Baker, and Harry Stuchell, who came in 1902 to build the Eclipse, which he managed with his sons.

Though these men might compete for quality, and though some of them would not hesitate to grab off a quick profit while the others fumbled, the various members of the larger Everett family never really confronted each other as economic enemies. It was natural that the major industrialists in the city should develop a community of interest, and if they were occasionally ruthless to outsiders, they would not casually violate the values of loyalty and friendship. It was, moreover, obvious to them that in any direct or enduring individual challenge among them, the community had too much to lose and the individuals had too little to gain. Their logs came usually from the same sources, and there were usually enough to go around. They all produced for the same distant markets which they could seldom anticipate and never control. For Clough to have cut Baker, for example, when there were so many hundreds of competitors beyond his reach, would have been shocking and thoughtlessly vicious. If these men used cutthroat techniques, as surely at one time or another they must have done, their intended victims were the hundreds of smaller producers whose cyclic existence and price-cutting so often led the timber industry toward endemic frustration.

Of those outside the blood and marriage lines of the Clough family, Joseph Irving probably developed the closest relationship with the patriarch and his many interests. Irving left the management of the Monte Cristo and his own teamster busi-

ness and became variously the president or vice-president of
the Standard Railway and Timber Company, the Sultan Railway and Timber Company, the Monroe Logging Company,
the South River Lumber Company, the Irving Shingle Company, and the Irving-Hartley Logging Company. Some of these
were, of course, short-lived partnerships formed to cut specific
stands of timber and then forgotten. Others employed as
many as four hundred men for as long as a decade. Irving was
a huge, powerful, roaming terror of a man who could drive
four hundred loggers to unprecedented performances. He
was also a warmly personable and intelligent man, and he
moved easily toward the upper circle.

Though Jim Hill and McChesney encouraged these men
with free mill sites, cheap timber land, and reduced rail rates,
Hill was not their financier. As they felt a need to buttress
their investments or expand their operations—and they were
usually expanding or contracting at a frenzied pace—they
became increasingly dependent upon William C. Butler, who
was in many respects the most imperious of Everett's new
rulers. Butler, like Irving, was a significant survivor of the old
era. From mining engineering to smelter management to adviser to F. T. Gates, he had participated in the rise and fall of
the Rockefeller interests. A Rockefeller protégé, he not only
came from a prominent New York family, he married into
another. Though he was only twenty-seven years old when
the depression struck, Butler had maybe one hundred thousand dollars to invest after 1893. He emerged from the lean
years as the president of two financial houses, the Everett
First National Bank and the Everett Trust and Savings Bank,
and was soon a very wealthy man.

When almost everything in Everett was new and built on
borrowed money, Butler had the money. And when most
loans were short-term notes of demand, subject to renewal at
the discretion of the banker, Butler held a kind of power that
Renaissance princes might have envied. Though inevitably he
walked behind the image of a cold, hard, bloodless tyrant and

was widely regarded as the meanest son-of-a-bitch in town, he accepted this image with a certain pleasure. A fine indifference to popular fancy was but one of his many personal resources.

The millowners likewise cultivated their own individualities. They were, however, with the exception of the older Clough, all about forty years old, all proud, vigorous, and highly motivated toward measurable success. As a group, they presented an easy congruence of interests and backgrounds that invites a close sociological portrait.

With the Everett millowners, however, there are specific hazards to group portraiture. In the first place—and this is the first stroke of a portrait—they left no records. There is today no remaining archival evidence of their milling or logging operations, no private papers, no public papers, no correspondence, no day books, no diaries, no autobiographies. For the most part they kept few such records even while they were active. Clough, whose operations were perhaps the most complex, kept his short- and long-term records in his head and in his vest pockets. The others cared as little for bookkeeping or any other tools for analysis, and they systematically avoided them. And whatever they did leave behind them was methodically rather than casually destroyed. They were men to whom privacy was a proof of character. They regarded their various business ventures and industrial operations as ultimate expressions of their very private lives, and they took steps to determine that these lives would not be open to contemporary or future curiosity.

Of the principals, Roland Hartley was most in the newspapers—as industrialist, then as mayor, as legislator, and in the 1920s as governor of the state. He was always an articulate and even flamboyant spokesman for the cast-iron Republican industrial conservatism he chose to defend. He never hesitated to give his opinions or attitudes about business, labor unions, social workers, reformers, society, the state, or the nation. But even so, he was at best devious in his self-revelations. He always claimed proudly to be a "self-made" man, though surely his marriage to Nina Clough and the paternal instincts of her father had been significant factors in his advance to fame and fortune. He claimed a political experience and popularity in Minnesota which today cannot be documented. During his mature years, he always presented himself prominently for military and patriotic honors, and he wore the title "colonel" with a pugnacious pride. But his appointment to that rank was largely a ceremonial gesture by the governor of Minnesota, his father-in-law, and it never brought him a command or took him to a field of battle.

For a quarter of a century Hartley demanded to be heard and respected as a business and industrial leader whose long experience in vital matters had prepared him to govern in a businessman's society. Yet he was never president or even manager of any of the companies with which he was associated. He worked, to be sure, but it was Clough who made the major administrative decisions. In fact Hartley showed no apparent interest in the processes of business or in the dynamics of industrial management. His life moved in a line toward wealth and then toward political power. There is, however, no hard evidence to mark this line. Upon his death, his son David destroyed the full truckload of private papers that had survived Hartley's years in Everett and the statehouse. Quite deliberately, the historical substance of his character and personality was buried with him.

As a corollary to such principles of inviolable privacy, these men held to an equally fierce individualism and were similarly determined to prevent any personal or institutional interference with their conduct of their own affairs. It was said of Governor Clough in Minnesota that "men who sought to change his mind were often disappointed." This was no less true in Everett, where this quality became a distinguishing characteristic of his closest associates. The Clough family ideals were personified in the career of Weyerhaeuser, or, more warmly and dramatically, of F. Agustus Heinze of Montana, who would fight even Rockefeller. They admired this pirate of the copper wars because of what their Everett newspaper called his "unlimited physical and financial nerve," because he demonstrated the moral glory of uninhibited courage and energy.

Clough, who was as strong-willed as Weyerhaeuser and as ambitious as Heinze, would have duplicated their accomplishments if he had only been given the opportunity. He had fled the bleak future of a New England farm to make his way in the West, and no man, no tradition, would stop him. Hartley had left Canada; Baker, rural New York; Stuchell, Pennsylvania. Their folk hero was a giant who honored no home and no master. They had, they felt, escaped a hard grip of poverty and ignorance, seized the circumstances of their own existences, and found identity in being free to make the most of bonanza. This was the freedom they were so determined to keep. It was against men like Clough, Hartley, and Butler that the Populist revolt had been directed.

Theirs was also an individualism that settled easily into a stiff class-consciousness. Believing that they had won both their responsibilities and their prerogatives on individual merit, they were impelled by an almost sacred obligation to protect their achievements from the envy of those less meritorious. In what they did and said there was an implicit paternal contempt for those who never rose above the level of the semi-skilled labor they demanded in their mills; it is clear that they hated labor unions and all that unions represented. Their attitude toward wage earners was well reflected in the basic rules for the Weyerhaeuser logging camps: no liquor—for workers are irresponsible; no weapons—for wage earners cannot reason; no conversations at meal times—for common men have no discipline; no thermometers in the camp—for what they don't know won't hurt them. To keep an edge on tradition, George Long of the Weyerhaeuser Company would arbitrarily fire groups of his loggers in 1908 as a warning to others who, he thought, were becoming too independent. During several crises the Clough group established their intention to close their mills forever before recognizing that their employees had any legitimate interest in the administration of these mills. It was their misfortune, perhaps, to live in an age when men confused property with character.

One factor in these harsh attitudes may have been that the mill barons of Everett were men of little formal schooling, and that they took an arrogant pride in achieving so much without the standard equipment of educated men. The senior Clough, even when governor, was at best semiliterate. He overpowered grammar with his clarity of purpose and presence of command, and no one of his friends or enemies ever thought this a disadvantage. Hartley's education did not extend beyond several primary grades. At the age of fourteen, he had been a hotel clerk; at fifteen, a cook's helper in a logging camp; at sixteen, a logger driving four-horse teams. In his early twenties he had spent part of a year at the Minneapolis Academy studying bookkeeping and penmanship, and thereafter it never occurred to him that he might not appropriately correspond with university presidents. Irving, likewise, had no more than a few grades, and he never went to an academy. Baker and Stuchell were unusual in that they had graduated from American high schools. They were all, like Weyerhaeuser, organizers and administrators, not technologists and never innovators. They used the existing system. Their achievements came through the convergence of personal discipline, tight organization, and fantastic luck. Part of the luck was that intellectuality was not demanded of timber men of their generation.

In fact they could with impunity hold education in contempt. Somewhere in the Clough-Hartley configuration of values was a sort of Latin *machismo*—the assumed necessity for a man to test himself and define his worth through demonstrations of masculine will, courage, aggressiveness, sexuality, and physical prowess. Joe Irving, six-foot-one and 250 pounds, roared through his camps on an apocryphal two quarts of whisky, two women, and twenty-five cigars a day as he hired, fired, and knocked heads, bought, sold, traded, cut, or burned at a moment's decision. He did the work of ten men, all the while cursing unions, professors, taxes, lawyers, and politicians. Herbert Clough once grabbed a planer's knife and almost killed a man who had been drunkenly insubordinate to him in his uncle's mill. Hartley, a diminutive five-foot-six and 140 pounds, cruised the woods with a speed and gusto that, to his pleasure, exhausted larger and younger men. In his fifties he swore that he never gave a worker a job that he could not do better himself. A man who could not earn a living with sweat and muscle, he would say, "wasn't worth a shit." His more public profanities later scandalized state legislatures and even shocked newspaper editors, who had to censor almost everything he ever said.

There is yet another expression of values to be seen in the organizations with which the Clough group affiliated. They were, without exception, Masons, Elks, members of the Country Club, the Cascade Club, and the Republican party. Their religious affiliations cannot be identified, except that the male Cloughs and Hartleys never associated themselves with any organized church. Theirs was, in a sense, the religion of the White Anglo-Saxon Protestant ethic as defined in what Clough did and said, and as ritualistically celebrated at the Elk's Club or in the more sacrosanct rooms of the Cascade.[2]

This ethic—especially the premium value of physical and financial nerve—was reinforced daily by the industrial conditions which the Clough group was in part creating. They had brought with them to the Northwest a heavy indebtedness for their capitalization, which meant that their operations had to pay, and pay well, according to a rigid schedule. There were at the same time and across the entire region similar groups in similar circumstances, all in riotous competition. Even around Puget Sound there were too many groups and too many trees. The sheer abundance of the frontier made industrial capitalism a sick system.

After 1900, Jim Hill had brought so many timber men and opened so many forests that the industry was fearfully overexpanded and afflicted with chronic overproduction. When prices dropped, most operators had to cut more wood than before to pay their debts. It was a mad world in which a diminishing demand for their products and a falling price level forced hundreds of millowners to produce twenty-four hours a day until a glutted market refused to take another stick or shingle.

Only the Weyerhaeusers had any degree of control over the vertical scope of the industry. Their two million acres of timber, their command of the capital necessary for increasingly efficient technology and, occasionally, for nonprofitable production, their accumulated sophistication of managerial talent—these advantages allowed them to plan grandly for the sustained yield of centuries. They were almost postcapitalistic from their beginning in the Northwest because they produced their own raw materials and had the capacity to develop markets while they absorbed losses.

But in the timber industry outside the Weyerhaeuser compound, the American system of free enterprise meant twenty years of predatory capitalism and the relentless costs of the shakedown—an environment that encouraged aggression, ruthlessness, conspiracy, desperation, social turmoil, and individual disaster. The very survival of the Clough group during these twenty years indicates their strengths and their keen understanding of the components of the timber industry—logging, shingle milling, and the manufacture of lumber. Of the three, lumber was the healthiest because the entrance requirements were higher in terms of investment, talent, and technological skill. With so much lumber suddenly available to a world market, the quality of the machinery, the men, and their products assumed vast importance. When, for example, Edwin G. Ames of the Pope and Talbot Company visited Everett in 1910, he noted enviously that of all the operations he had observed that year, only Stuchell's Eclipse Mill was making a significant profit, and that this was because Stuchell was turning out the best lumber Ames had ever seen.

In his methodical and orderly control of quality, Stuchell was an extraordinary exception to what Ames had come to expect from the lumbermen of Washington and Oregon. Even with the higher demands at entrance, there were hundreds of millowners around the two states to whom even simple bookkeeping was an esoteric art. Their manufacturing plants were simply a series of rusty saws in leaky shacks, powered by belts from steam engines, locked in a dreary rhythm of overproduction and close-down. Most of them could make good profits only by building a speculative inventory against a rising market, but the risks of stacking either lumber or logs were appalling. A millowner who bought logs for a season might awaken one morning to find that the collapse of a price trend had reduced the value of his log pile by thousands of dollars overnight and doomed him to make cheap lumber from expensive raw material.

Even with the best of prices, the lumber millers were always vulnerable to a major predator—the railroads that had brought them into existence. In good times, there were shortages of freight cars, and this taught men confusion, bribery, and fury. And if they had the cars, the apparently promiscuous fluctuation of rail rates could wash away their most carefully anticipated profits. Lumbermen in the Pacific Northwest had taken Jim Hill's word that they could easily compete with the moribund mills of the Midwest and South, and Hill had in fact reduced his rates from Puget Sound to St. Paul after 1900 and had put steamers on the Great Lakes to haul wood to Cleveland and Buffalo. Yet by 1904 most lumbermen felt that Hill's monopolistic rating and arbitrary scheduling were subjecting them to poorly concealed plunder.

It was that year that the timber industrialists of the state of Washington were so disturbed that they set out to get what the Populists had deeply desired but never obtained—a state commission with the power to regulate rates Jim Hill could charge them. After a great organization effort and a funding for political action, they identified candidates for the legislature who would vote for the commission, and they pushed those candidates to Olympia with a hundred thousand pieces of campaign literature. They got their legislature, they got their commission, and they got their war with Jim Hill. The Empire Builder punished the rebels by advancing his rates and by creating a shortage of cars and a degree of traffic congestion that worked a virtual embargo on Washington lumber. While their lawyers filed suit against the Great Northern and the Northern Pacific before the Interstate Commerce Commission—a suit which they ultimately won and which was acclaimed as a major trust-bust by the Roosevelt administration —some lumbermen were so furious at Hill and his power that they openly advocated the government ownership of all railroads.

Though they were learning the ways in which "progressive-minded" governments could serve them, they also learned what there was to fear from "progressive" energies. Taxes, which they had not studied much before coming west, could rise up to rob a millowner or logger who thought he had found hope and confidence. In Snohomish County, the rate of $.31 an acre on forest land in 1905 rose to $1.40 an acre in 1907, and it did so in the hands of the same legislators who had created the railroad commission. This increase of over 300 percent so alarmed landowners that they were frantic to log their timber immediately and sell out rather than accept the progressive principles of conservation. The logs consequently dumped on the market were a distressing stimulant to the overproduction and falling prices of that year.

To protect themselves from a host of furies, the lumbermen in Everett had joined the West Coast Lumber Manufac-

turers' Association when it was organized in 1901. This association intended to fight railroads, persuade politicians, find
ways to control costs, and establish prices. It functioned well
in tax litigation and in suppressing labor unions, and it worked
with uneven success toward negotiating with logging companies and fixing the lumber prices at which members would
sell. In the good years—1901, 1902, 1905, 1906—the association's work to prevent price competition was so successful and
so obvious that the phrase "lumber trust" joined "railroad
trust" in currency among certain reformers who could gain
the attention of Theodore Roosevelt. Thereafter a more subtle
cooperation among the informal committees produced lists of
"prevailing prices" in place of the old "official price list," and
Roosevelt's attention did not endure. But in the lean years
following 1906, members of the association were sorely
tempted to cheat on each other; most did, and the industry
was without protection or discipline.

The milling of red cedar shingles was potentially even
more lucrative than lumber, and several of the Everett mills
represented major capitalizations. Clough-Hartley cost more
than a million dollars; it employed 165 men and produced over
a million shingles during a ten-hour shift. At the other extreme, this was an industry in which any illiterate could get
his saws and a shack for a few hundred dollars, hire a crew of
half a dozen men, wrestle a few logs, and call himself a manu-
facturer. Such marginal operators—and there were hundreds
of them from Oregon to Puget Sound—could glut the market
in good times as well as bad. Such entrance requirements extended the inevitable period of shakedown across two decades
of brutal competition.

Few of the millers could, like David Clough, keep sufficient
money and enough relatives in logging companies to influence
the price they paid for raw cedar. Those less fortunate faced
the frustrations of wildly variable log prices and had to gamble recklessly on log inventories or simply pay whatever they
must from day to day to stay in business. Then with their

shingles bound and baled, the millowners had no control at all over the prices their bales would bring when they were shipped out to a world market consisting of thousands of independent suppliers whose demands they could never predict. Normally the mills sold to a wholesaler who had connections in the most populous states. The typical wholesaler cared little about prices so long as he could sell for more than he paid in Everett. He enjoyed and even encouraged overproduction, for at rock-bottom prices he could build inventories and be in a strong position for the beginning of the spring building season.

The shingle mills in the Pacific Northwest usually ran wide-open from April to November amid incredible risks. Fire hazards were so persistent that most mills sooner or later burned to the ground. Insurance, if available, was subject to larcenous premiums. Within the daily routines of the mills, industrial accidents were seemingly inevitable, and they inevitably threatened serious litigation. And if the workers did not sue, they called strikes. Of all the unions in the timber industries, the shingleweavers were traditionally and consistently the most radical and the most militant. They worked with a grim dedication toward denying the operator his freedom to hire and fire whom he pleased and pay what he would or could. Outside the mills, the wholesalers sulked in devious conspiracies to rig prices and rob the millowners of any profits the railroads had inadvertently left them. There were no normal years in this industry. Most years ended in a shutdown of three or four months, followed by an annual realignment of the same painful circumstances and confusion.

In an attempt to hold some control over these risks, the millers organized the Shingle Mills Bureau in 1906. This was the year of their most satisfying prosperity and their happiest cooperation, for they did successfully refuse to recognize the union, and, with the high demands of the season, they did reduce some wholesalers to begging for shingles. But the field was too loose for such discipline to endure for long. There were simply too many marginal mills, and the larger competitors could never effectively curtail production to sustain the demands that would have protected their prices.

At the base of the entire timber industry, logging operations were the most speculative and most chaotic, but they were also the most promising for the short-run bonanza. Though the woods sometimes swarmed with small-time tree choppers from the pre-industrial period, there was no future after 1900 in a man's chopping out his own homestead. After the Great Northern came, capitalizations of fifty thousand dollars to one hundred thousand dollars in logging were common —in land leases, timber rights, machinery, and initial payrolls.

There were few capitalists, however, who had the entrepreneurial nerve to shoulder the full risks of such investments. Logging companies were commonly formed as loose partnerships to spread the dangers among groups of speculators who knew the market and the chances of total ruin. The Brown's Bay Logging Company, for example, was organized in 1906 to log off a large tract of timber south of Everett. The principal owners wanted to get their land out from under county taxes as soon as possible, and they knew they could sell the timber to Clark-Nickerson. They invited friends in at $100 a share, and after four years of cutting, they raised the capitalization to $210,000, or $210 a share. When the company had stripped the tract and liquidated in 1916, they paid off these shares at $650 each.

Some profits were even more spectacular than these, and E. G. Ames of Pope and Talbot grieved during the good years to see his company pay out big money to men who, he felt, rarely deserved it. "Men of little ability," he wrote to the San Francisco office, "have tumbled into a fortune." During the great boom of 1906–7, he watched one individual clear three hundred thousand dollars from logging, then saw another take four hundred thousand dollars. This kind of return brought a more special and private jubilance to the loggers who sold to themselves rather than to Pope and Talbot. Thus David Clough could make millionaires of his relatives. With another period of prodigious acceleration during World War I, Roland Hartley and Thomas Hartley, a cousin, outbid the Rucker brothers for the timber rights to the Tulalip Indian Reservation. This was one of the really plush remaining stands of prime timber. The Hartleys themselves capitalized heavily, forming a very limited partnership but risking most of their assets. Within four years Roland Hartley alone had bank deposits representing clear profits of nearly a million dollars.

It was Joe Irving, the boss for the lumber camps financed by William Butler and the Clough group, who tried hardest to formulate some degree of control over the selling price of logs. He helped organize the Washington Logging and Brokerage Company, a group of loggers who tried to regulate the cutting of timber and consequently the number of logs affecting the price at any given time. This attempt was never effective because loggers, who were even more numerous and more independent than shingle millers, were never willing to accept any rational control.[3]

While they were learning the whims of an erratic economy, the Everett industrialists did not find the years from 1902 to 1905 particularly rewarding. The going was rough, but those who survived learned the vagaries and the terrors of turning raw wood into substantial profits. By 1906 they had gained essential experience, and that year the earthquake in San Francisco suddenly opened the full scope of opportunity in the Pacific Northwest. The fires of San Francisco created the markets for Everett. The prices of logs, lumber, and shingles leaped to figures twice as high as those of the year before. The Clough mills alone turned out an annual total of over one hundred million feet of lumber. Most happily for Clough, the railroads and Jim Hill could not pirate this, for it all went to California by water. In a matter of months the extended family made its first Everett fortune.

By December, 1907, San Francisco was smothered with lumber and the mills of the Pacific Northwest closed in a panic of high inventories and deflated prices. This shut-down was concurrent with the congestion in rail cars and with Jim Hill's embargo on Washington lumber, and it began a period of general unemployment and deep community distress that lasted for several years. For the Clough group, however, the money was safely in the banks of Everett or St. Paul. Prices of lumber did not reach the glory of 1906 for another decade, but after 1909 conditions for the industrialists were never really bad for long. Prices fell, but not below the level of 1905, when they had made a reasonable living.

During these years David Clough built his great house on the bluff overlooking the bay. Roland Hartley, who had until then lived with his father-in-law, built a spacious colonial with five bedrooms, a sweeping lawn, and servants' quarters on the back properties. Stuchell built a fenced and secluded mansion in the Pennsylvania style on the hill above the city. The San Francisco quake had stabilized the Puget Sound baronage.

Clough had come to Everett to make a second fortune after the depression of 1893 had stolen the rewards of an already full career. He had taken money where he found it—from friends like Melvin S. Clark, L. W. Wolcott, and W. C. Nickerson—and he made himself a multimillionaire before he died in 1924. In so doing, he also repaid his friends handsomely and allowed his relatives to become very wealthy indeed. Roland Hartley was foremost among these, and he had become at least a millionaire when he left the business at the time of his father-in-law's death.

These figures do not suggest unusual profits for American industrialists during this period. Some made more, many made less, and few faced such relentless risks of losing everything. In this regard, the figures suggest entrepreneurial skills and energies of an exceptionally high order, and any study of Everett would be of less significance if this were not so. These men contributed vigorously, shrewdly, and perhaps indispensably to the industrial exploitation of the resources of the American frontier.

What these figures also suggest is an often ruthless extraction of maximum profits. Because they could never achieve the kind of market monopoly that allowed other industrialists to rob the American public, they cut their gains away from potential wages in Everett and potential contributions to communal self-respect and security. David Clough—and most of the others followed his example—never spent a dollar on his mills that did not promise an immediate yield, not on wages, research, innovation, or safety. His attitude was about the same toward the city he had helped to create. In his inexorable determination to win a second and then a third fortune, he wore out his machinery, infuriated the men who worked it, and alienated an entire community. What the naked figures of Clough's profits do not reveal is their burden on the lives of individuals less fortunate than he and a long history of collective anxieties.

V

The Search for Community

!!

Each year after the opening of the Weyerhaeuser Mill, the Great Northern brought thousands of migrants to its new depot on the ridge above the harbor. These were wage earners and businessmen, real estate operators and saloon-keepers, farmhands and millworkers from the Midwest and New England, men, women, and children from Canada, England, Germany, and Scandinavia. Each trainload of them probably represented a cross section of the energies and ambitions that James J. Hill had released by opening the West to industry and to the ambitions of people everywhere. The population of Everett grew from eight thousand in 1900 to more than four times that number in a decade. Even the collapse of lumber markets in 1907, disastrous as it had been to so many lumber and shingle mills, did not discourage the migrants, to whom Everett meant an opportunity to find a new identity.

From the passenger platform, a newcomer could look down over the industrial area of the waterfront that began to the south with the docks, mills, warehouses, and railroad sidings. Then crowded to the north and east were mills and plants that sprawled eight miles around the beach from bayside to riverside. By 1910 there were ninety-five manufacturing plants in Everett, including eleven lumber mills, sixteen shingle mills, seventeen combination lumber-shingle mills, a paper mill, an iron factory, several makers of logging and milling machinery, shipyards, an arsenic plant, breweries, and dozens of minor industries subordinate to the sawdust economy. The city of smokestacks had become a reality, and it was a distinctly urban reality. Over five thousand of the thirty-five thousand men, women, and children in Everett in 1910 earned wages in mills and factories—a ratio more comparable to the urban East than to the urban West.

Yet the frontier was everywhere evident. If the newcomer came by boat, he could see from Port Gardner Bay that Everett, shining white in the sun, was still a clearing in a dense wilderness. From the industrial maze of the Clough-Hartley yards, he could see across a sandbar to the shores of Tulalip, where the Indians fished and smoked salmon as they had done for centuries. Beyond the industrial noise, he could hear the rifle shots fired almost daily by hunters within the limits of the city. Across the river he could have logged-off land almost for the asking—twelve dollars, less than a week's wages, for an acre of stump farm, and seventy-five dollars an acre for improved farmland. Within the context and the tensions of these two realities—urban industrial and primitive frontier— the newcomer would find a city searching for order and community.

At the vertex of these realities was an expanding population which on the surface seemed remarkably cosmopolitan. A fourth of the people were foreign-born, another fourth were of foreign parentage. First or second generation, they had come from Canada, Norway, Sweden, Germany, and England, in that order, and from all over the United States. Almost any day on the streets of Everett one could hear Norwegian, Swedish, and German, and sometimes Italian and Greek. In this diversity of national origins, the clubs and saloons, neighborhoods and churches found their characters. National loyalties could sometimes erupt momentarily in ugly passions that might, for example, send Norwegian rocks through the stained-glass windows of a Swedish church, but as the years went by these differences subsided into an easy rapport.

Despite its initial linguistic multiformity, Everett was essentially white and Anglo-Saxon in its values. The native American was clearly the dominant culture. Because the European languages carried with them no deep cultural differences, they soon lost their social significance. The Canadians, English, and Irish blended easily. Northern Europeans might cling tenaciously for a while to native-language church services, but after a few years of adapting and adjusting to new ways of realizing common goals, they usually relaxed their hold on old-country customs. The Norwegians closed their private school in 1909 when the public schools included the Norwegian language as a regular part of the high school curriculum. On the other hand, the Catholic parish supported a parochial school which never lost its vitality, but this school was not national in its focus. So strong and so general, in fact, was the sense of a new and American identity that citizens from almost every background united in 1904 and again in 1907 to drive out the few "un-American" Japanese and "Hindu" workers David Clough wanted to place in the Clark-Nickerson Mill.

Thus, in this notably urban community of newcomers, the homogeneous character of the population was far more striking than its cosmopolitanism. Everett was becoming a city of families and family residences. The migrants had come seeking more than just money: they wanted a permanence, a stability, and the institutionalization of their ideals. In 1910, the census takers found that among the 24,814 people living within the formal boundaries of the city, there were 5,314 families and 4,953 residences. If the Everett families conformed to the state average of five members, then just about everybody was living with a family in an individual family dwelling—a ratio significantly higher than that of any comparable urban-industrial area.

They built on the twenty-five-foot lots of the Everett Improvement Company, or on two lots if they were affluent, three or more if they were rich. Most houses were designed by the carpenters who built them. They were more often than not a thoughtless imitation of the more severely unimaginative midwestern residential styles. Crowded together, invariably oriented toward the sidewalks and streets rather than toward the bay and mountains, they covered block after block without variety or distinction.

But if his house were crowded against others, the worker had only a mile to walk to the mill. His wife and children had no geographic barriers to neighborliness and assimilation. If his living room faced the street instead of the bay, it was because he wanted to watch people, not meditate on nature. He had come to exploit, not to contemplate, and his new life demanded associations with humanity, not wilderness. The least of these homes offered the luxury of bedrooms for the children. If they were made with scrap lumber and covered with cheap paint, they were new and clean, and a man could find pride in appearances. And most importantly, he could plan to free himself from rent and debt. Most real estate sales were to wage earners, and most of the bank accounts in Everett represented the deposits of wage earners who were saving to pay off a mortgage in five or ten years. Owning real property was probably the most easy, most desirable, and most conspicuous evidence of social mobility that the newcomer could acquire.[1]

In the good years, life in Everett could be a satisfying

rhythm of work and leisure that allowed a man or a child to pass his days in the confidence that society was stable and progress was real. Max Miller, who grew up in Everett and became a nationally famous journalist, recalled his childhood with a nostalgic warmth that suggests the security of these rhythms. The mill whistles, he remembered, blew at six in the morning, giving a man an hour to build a fire, have his breakfast, and maybe smoke his pipe for a reflective moment before he joined the procession of workers walking over the ridge and down to the waterfront. The whistles blew again at seven, when the shift began. Each whistle was subtly distinct, and young boys found an early achievement in being able to name them—the Ferry-Baker, the Clough-Hartley, the Hulburt, the Eclipse, the score of others. They blew at noon, when many boys too young for school stood outside the mills with their fathers' lunch pails. A one o'clock whistle sent the men back to work, then the six o'clock told that the men would soon be coming back up the bluff, covered with sawdust, carrying bundles of kindling over their shoulders, predictably tired, hungry, and curious about the world outside the mills.

To the young boy, Everett was an orderly and comprehensible universe of constant fascinations. Max Miller's ambition was to be a logger and jump heroically across the rafts of logs that came down the Snohomish River. His parents forbade him to go near the river, which was but a short walk from his home, but their words could not restrain his youthful energies. There was a sandbar in mid-channel, and in the brilliant warm heat of water and sun, he and other boys played through the long afternoons of a northern summer.

He prowled cautiously around the hobo jungle along the Great Northern tracks on riverside. He even saw the great Jim Hill step from his private car in the switchyard and lecture solemnly to a boy who had been caught stealing a small electric fuse from a deserted caboose. ("Do you realize, young man, that the Great Northern Railroad is in debt the sum of $4,300,092 and can't afford to lose a single fuse?")

And he knew the block on East Market Street that was fenced with high boards like a ball park but was not a ball park. He had held his eye to the knotholes and seen the rows of tiny rooms where certain ladies lived. These ladies had stood on the fence and waved and cheered to Theodore Roosevelt as he passed in a limousine, but they were ladies who, he knew, were all going to Hell.

Miller grew up free to roam the growing, changing town and to explore its many dimensions. He could peek in the saloons, hitch rides on the backs of streetcars, wander around the woods, the lakes, the islands, the rivers. Like many of his contemporaries, he tended the cows his family kept in a vacant lot as a modest shield against the sometimes brutal business cycles, and he worked each morning before school in a bakery. A career in the mills seemed to him inevitable and not undesirable. More serious boys argued over which was the best mill and who would make the best foreman. They all looked forward to a man's work and store clothes and money in their pockets, and the freedom of a night downtown. As they reached fourteen or fifteen years, most of them slipped away from school and into the lumberyards, the factories, the logging camps, or the mills.[2]

The high school building they avoided was a heavy, Romanesque cube of masonry which was the pride of the city when it was completed in 1910. The curriculum, in its stern application of directed study and recitation, was ruthlessly academic. Almost half the grades given in all subjects were below "C." With dismal regularity, half the students failed algebra, a sixth failed English, a fourth failed commercial subjects, and even a fifth failed manual training. Maybe a third of all students dropped out of high school before graduating. The faculty dismissed these failures as a reflection either of the low ability of the students or of the circumstances that forced them to leave school and earn wages.

The school board was probably responsive to popular demand when it insisted that the teachers of the high school re-

quire hard work for the sake of hard work and discipline for
the sake of discipline. This elected board was constantly alert
to "the alarming and growing evils associated with the ath-
letics and other extraneous functions [of the school] . . .
profanity, vulgarity, rowdyism." In regard to these threats,
it demanded strict regulation and curtailment. The schools
were there to teach the values of work, respect, and decency,
to inculcate without compromise whatever was necessary for
social adjustment, and then mobility.[3]

Throughout the city, a galaxy of independent organizations
—many with national identities—worked to equip the parents
for the same adjustment and mobility. Everett was complexly
organized, even overorganized. In 1909 the city had forty
fraternal lodges, most of them with women's auxiliaries. There
were twenty-five labor unions with auxiliaries, dozens of reform clubs, political clubs, women's clubs, book clubs, historical societies, and professional organizations, each holding
regular meetings, picnics, smokers, clambakes, dances, and
parties.

A Norwegian immigrant family, for example, might find
friends immediately in the Sons of Norway, a fraternal club
that held its members and their families together in its social
events and secret ritual. The family would probably join
one of the Lutheran congregations, and while working in the
church's many activities become acquainted throughout the
Lutheran fellowship, which was, by and large, the Norwegian
fellowship of Everett. If the father joined a labor union, the
auxiliary clubs and societies of this organization would be an
easy extension of the family's associations and interests beyond those that were strictly national. All in all, maybe a
dozen committees could involve every member of the family
in cooperative work, schooling, or recreation every night of
the week. Young people or adults could, in addition, attend
YMCA courses in English, bookkeeping, or arithmetic. Joining
the Eagles, a service club, or a reform club might in a sense
climax their integration into the larger community of Everett.

In this process, there was no lack of leadership or encourage-
ments. Almost everyone, for example, knew Hans Solie, who
had come in 1901 to work at Weyerhaeuser. He joined the
Sons of Norway, and he and his wife served faithfully on its
many committees and worked their ways to leadership. They
organized a Lutheran congregation. A measured step in Solie's
progress was that he soon quit the mill, joined the carpenters' union, and became active in the Trades' Council, which
represented all the labor organizations in the city. Later he
joined a Socialist club "to help make a better world" and
served the Socialists in a variety of official capacities. By 1909
he and his family were in the fullest sense rooted in the community. They were always ready to welcome new residents—
to the lodge, the congregation, the union, the movement—
and show them the routes of integration.[4]

Of all the organizations, the forty churches were among the
most vital. Their differences were more often national than
theological. Of the six large Lutheran congregations, only one
held services in English. Among the five Methodist, there were
services in German, Norwegian, and Swedish. These churches
were the obvious landmarks and neighborhood centers, and
their Sunday schools and week-day associations were effective
agencies of social confidence and harmony. Even the smallest
could offer a depth of involvement that would bring the newcomer to ease. The Svenska Evangeliska Mission-församlingen,
for example, first met in 1902. As a non-Lutheran Swedish
fellowship, it never included more than fifty members, but
these men and women finished a new church building in 1908,
praising that "wonderful time of life and spiritual warmth"
("härliga tid of liv och andlig värme") that brought them
together at this place for constructive and richly satisfying
achievement. Another evangelistic group, the Deutschen
Evangelischen Zions Gemeinde, enrolled only twenty-two
German families in 1909, but they had raised two thousand
dollars to buy a used one-room building. The *Jungenverein*
earned another fifty-five dollars to buy an organ. Almost

everyone worked at improving the property, rejoicing ("der sind wir Fröhlich") in progress and fellowship.

This was indeed a good year, the more so because the mills were running again after the idleness of 1907, and the economic health of the community had immediate social manifestations. The churches became even more vigorous and confident. The Catholic parish grew to a thousand members, expanded its church and hospital, and even went on to organize a second congregation. Members of the First Congregational Church recalled this year as a period when "the spiritual life of the church intensified and deepened, and there was a noticeable outgoing into the life of the community and country."

The most striking exception to this concord occurred within the old and firmly established Trinity Episcopal Church. In 1909 this congregation received the Reverend Louis Tucker as its rector, and it was his unhappy fate to preside over a period of disunity and dissension. Father Tucker had been born in Virginia and had spent most of his life in the deep South. He came to Everett equipped with a superior education and the finest of southern sensitivities. Articulate and cultured, he was a man who enjoyed vintage wine, a good cigar, and light verse as well as Spenserian sonnets. Furthermore, he thought these things were important. As a priest he had most recently become accustomed to the subtleties of prestige, good living, influence, and power in Baton Rouge. He had, perhaps, known more power in Louisiana politics than was appropriate to his position, and a crush of political circumstances, as well as malaria, had encouraged him to accept a new life in the West.

In a sparkling autobiography written years later, Tucker estimated that when he arrived in Everett there were about a thousand Anglicans on the parish rolls, though only about a hundred of them were in any way involved in parish affairs. He found himself trapped in a "dingy, vulgar, tawdry building" and torn by the animosity among his communicants, who argued heatedly over whether Trinity should be high or low in its ritual. He could satisfy neither, and he saw no redemption.

Beyond the altar, he explored a city which to him was utterly without social graces. People did not call on him at home. No one seemed to have an education. Had he tried to discuss English literature, he later wrote, people would have regarded him as a "raving maniac." There were indeed good men in Everett, he thought, but they cared for nothing "except grim, hard work." He felt isolated in a materialistic culture of the most solemn and single-minded dedication. The only topics men took with any real seriousness were work, possessions, and money.

The functional priests of these values were, he said, men who in Virginia would have been called "lesser gentry." Their altars were in downtown businesses and real estate. Tucker came to see the businessmen as "half-educated commoners" who had grown disgustingly fat on the lumber and land bonanzas of 1906, and, since then, had become predictably conceited and exclusive. They would have nothing to do with the poor, he noted bitterly, and the poor in 1909 included the Reverend Louis Tucker.

He felt constantly and mercilessly criticized because he could not "keep up appearances." He could not possibly afford the servants he had taken for granted in Baton Rouge. He had four children and a wife who had never done housework. Tucker himself was up before dawn, chopping wood, helping to dress the children and to cook and clean. He was out until dark, bicycling through the rain and fog as he made his rounds from church to homes, hospital, and jail. By nightfall he was exhausted, but there was still no respite. Though he had never worked with his hands, he had to make his own furniture in Everett. He had no money to buy clothes, he said, or even to keep his shoes shined. His three dollars a day —less than a carpenter's wage—came grudgingly. "The treasurer at Everett," he wrote, "was a baptized Jew," who, Tucker lamented, "had retained all of the worst Hebrew char-

Port Gardner Bay, 1908 (Photo courtesy of Everett Community College Library)

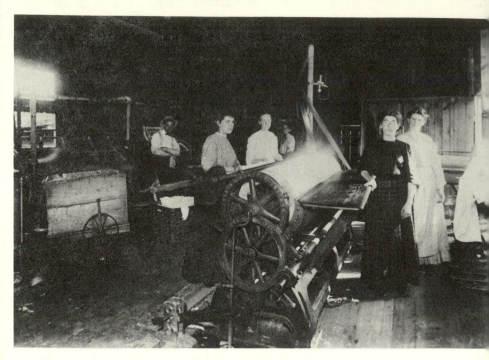

Women in industry, 1908 (Photo courtesy of Everett Community College Library)

Street scene, 1908 (Photo courtesy of Everett Community College Library)

acteristics without adding any Christian ones." This was Albert Brodeck, the clothier, whose personal qualities, whatever
their origins, did seem to Tucker to have been maliciously
blended with a view to the rector's destruction. Brodeck never
allowed the priest to audit the church books.

Seldom, perhaps, had a sincere rector been so alone in his
battle with materialism, and seldom so grievously defeated. In
one representatively sad episode, recorded in the minutes of
the Snohomish County Ministerial Association, Tucker tried
to arouse his colleagues to the defense of a man fired from
Stuchell's Eclipse Mill because he refused to work on Sundays.
The ministers discussed the matter discretly, then, ignoring
Tucker, abruptly dropped it.

Dejected by financial, cultural, and spiritual poverty,
Tucker was driven toward ultimate despair by the gloomy
weather of Puget Sound, by the endless "mists and drizzles
and sprinkles and sobs and fogs and snivels." When he fled
across the mountains to vacation in Yakima, where he could
refresh his soul with the sight of sun and stars, the parish
gentry complained of his taking days off with pay. Harried
and threadbare, feeling that he had "failed abjectly in Everett," he suffered a nervous collapse. The vestry, he said,
was then afraid that he would die before they could get rid
of him, so they gave him two weeks' notice. He negotiated
for a rail ticket to Louisiana and left Everett with thirty
dollars in his pocket. Three decades later, he could not think
of Everett without reviving the lingering spirits of contempt
and bitterness.

What Everett lacked as a human community, Tucker
reasoned, was a communion of men and women who, like
the gulf fishermen he had known, were in "close contact
with life and death, and the romance of both." Such people
lived by strength of character and passion and tragedy, and
these qualities he could understand. To live by money-
grubbing alone, he felt, deprived life—and Everett—of fundamental dignity.

It was this longing for the romantic, more than the refinement of his tastes and education, that alienated Tucker from the people of Everett. He was surely right to feel that the values by which gulf fishermen lived and died were singularly lacking in Everett. By this measure, the spiritual dimension of Everett was indeed flat and shallow. Yet if Tucker had known Karl Marx, Henry George, William U'Ren, or Eugene Debs as well as he knew his Victorian novelists, and if he had attended union meetings and talked with shingle weavers, he might then have understood why romantic fatalism was not to them a cherished value. With this understanding, he might have found friends. He might have uncovered a growing sense of community that was qualitatively different from any he had known before.

Gulf fishermen may have accepted their fate, but mill-workers were determined to control theirs. Because the fishermen Tucker had known could not control the sea, they may have looked to religion for guidance toward some personal harmony with the sea's ebb and flow and threat and promise. But the millworkers in 1909 would accept nothing eternal about their mill or their working conditions. These could be changed, and in changing them men could achieve more dignity. Money-grubbing was but one expression of the millworkers' conviction that they should not accept this world as it was. They should try to build a better one.

The millworkers were impressed by potential as much as by reality in 1909. They would not see themselves as lost sheep in a mixed-up cosmos of frontier and industry, nor would they consider that the honest devices and desires of their own hearts were in any way inconsistent with the godly, righteous, and sober life. Gulf fishermen, as Tucker remembered them, may have accepted the tragic flow of life and death, and sought a faith to explain it. Millworkers in Everett, sustained by a different ethic, sought purposeful action which could reassure them that tragedy was not eternal. They found confidence in a broad range of active institutions.

Though Everett still drifted somewhere between the machine and the wilderness, the time had passed for the romance of pure passion, of easily symbolic good and evil, or of man against the natural elements. Yet when men began to react with passion against an industrial system that resisted their deepest longings for dignity and opportunity, there would be tragedy. It was in not sensing this conflict that Reverend Tucker most abjectly failed.

Other clergymen were more fortunate. In the developing patterns of integration routes and urban geography, some churches became congregations of wage earners and union men, and their ministers took considerable pride in this identification. The First Congregational Church for six years had the Reverend R. B. Hassell, a Populist-Socialist orator and pastor who built a tradition of congregational resolutions on social problems. His church brought Booker T. Washington to its pulpit, and it invited labor leaders to preach in the most secular terms. The Grace Methodist Episcopal Church, located in a precinct which was returning a heavy Socialist majority by 1910, regularly presented union speakers, and its minister often appeared before the Trades' Council as a friend of labor. The Everett *Daily Herald* boasted in 1909 that "our most influential ministers do not hesitate . . . to speak with definiteness upon the great questions that affect the welfare of laboring men." [5]

Such churches informally but effectively harbored a host of reform organizations that cut across traditional economic, political, or religious loyalties. Everett was beginning to vibrate with reform sentiment. The clubs were everywhere: direct legislation clubs, women's suffrage groups, societies for the public ownership of utilities, for direct primary elections, for the public ownership of major natural resources and major industries. The Anti-Saloon League used some congregations as precincts for political action. Groups that

favored local option on the saloon question were organizing
in every neighborhood. By a contemporary estimate, at least
half the businessmen and half the wage earners belonged to
at least one such organization. It seemed to some participants
that just about everyone was eloquently eager, as Hans Solie
was, to "improve society." The pulse continued to rise, and
in 1912 the *Labor Journal* took note of the bylaws of a
"Hysterical Society" of Everett, affiliated, one might suppose, with the Trades' Council: "No more than seven members shall speak on a subject at any one time. . . . Criticism
of the city administration and of William H. Taft takes
precedence over all other business of this society."

Everett was a church town, a reform town, and a wage
earners' town. It was an American Federation of Labor town,
among the most highly unionized in the country. After
1906, there were more than two dozen local unions with
regular representatives on the Everett Trades Council. This
group provided a forum for discussion and an agency for
action, and members took noisy positions on every social
issue. Since at this time there were no more than six formal
union contracts or closed-shop agreements in all of Everett,
the fraternal function of member unions was at least as important as the economic. Union men addressed each other
sincerely as "brother," and each union hoped to "pension its
workers, bury its dead, and care for its unfortunate." If
"Sister Johnson" were ill and needed assistance, fellow
workers and sisters would read about it in the *Labor Journal*,
which was a constant stimulant to a sense of community.

The most militant and articulate representatives on the
Trades Council were the shingle weavers, whose union was
by far the largest and strongest. They had organized in 1901
during a strike for higher wages, had joined the International
Shingle Weavers Union of the American Federation of Labor,
and had continued to grow as a dominant labor power in
the Puget Sound region and the state. In 1904 a second strike
won them a union scale of wages. During the great boom of

1906 they demanded a third raise and clashed with the Shingle Mills Bureau, which spent fifty thousand dollars to coordinate a lockout and transport strikebreakers from mill to mill. The union extended the strike throughout the shingle industry in the state, and as market prices soared upward, the bureau and the union drew a compromise which provided for the wage increase without union recognition. Therafter, even during the 1907 collapse, the shingle weavers in Everett were fully organized in every mill. These mills were soon shipping out six million red cedar shingles a day, more than any city in the world. As the mills grew, the union also grew, and Everett became a regional nerve center of union consciousness.

The term "shingle weaver" was generic, and was applied alike to the sawyers, filers, and packers who worked as a crew in the mills that produced these shingles. Stacking the slices of cedar into overlapping bundles, a skilled packer worked so rapidly that he appeared to be "weaving" the shingles together, and hence the name. After 1900, mill technology advanced significantly with the introduction of new upright saws that allowed a cleaner and thinner cut. The product was then so uniform and so versatile that red cedar shingles came into demand as roofing material of the highest quality. Everett grew on this demand. The new saws, however, did not increase the productivity of the individual worker. They may, on the contrary, have diminished his productivity, for they quite suddenly made shingle sawing a mercilessly bloody vocation.

The brotherhood of shingle weavers was bonded in the grim realities of blood and sawdust. The bolter saw was a circular blade that stood fifty inches in diameter and gleamed with three-inch, razor-sharp teeth. To cut a cedar log into bolts that would fit the carriage of the shingle saw, a man pushed the log forward at waist height with his knee and hands. He could too easily fall or be pulled to certain slaughter. Nearby the sawyer on the upright machine faced two whirling blades. To his left, one saw sliced the blocks that came automatically from the bolter. The carriage could be set to rip off fifty to sixty slices a minute. With almost incredible dexterity, the sawyer cleared this saw with his left hand, then passed the slices of wood over to his right hand, with which he then shaped the shingle on the trimmer saw and passed it down a chute to the packer. While his hands moved faster than the eye could follow, sawdust clouded his vision and clogged his throat and nose. Driven by the bosses until he took a sullen pride in his speed, a good sawyer could cut and trim thirty thousand shingles in a ten-hour shift. This meant thirty thousand chances to feed the steel with flesh and bone. Sooner or later, the sawyer reached too far or not far enough.

These sawing machines made possible a new industry. But they were conceived by a mind that worshipped efficiency more than humanity. They could very well symbolize the machine as an implacable enemy, or industrialization gone utterly mad. For more than half a century after these machines were in regular use, a shingle weaver was easily recognized by the grotesque irregularities of his torn and broken hands and arms. A sawyer who had lost four or five fingers was not uncommon. There were men around not yet thirty years old who had lost as many as eight fingers in that many accidents. A State Bureau of Labor survey during this period showed that over 50 percent of the shingle sawyers had already suffered serious injury, and that among these men industrial accidents were the primary cause of death. Of the 224 people who died in Everett in 1909, 36 were killed in the mills.

Such butchery often condemned a man to stay with the saws rather than flee them, for there were few jobs open to men without fingers or thumbs. And besides the saws, the inevitable afflictions from cedar dust and vapor were cedar asthma, nervousness, and stomach disorders. Shingle-mill workers were thus linked by their common physical and psychological hazards, by their lack of occupational mobility, and by their casual disregard for craft differentiations. These factors—almost classic symptoms of class-consciousness—also encouraged them to extract from the mills as much security as they could possibly gain. Their average wage in 1910 was $4.50 a day, significantly higher than the $2.25 that lumber-mill workers made, and they had won this level by their solidarity and militancy. Every shingle weaver in Everett paid dues to the International, even though the millowners refused to recognize its authority.

The weavers' executive secretary in 1909 was Ernest P. Marsh, a young man who had come to Everett several years before, worked in the mills, then risen in the union ranks to lead the local, direct the Trades Council, and edit the *Labor Journal*. Then in his late twenties, Marsh was from the Great Lakes region, his parents from England. Photographs of him during this period show a clean-shaven young man with steel-rimmed spectacles, a sincere face whose mild countenance draws attention away from the millworker's hands and shoulders. These pictures suggest, perhaps inevitably, a younger, more scholarly, and less passionate Eugene Debs. Married and with two children, Marsh was in his age and circumstances probably representative of many men in Everett. He was distinguished, however, by his curiosity, his warm personality, and his intelligence. He was a man of broad interests and deep energies that could be a source as well as a reflector of the enthusiasms generated by the community. And unlike some of the brightest young men who emerged from the mills during these years and became spokesmen for the radical cause, Marsh was the soul of moderation.

When Marsh wrote, as he often did, that "there is nothing more noble than true unionism," he meant Sam Gompers unionism, the American Federation of Labor, and fellowship in a spirit that was moderate, decent, reasonable, and in every way middle-class. He glorified the bustling growth of Ev-erett, delighted in the endless activities of speaking, organizing committees, assisting ladies' auxiliaries, promoting union buttons and union smokers, picnics, and fishing parties, and publishing special editions. His values were clearly expressed in church life, civic pride, democratic institutions and practice, loyalty, modesty, fraternity, family, and reason.

Marsh was never afraid, for example, to say that businessmen should not be unreasonably restricted in their drive for profit. The capitalist system, he felt, could accommodate the best interests of both employers and workers. Class differences, he cautioned, should be discouraged. Labor unions should be democratic and set a mood and tone for the entire community. Labor leaders—and he surely included himself—should educate and mediate, and they should demonstrate that education and reason are the tools of progress.

When he became editor and publisher in 1909, three years of industrial peace had softened the militancy born with the shingle weavers' union and spread by them through many unions in the city. The compromise which the union and the millowners had agreed to in 1906 still functioned. It was an informal agreement, and, Marsh believed, the achievement of men of good will. The personal understandings involved in this arrangement were, he felt, the essence of community health, and he saw no reason to suppose that they would not endure. Marsh knew the nature of the timber industry, and he watched the prices of logs and shingles as closely as did any millowner. When the mills closed down occasionally to squeeze the brokers into raising prices, Marsh was not critical. He accepted the several unhappy but obvious facts of life in Everett that he could not hope to change immediately. But so strong was Marsh's faith in Everett and in progress that even William C. Butler advertised his banks in the pages of the *Labor Journal.*

Marsh's editorship justified the banker's confidence, for in his optimistic way, Marsh made the *Journal* responsive to the needs of the community. His editorials reflected an idealism that must have been shared by the many men his age who also shared his excitement about the twentieth century. Marsh thought that every able-bodied man could and should provide for himself and his family, and that the way to personal success was through ambition, modesty, cooperation, thrift, sobriety, and responsibility. If such a man were unfortunate, then a strong union could and should take care of him. Marsh had a vision of every family on its own five acres, growing its own staples and drawing strength from the traditions of agrarian morality. With such a base of security, a man could take advantage of the seasonal cycles in mill work to lift his material ambitions as high as he would have them soar. Profoundly drawn to the agrarian past and the industrial future, Marsh in these early years was convinced that reasonable men could integrate industry with the frontier and thus open opportunities and securities never before known.

At the same time he was not blind to the inhumanity of the system he saw around him, nor was he ignorant about the extent of unreason. He could turn to wrath when he examined the issues of child labor, monopoly, poverty, crime, working mothers, the ten-hour day, or cheap immigrant labor. His outrage over the conditions of industrial safety and industrial health marked him as a leader of real potential. As a favorite speaker across the state, he told union audiences that industrial abuses were unreasonable and that reasonable men should not rest while such abuses continued.

Though he sometimes expressed a vague feeling that socialism was not Christian, Marsh was willing to explore most ideas without prejudice. As a good union man, and one who read widely, he was in 1909 beginning to admire Eugene Debs. Among his own shingle weavers there were many who took their socialism religiously, and Marsh always regarded them as good men. He could not, however, understand that socialism was relevant to Everett, where, he believed, the problems would have to be solved by good will, not by doctrine. And he was obviously uncomfortable with the Socialists' disdain for craft unionism. He would admit by 1909 that industrial patterns of organization were appropriate to some industries, maybe even the timber industry. He admired Debs's activities among the railroad workers. Part of his idealism was that he thought he could make the AFL flexible enough to accommodate such unions. The two great enemies of true unionism, he wrote in 1910, were "open-shop employers and radical socialists."

He was especially disturbed by Big Bill Haywood's Industrial Workers of the World. These men referred to themselves as the "bummery," even with pride, and they had been around in the woods and mills since 1905, voicing their uninhibited and sometimes wildly poetic contempt for capitalist trade unionism. They were also contemptuous of Christianity, patriotism, politics—anything that supported the capitalist system, which they cursed or ridiculed as inhuman, corrupt, and doomed. In a rotten system, they were saying, reason is not effective; only threats or coercion can advance the cause of the workers. To Ernest Marsh, such a dark view of the world was a denial of everything he believed.

The Wobblies wanted to organize all the wood workers, and so, really, did Ernest P. Marsh. He thought for a happy moment that the IWW had starved out in 1907, but they were coming back in the lumber camps and mills by 1908. Marsh was at least grateful that there were no more than a dozen red cards in Everett. He described the IWW as loud-mouthed, foul-mouthed, irresponsible, irreligious, and unpatriotic fools, directed like puppets by a handful of dictatorial "slum angels" from Chicago who shamed the union movement. This was, of course, the view of the middle-class trade unionist. An equally articulate Wobbly might have replied—and with equal evidence, sincerity, and conviction—that the foul words rendered no harm comparable to a lice-ridden bunkhouse, that a responsibility to humanity was not always responsibility to capitalists, that the leadership of the IWW was decentralized and democratic, and that the movement these leaders represented rose inevitably out of the industrial environment of Coeur d'Alene mines and Puget Sound mills, not out of the slums of Chicago.

And it is clear that Marsh, like many other trade unionists in the West, knew from his own experience the industrial conditions which gave Wobbly words a reality no working-man could ignore. As a union leader, Marsh repeatedly warned the millowners of the state that the IWW would indeed flourish in depraved industrial environments, that industrialists themselves were giving a hard currency to the talk of sabotage and the wisdom of "a poor day's work for a poor day's pay." He urged capitalists and the AFL to take these words seriously, to cooperate, and to improve working conditions before the IWW generated class hatreds that could rupture the whole society. He predicted several times that the hot-headed determination of some bosses to exterminate the Wobblies with clubs and guns could force all working-men into final loyalties and ignite the very class hatreds that Wobblies planned to use as fuel for revolution.

He could sense the ominous reach of the problem even in 1910, when city officials in Spokane were herding Wobblies to jail by the hundreds simply because they had held meetings on the city streets. As the jails filled and overflowed with tattered and impudent martyrs who did not even care if they were treated like criminals—and still more came each day—polite society in Spokane shuddered. But the shingle weavers in Everett collected cash contributions to send to the Spokane jails.

Marsh was deeply disturbed because he believed that the people of Everett were engaged in a profound and delicate undertaking—the adjustment of industrial capitalism to their values of democracy, cooperation, and social responsibility. Probably most people in Everett in 1910—certainly those in the conservative unions and even many of Marsh's friends who were Socialists—shared his belief in moderation and reason. They knew very well the lice and the dreary brutality of the logging camps, the drudgery of the ten-hour day, the bloody saws and the asthma, the rigidity of wages that never rose as fast as the cost of living and that promised a new life but always in the future. They knew the layoffs, the hunger, the loss of self-respect, the desperation. Yet they had come to Everett in hope, and they had gained much. They, like Marsh, believed that they could some day be masters rather than victims of the system.

The Everett of Ernest P. Marsh between 1900 and 1910 suggests in many ways the America that Alexis de Tocqueville had found seventy years earlier. People were building, buying, selling, organizing, meeting, and moving. They were talking endlessly of individuality, freedom, reform, and progress, and these topics seemed to them entirely consistent with money, property, and conformity to the patterns of social advance. They were builders, joiners, materialists, optimists, imitators, and creators. They were vigorously engaged in knitting together the fabric of a new life and a new sense of belonging. For a while—during these years of growth and general prosperity—they found a sense of community in feeling that they could integrate their diversities and control their circumstances.

Men and women had come to Everett seeking economic opportunity, and they had, to an encouraging degree, found it. Most of them probably felt that. the system was giving them a considerable part of what they deserved. Hard work, thrift, sobriety, and common sense usually did yield success. A man could own his house, send his children to school, and find acceptance at his own worth in an ever expanding network of social connections. Private property was widespread enough to balance the dangers of absentee ownership. As Weyerhaeuser and Hill maintained their obscurity, people could believe that the important decisions for Everett were made by the men who had built their lives in and of the city.[6]

VI

Radicals of the New Order

||||||||||||||||||||||||||||||||||||||||||||||||||||||||||||||||||||||||||||||||

THE Reverend Billy Sunday came to Everett in 1910 to beat the devil in the devil's own backyard. And Sunday wanted the people to realize that he had come just in time. As he explained how this yard was rotting in a stinking heap of discarded promises and foul deceptions—rotting so that a decent man could not find a clean place to put his feet— his voice would mount in masculine contempt. He would throw aside his coat and tear open his collar. Working for the Lord, he would have the people know, took clean strength and honest muscle. Billy Sunday had a country boy's respect for God's warm sunshine, a serious man's disdain for pretense and polite convention.

With sweat dripping from his face, he would tilt back for the pitch, then lunge out toward his audience to hurl a terrible if invisible missile over their heads and beyond infinity. It was his curve ball for the devil. Hunched forward in his follow-through so that his face seemed to project far beyond the platform, eyes blazing, he pointed at individuals whose desperate gaze could not escape his long athletic arm and fingers. Then his sharp voice would fill the Everett tabernacle. "You dirty dog!" he would shout, as if in a moment of discovery. "You dirty dog . . . your *heart* is *wrong*. You have a nice *outside*, but you have a *rotten heart*. A lot of you people are like unwashed hogs and sows. You say that is *vulgar*, but I say *you* are. You are dogs licking your own vomit!"

As men and women alike wept and trembled, Sunday would continue his assault. They were stupid: "If some of the guns that you young bucks carry in your hip pockets were to explode, it would blow your brains out." They were hypocritical: "The so-called Christian homes," he gloated, turned out "eighty percent of the whores and gamblers" that infested the dens of Hewitt Avenue. Card playing and dancing, in so-called Christian homes, "ruined more young men than all the saloons the Devil has ever licensed." And this, he would thunder, was because the parents in these homes had worshiped the dollar, new furniture, fancy clothes, and shiny shoes, and in their stupidity had forgotten to teach and to act on the basic truths: "Jesus was either the Son of God or a liar. He was either the Son of God or a bastard, the illegitimate offspring of a Jewish harlot."

While Unitarians blanched and saloonkeepers lowered their prices, Sunday convulsed Everett with spasms of righteousness and repentance. Ernest Marsh, who had commented sarcastically in the *Labor Journal* about the amount of money Reverend Sunday was making as a dramatic actor, wrote after the crusade had begun that "there are happier, better homes in Everett" because of Billy Sunday. Marsh called the tabernacle sermons the occasion for "the greatest moral awakening in the city's history."

The Protestant churches, arming themselves for a battle to

vote the saloons out of Everett, had sponsored his coming. Volunteer labor had built the tabernacle to seat sixty-five hundred souls. Sunday's first sermon was titled "Home, Booze, and Native Land," and he delivered it three times that first day in June 1910 to over twelve thousand people. When he left Everett five weeks later, he was disappointed, he said, in the city's lack of Christian spirit. But he had increased church membership by twenty-five hundred.[1]

It was a sensitive moment for Billy Sunday to cry out a harsh moral judgment upon Everett's energies and directions. The trend toward good markets for lumber and shingles after 1907 had no doubt produced a veil of smugness that had blurred the community's perceptions of its own unkept fringes and allowed individuals, for a while at least, to ignore the terrors of their own personal worlds.

But of even more pressing concern to the churches was the development of circumstances which had once again torn the moral lid off in Seattle. The fumes were carrying up-sound for more than twenty miles. Seattle Mayor Hiram Gill had promised his business friends to restore prosperity by luring loggers and millworkers from the entire Puget Sound region to the flesh pots of the Skid Road district that had been notorious since the days of Klondike gold. And he was doing it. The saloons of Seattle roared twenty-four hours a day, seven days a week. The full magnificence of Mayor Gill's conception was dazzlingly clear when the Midway, a house for seven hundred women, opened its doors. The word went out, and the interurban rail lines were suddenly crowded on every run. The Skid Road district swarmed, the Everett papers reported, with "men of every station of life."

Elsewhere, businessmen suffered. Those who depended upon the payrolls from the logging camps were the first to cry, but soon almost all of them felt that they were being left cold and dry while Seattle bubbled and burned. The Everett *Tribune's* estimate that maybe 30 percent of the wages earned around the city were being spent in Seattle suggested to many

business leaders that the local saloons and resorts should respond in kind to the competition. Months before Billy Sunday
lay siege there things had indeed gone from bad to worse:
saloons never closed; some sold openly to minors; others
brought in the customers with gambling, prostitution, and
narcotics.

These lurid dimensions of Hewitt Avenue were no secret
—the idea was that they not be secret—and they were soon
offensive even to many of the most tolerant citizens. The
majority had come to assume that with forty saloons in the
city, a few grubby ones were inevitable, and to believe that in
a timber town a few brothels were a social necessity. But
many were not able to understand that the honest interests of
businessmen demanded a carnival of whores and drunks from
bayside to riverside. In the summer of 1910 they were wonder-
ing where it would all end.

The city's earlier experiences with a politics of morality
had not been promising. When the mills had begun to prosper in 1902, so also had the saloons and whorehouses. Competition, even during these years, encouraged a methodical
amplification of private and public indecency until in one
week in 1903 police found twelve boys drunk in one saloon
and seventeen dead-drunks stacked up in another. The saloonkeepers involved were even inviting retribution with increasingly ribald frescos, gambling and dancing, and prostitution.

In that year Mayor Jacob Hunsaker responded to public
concern by appointing Peter Kraby, a former Pinkerton, as
chief of police. In this appointment Hunsaker probably had
the concurrence of John T. McChesney of Jim Hill's Everett
Improvement Company, for Kraby was at the time employed
by that company in a confidential position. Because Kraby was
a severe and dedicated man who took seriously his orders to
clean up the town, and because he performed so well, many

businessmen were appalled by the loss of hundreds of week-end customers from the mills and surrounding camps. "What's the difference?" one merchant implored, "if a logger comes in and spends $50 in a dive? Doesn't the money finally get into circulation in more respectable places?" Soon dozens of similarly aggrieved merchants joined the saloonmen in peti-tioning for the dismissal of Chief Kraby.

The issue suddenly opened to an unexpected depth of conflict when the major employers in the city moved to define their own interests. Joe Irving was outraged because he wanted his men to be able to come into town on Saturday nights, find a girl, and get drunk. It was easy enough for him to pick his men out of the saloons or the city jail each Monday morning, but if they went to Seattle he had real trouble filling his crews. The millowners stood with Irving, and they may have seen some advantage in keeping around town the kind of casual and cheap labor—always a useful threat to the unions—that drifted in and out of the dives. The industrialists supported the downtown merchants, and when the petitions failed to move Mayor Hunsaker, his in-surance business fell off disastrously. By the summer of 1903, he had decided that he could no longer afford to stay in politics.

That fall, Nelson Craigue, a Republican legislator, endorsed the Hunsaker "clean town" and filed for mayor with the obvious backing of McChesney and the EIC. His Republican opponents included, among others, Albert A. Brodeck, the Episcopalian clothier who had so closely guarded the treasury of Trinity Church. Brodeck had the saloonmen behind him in a concerted effort to keep the nomination away from a "clean town" man, but he saw more at stake than girls and saloons. He soon turned the campaign into a businessman's attack upon Jim Hill, John McChesney, and the Everett Im-provement Company.

For weeks Brodeck published the *Daily Bulletin*, which ventilated all the sour feelings that businessmen had for years concealed. The policies of the Everett Improvement Company, Brodeck made clear, were a constant threat to them because McChesney encouraged more business to locate in Everett than could profitably compete there. He forced businessmen to cut each other's throats on the one hand, Brodeck noted, while he denied them any advantage of competition on the other. The EIC had an absolute monopoly on the rates for gas, electricity, water, wharfage, and land—even graveyards. Businessmen could appeal these rates to no one. Furthermore, Brodeck complained, the EIC received favored tax treatment because it could control the assessors. For example, he pointed out, the EIC electric company was bonded for a million dollars and insisted on squeezing 6 percent of that amount out of the city each year, yet it was assessed at only $140,000, the figure upon which it paid local taxes. And finally, Brodeck said, the EIC's man Kraby had driven away the customers that businessmen depended upon for their incomes.

Unable to deny such charges, Craigue and his "clean town" supporters moved awkwardly. They advertised the integrity of John McChesney, whom everyone knew as the silent and imperious agent of Jim Hill. They tried, with even less success, to denigrate Al Brodeck as a disguised Jew. In a delightful exchange, they caused Brodeck, almost casually, to admit that he was the only Episcopalian Jew in the city who had volunteered to fight with the United States Army against the Nez Perce Indians and who had been decorated and promoted to officer rank in the field of battle. In blunder after blunder, the Craigue forces learned that the businessmen were not with them, and that rail freight pricing that year had caused major industrialists to lose their regard for anyone associated with monopoly or Jim Hill. But before the mill-owners could protest effectively, McChesney had demonstrated the considerable power of the Everett Improvement Company by hand-picking the delegates to the Republican city convention. These delegates dutifully ignored Brodeck and handed the nomination to Nelson Craigue.

With Brodeck so blatantly the victim of the EIC, the Clough-Hartley group moved smoothly into political action. Without difficulty, they placed a Clark-Nickerson book-keeper, Thomas E. Headlee, as the Democratic candidate against the Republican Craigue. From a platform based shakily on "enforcing the law," Headlee took Brodeck's following among dissident businessmen as well as the votes of regular Democrats. On election day, 1903, in an unprecedented act, Clough's Clark-Nickerson Mill gave its men time off to vote, and Headlee won by a three-to-two margin.

Mayor Headlee served the establishment well. He dismissed Peter Kraby and almost immediately renewed the license—in the words of an opposition newspaper—for one of the worse "doping and robbing" saloon–dance halls. The loggers returned, Joe Irving ressembled his logging crews, and Hewitt Avenue was again an untroubled shelter for the weaknesses of spirit or flesh. Despite petitions from various church groups, Headlee began fining prostitutes ten dollars a month, a device which produced so much revenue that he could reduce city business taxes. Everett's "moral element" had without warning been caught and mangled in a revolt against the Everett Improvement Company, and it did not easily recover its equilibrium. The Clough-Hartley industrialists had found that the mayor's office, which paid no salary, was easy enough to staff with good open-town men until Roland Hartley himself was ready to take charge in 1909.

In 1910, even after Billy Sunday had renewed the cries of clergymen and aroused the public, Mayor Hartley and his administration were reluctant to assume a moral posture. To the surprise of some, they had appointed as chief of police the formerly stern Peter Kraby, who served Hartley as well as he had before served the closed-town forces. Under Mayor Hartley, Chief Kraby maintained the peace and kept city revenues flowing from a consistent application of "license by fine." The city council showed that it planned no restraints when it voted down a mild proposal for an ordinance against free lunches in the saloons.

But by 1910, the people of Everett were unwilling to be rebuffed in this manner. As were many people across the state and nation, they were increasingly impatient with a political system which allowed men in power like Roland Hartley to be so rigidly unresponsive to what most of the voters wanted or feared. The mood of reform that so distinguishes this period in American history had already blended the currents of moral and political revolt. It was certain that the people would have their way in matters of public morality. In the state of Washington, antisaloon sentiment had raised a major issue in the state legislature of 1909 and produced a local option law which gave towns and cities the opportunity to vote yes or no on the question of saloon licenses. Almost immediately, churches all over the state had organized Local Option Leagues which prepared petitions and rushed the question toward the November ballot.

In Everett, the Local Option League used the organizational techniques with which the city was so familiar. It formed "prayer-meeting districts" in every precinct and appointed captains to hold weekly meetings and to register all the unregistered voters. Following Billy Sunday's long attack upon the city's moral inertia, the league sent speakers into every neighborhood. Months before November, the saloon question had obscured every other issue of community concern. And with a devastating acceleration, it was rending the very fabric of community life.

The delicate seam of religious unity was the first to break. Leaders of the powerful Scandinavian Lutheran congregations, along with the Methodists and Presbyterians, marshaled for a holy crusade. With equal fervor, the Reverend William A. Wasson, a former rector of Trinity Episcopal, warned that local option would explode in religious conflict. He was right, for the Catholic, Episcopal, German Lutheran, and Jewish churches refused to support the campaign for no-license. Wasson himself led the defenders of the saloon by speaking almost every night. The saloon, he said, was the "poor-man's club." It had for centuries offered workingmen centers for recreation and fellowship that were not inconsistent with God's commandments. He would, he said, attack the saloon's abuses as well as any other man, but he would not help abolish the institution.

While Wasson preached and wrote, the newspapers reflected the division among the city's businessmen. The editor of the Everett *Daily Herald* advised that the saloon was no longer "essential to the city's development" and that the political and moral offenses of the saloon had "brought this storm down upon its own head." He urged an antisaloon vote as a moderate and reasonable solution to a festering social infection. He took care to note that Everett's proposed law would not be a fanatic's prohibition law. It would not attack the use of alcohol by reasonable men in their homes, but it would abolish the saloon.

The editor of the *Morning Tribune*, on the other hand, saw a no-license vote as "a mistake which the city cannot afford to make." Without defending the saloons, he predicted that closing them would severely inhibit the growth of the city and shift a crushing tax burden to other businesses. This thought was also the worried theme of the Everett Taxpayers' League, whose leaders included David Clough and A. A. Brodeck. In street meetings and in letters mailed to every taxpayer, this league warned that abolishing the saloons would increase other city taxes by 50 percent.

Toward the climax of the campaign, the Taxpayers League brought in Clarence Darrow, whose name and fame they thought might rival Billy Sunday's. Before a crowd of twenty-five hundred, Darrow spoke on "Prohibition, A Crime Against Society." He called for a defense of personal liberty and urged sincerely his own conclusion that local option was a "movement of the rich to deprive the poor of certain pleasures they enjoy."

To counter Darrow at this last moment, the Local Option League brought George Cotterill up from Seattle and found him an audience of four thousand. Cotterill in 1910 was a persuasive spokesman for the reform sentiments of the state. He was a leading legislator, a friend of labor, and the state's most vocal advocate of women's suffrage and direct legislation. The son of an English gardener, Cotterill spoke of the emigrant's just desire to build a society free from vice and saloon corruption.

The conflict between Darrow and Cotterill personified the dilemma facing Ernest P. Marsh as he explored the issue for the Trades Council and for the readers of his *Labor Journal*. He was aware that Clarence Darrow spoke for the cause of the wage earner in an industrial society and from a deep concern with the social reality of industrial conflict. Darrow's defense of the heroes of militant unionism and his association with men like Peter Altgeld, Eugene Debs, and Big Bill Haywood had brought him to the center of a national drama. From this position Darrow was saying that he could see the moral crusade against saloons as almost maliciously designed by the great vested interests to dissipate the energies of progress. The nation was progressing toward more freedom, not less, he said. His own desire was to liberate men from oppression, including the oppressors who would "banish all real enjoyment and entertainment from the earth" and those who from "religious and social bigotries" wanted to "destroy the liberties of American citizens."

But as a labor leader already caught up in the politics of state reform, Marsh knew also that George Cotterill was no less eloquent than Darrow when he spoke to the hopes of wage earners for a more human environment. To Cotterill, the reform of public morals was the essence of progress. He believed that measures such as local option would begin to shape a society in which the abuses of industrial power could not long endure. To men schooled in the power politics of Chicago or the industrial environment of the steel mills, Cotterill may have seemed a soft-headed and naïve provincial. Yet in his home state he reached out to those for whom Chicago represented the environment they were most determined to avoid. Cotterill wanted the new citizens of a new state to build new moral foundations for a new society. In this regard he was more a leader of community-consciousness than of class-consciousness. Yet he would liberate the unions. Close the saloons, Cotterill believed, and the workingmen would march to the union hall in a fierce, wide-eyed sobriety to demand their share of the world's wealth.

Both men held views close to Marsh's own ideals. With considerable misgiving, he saw the local option movement divide the labor movement as community moral consciousness transcended even union loyalties. Marsh was finally trapped in opposition to local option because closing the saloons would destroy the unions of bartenders, brewery workers, and musicians he was obligated to defend and whose strong conservative principles had always supported him when he moved to restrain the Trades Council radicals. With an edge of bitterness that had not before cut into his editorials, he wrote of the local option movement as the work of a "handful of fanatics."

To Marsh's sorrow, the city became a moral battleground. Women led boycott campaigns against merchants known to favor continued license. The Trades Council was working against its supporters in the churches. While church leaders were attacking each other as well as industrialists and businessmen, neighborhoods and even families became camps of heated hostilities. In the downtown area men expressed their feelings with fist fights every day for a week before the election. On Sunday, November 6, while groups of gloomy saloon regulars and contributors to the Taxpayers' League watched in silence, a great army of children marched with a temperance band through the streets of Everett, pleading for a new moral order.

On Tuesday the early returns were heavily wet, but the six o'clock whistles released the millworkers, whose votes brought a victory for the drys, 2,208 to 1,933. Precinct totals show a clear division between the downtown areas, where the presence of the saloons and the pressures of wet business-men held up the wet vote, and the residential areas, where the vote was dry by a margin of three to two. The workingmen of Everett—in this last city election before women could vote—had endorsed a reformer's vision of a better world. They had, of course, voted from a bewildering variety of personal and impersonal motives, not the least of which was one far more radical than Clarence Darrow could admit: the sober society would be a rational society, and a rational society would build a radically rational economic system.

The local option vote was a vote for a moral environment and the first passionately ideological vote the people of Everett had made. It was a vote that shattered a sense of com-munity which would not easily come again.[2]

The conflict had taken from religious groups a large measure of their social vitality. Within the Scandinavian denominations, individuals began to change congregations, and congregations divided to form new synods. These realign-ments tore across the network of friendships and group associations that had contributed so much to a sense of com-munity before 1910. Hans Solie, the carpenter who had organized a Lutheran fellowship when he came to Everett, saw this group disintegrate in the sour feelings that followed local option. New cliques formed and isolated themselves, and he felt a sad erosion of the communal spirit among Nor-wegians. This disunity and unrest around 1910 encouraged him to give more and more of his time to the Socialist party.

Not long after the local option battles, the Reverend W. H. W. Rees of the First Methodist Church fell into a deep sense of dejection. He had arrived in Everett during the summer of 1910 and had driven himself to exhaustion as a leader in the crescendo of local option emotions. Having won the battle in 1910, he had to defend the peace, and then fight again in the repeal movement that commenced almost immediately and pressed toward another climax at election time in 1912. Soon ill and despondent, he wrote to his bishop that the "moral reform tide" that had been driven high by the "great Billy Sunday revival" was fast receding. Those who had been most dedicated in 1910, he wrote, were "notable for their absence." His congregation was divisive and querulous. In their growing anxieties, some members compared him invidiously to Billy Sunday. Rees concluded that Everett had been morally and religiously burned out: "The worldliness of professed believers," he wrote, "the inordinate love of pleasure that has found its way into God's day . . . all have combined to make the work of the pastorate exceedingly difficult and loads down the faithful pastor's heart almost to the breaking point."

And it did break. Rees soon resigned, and the records of his church for a decade thereafter indicate no significant involvement of the minister or the congregation in the controversial issues before the city. This group, like most of the other major English-speaking Protestant congregations, was being unmoored by tides the members could not immediately understand. Most of these churches found new ministers after various intervals of discontent.

While Rees brooded, the editor of the *Morning Tribune* saw local option as "a gangrenous wound, sapping the strength and poisoning the system" of the community. He had earlier called for a moratorium on such conflict, a period of moral peace that would allow "hostilities and agitations to subside and bring the people again into unity."

He and others had expected that the rapid growth of the

city would continue to generate the kind of climate in which social lacerations would easily heal. But with an abrupt effusion of energies, the growth years had come to an end. In the first decade of the century, the population of Everett increased about 400 percent. But from 1910 to 1920, there was no significant increase at all. Labor and business leaders in 1911 dwelled on what appeared to be an obvious causal relationship between local option and economic stagnation, but they could not see that the timber industry itself had passed a significant mark. After 1910, the decline in railroad building deflated a prime market for lumber. At the same time the construction industry was turning more and more to concrete, steel, and composition shingles. As the national per-capita consumption of timber products decreased, the timber industry's sure instinct for overproduction kept prices in a steady decline. The people of Everett could perhaps feel these facts without seeing them, and sense that the limits of opportunity were no longer boundless.

To Ernest Marsh and the Everett Trades Council, the end of growth and the eruption of moral disunity were concurrent with a series of nasty labor problems. Each incident seemed to bring a heavier pulse of class-consciousness. When they could no longer feel the excitement of the crowds of newcomers at the Great Northern depot, carpenters and masons began to panic and rush toward any nonunion jobs they could find. Thus the building trades unions, which with the defunct bartenders and musicians had always been a conservative force against the radicals on the Trades Council, lost their discipline and influence. As if to rejoice at this development, the Chamber of Commerce then pledged to support the principle of the open shop.

Despite Marsh's efforts, the summer of 1910 opened a season of industrial warfare. The ironworkers and the electrical workers called strikes for higher wages and an eight-hour day. At the Sumner Iron Works, city police and private detectives protected the strikebreakers, and both disputes deteri-

orated into protracted bitterness. The two unions had the
support of the Trades Council, and in December the shingle
weavers announced that they would fine members who used
electric lights in their homes while the electrical workers
continued their strike.

Before the next month was out, the streetcar workers had
also called a strike against the utilities company, claiming
that the rising cost of living had made it impossible for
them to live on eighteen cents an hour. In daring to challenge
a strong monopoly, the union had the immediate support
of almost the entire community. Even the *Morning Tribune,*
which seldom offended any economic interest, recognized
that at least a 100 percent increase in their wages was necessary
for streetcar operators to obtain a "decent" standard of
living. The majority of Everett's businessmen, who paid un-
regulated rates for the water and electricity they could not
do without, felt little sympathy for the Stone and Webster
Company, an eastern holding company which leased the
utilities from McChesney's EIC.

Stone and Webster, with the monumental insensitivity that
usually characterized absentee ownership, brought strikebreakers into the city to operate the cars. When crowds of
people threatened to overturn these cars, the company
brought in a platoon of armed Pinkertons to protect its
operators. When Marsh offered to arbitrate, Stone and Webster refused him. The Trades Council then called for a boycott that closed down the streetcar system. With remarkable
unity, almost everyone in Everett chose to walk rather than
ride. When it was finally clear to the Stone and Webster
officials that the people of the city could and would get along
without them, the company granted a wage increase to end
the boycott. In the aftermath, the Socialists in Everett began
to publish a weekly newspaper.

The attitude of Mayor Roland Hartley during this Stone
and Webster war had given the Trades Council considerable
discomfort. Marsh had been willing before Hartley entered

politics to grant that he was a "man of honor." In 1909, though, Marsh advised union workers to vote against Hartley because "the colonel" was an avowed enemy of unions who would "put one class against another." As it happened, less than half of the city's voters turned out that election day to elect Hartley by a margin of only 321 votes. Marsh and the Trades Council soon had reason to wish that they had opposed the millowner more vigorously.

Mayor Hartley had found it convenient to absent himself from the city during the last weeks of local option fever. His low opinion of saloon reformers, however, was common knowledge. After his election he had favored the views of those businessmen who opposed restrictions on the rights of saloonkeepers to do as they pleased, and he made no serious effort to suppress the indecencies upon which Billy Sunday had so luridly capitalized. And when Hartley returned to the city, he was frank about his attitude regarding the dismal problems of municipal finance which the temperance victory had thrust upon his administration. He thought it outrageous that the city was obligated to refund thirteen thousand dollars in license fees. And he was furious because the city's anticipated revenues for 1911 were suddenly forty thousand dollars short of what they had been before local option.

Hartley's city council first considered a sadistically punitive occupational tax scheduled at five dollars a head on workers, three hundred dollars on bankers, and fifteen dollars on merchants for each thousand dollars worth of stock in their inventories. So high were the cries of opposition that the council abandoned this tax and passed instead a supplemental property tax, which was immediately challenged in the courts and declared unconstitutional. Under Hartley's direction, the members of the city council then turned to the task of cutting expenses, which they seemed to approach with a particularly vindictive gusto. They reduced the police force by one-third, ordered the street lights turned off, and laid off all city street cleaners. Stone and Webster magnanimously refused to turn off the lights, but the streets, in this age of horses, went without relief. Hartley even refused volunteer workers the use of the city's teams and wagons, as if to emphasize that a daily increment of horse manure was the inevitable consequence of the folly of banishing the saloons.

The city suffered. Finally in December Hartley called together a group of forty-six businessmen, labor leaders, bankers, lawyers, and ministers to discuss the future. Confronted with Hartley's inflexible righteousness, A. A. Brodeck of the Everett Businessmen's Association offered to raise voluntary subscriptions totaling forty thousand dollars—the equivalent of the loss in saloon fees—to carry the city through its first dry year.

At about this time, the streetcar workers left their jobs, and Hartley refused to offer the city's services in mediation. As protest grew against Stone and Webster, Hartley ignored the suggestion that he use his office to obtain lower utility rates for the city. Though he said he favored municipal ownership, he always qualified such statements with his phrase, "when it can be funded." This, said Marsh, was not honor but subterfuge, for everyone knew that next to unions, Hartley's most consistent hatred was for taxes. In his zeal to protect industrialists, Hartley had sometimes offended even friendly businessmen. In one argument over the utility company, a member of the city council had lost his restraint and called the mayor a "corporation tool." Hartley had ordered the police to remove that member from the council chambers. Following this episode, Marsh gloomily predicted that the people were sick of "corporation politics" and would probably vote for the Socialists in the next city election.[3]

The Socialists had prepared to make the most of this prediction. After the San Francisco boom years, men who could make a good speech vilifying the greedy millionaires and glorifying the radical unions were increasingly in demand, and by 1911 there were sixteen local organizations of the Socialist party around the mill towns of Puget Sound. Three of these clubs were in Everett, where members addressed each other as "comrade" at the dances sponsored each Saturday night at Liberty Hall by the Karl Marx Klub or at the meetings held each Sunday afternoon. In 1912, Eugene Debs drew a crowd to the Colosseum that overflowed into the streets.

The Commonwealth, a weekly newspaper which served the Socialist clubs of the county, released a steady flow of militant irreverence and Marxist statistics. One could read in this newspaper that Christian armies bred "syphilis among the unsophisticated heathen," and that because war was hell, this country should "let those who want it go there." But the editors often found their weekly lessons in their own industrial environment. When the Lowell paper mill gave a picnic for its workers in 1912, Socialists noted that the average annual value produced by the average Lowell worker was $2,471 and that his average annual wage was $519. For the difference—the surplus value—the wage slaves, like foolish children, got a free ride and all the candy and ice cream they could eat. Nothing, sighed *The Commonwealth*, could "compare in stupidity with the modern working man" who would vote for such a system.

To cure this stupidity, the editors argued, the Socialists must take over the schools. "The teaching of history in the Everett schools," one editorial read, "leaves the pupil with faith in the system of . . . wage slavery. History properly taught should leave the pupils with an understanding of the absolute necessity of collective ownership." J. E. Sinclair, a teacher and a Socialist, organized a Socialist Parents' and Teachers' Bureau in 1911, "the prime mission of which shall be to capture the schools for socialism." "Comrades," he wrote in *The Commonwealth*, "no crusade was ever more holy than this . . . the brutal injustice heaped upon the children by capitalism is too terrible for contemplation." It was absolutely necessary, he said, to teach that Columbus did not sail for God, that the Pilgrims did not seek freedom, and that the Constitution did not secure equality or liberty for all the American people.

Sinclair's plans for electing a Socialist school board were more than wild dreams. In 1911 the Socialists controlled three of Everett's seven wards, and they had every reason to suppose that they could expand these bases of power. J. G. Brown, president of the Shingleweavers' Union, was a Socialist, and so was Jay Olinger, then president of the Electrical Workers and soon to be president of the Trades Council. Several unions, especially the shingle weavers, contributed openly to the campaign funds for the Socialists who were running for city positions in 1911 and 1912.

The antecedents of this regional power went back at least to the sardonic James Frame and his urban populism in 1896. Many Populists, disgusted with the compromises of Fusion, found a new fellowship in the Socialist Brotherhood of the Cooperative Commonwealth. The mission of the brotherhood after the Bryan fiasco was communitarian: to colonize a state for socialism, to spread the gospel among its people, to elect Debs to the United States Senate, then to build a working model for a socialist state that would inspire a national democratic socialist revolution. In 1897 the brotherhood selected the state of Washington for their purposes. It was still sparsely populated but would soon, they reasoned, be predominantly industrial. It was a state won by the Fusionists in 1896 and already prepared for radicalism. It also offered cheap land and a mild climate. That year Socialist pilgrims founded Equality Colony on 280 soggy acres in the flat land of the Skagit River Valley, about thirty miles north of Everett.

For a while communitarians came eagerly to the West and to the Skagit wilderness. Equality had barracks-like family apartments, cabins, a common dining room, several shops, and a mill. It included about five hundred Socialists at the turn of the century, and there were a hundred or so more at the brotherhood's farmers' cooperative at Freeland, on Whidby Island, across the sound. Nor were the Socialists the only active colonizers who found the new state attractive during these years. Radicals of a more romantic persuasion could go to Home, an anarchist community across the water from Tacoma, where the newspaper *Discontent, The Mother of Progress,* advanced the cause of free love. There were in all twenty-six cooperative societies in the state by 1904. William McDevitt, a leader at Equality, claimed that these colonies made the state of Washington "the most radical state in political and social consciousness in the nation." This was no exaggeration. In 1912, Washington gave a higher percentage of votes to Eugene Debs than any other state.

The brotherhood, however, could not colonize for socialism as effectively as Jim Hill could colonize for capitalism. And, sadly for the brotherhood, the leaders at Equality argued dogma and ignored the economic realities of the Skagit Valley. Urban Socialists recently converted to communitarianism learned to curse the rain and fog, and by 1905 only the most fiercely dedicated stayed to argue in the cold mess hall and kitchen. In that year an arsonist of unknown faith put fire to the buildings and burned out the last of the brotherhood's hopes. Reduced to their own devices, the remaining radicals spread out among the Puget Sound mill towns to get a share of the San Francisco prosperity.

Whatever their new homes or circumstances, they never diminished the intensity of the arguments over the future of the Socialist party that raged between middle-class reformers on the one hand and revolutionaries on the other. Was the party—in Everett or the nation—to be moderate, compromising, and broadly based among wage earners, clerks and professionals, or was it to be thoroughly proletarian, anchored deeply in class-consciousness and honored only in the labor unions that were willing to fight for "industrial democracy"? Their internecine clashes were bitter and often ruthless, for the radicals were eager to purge those who expressed any

Hewitt Avenue saloons before the dry law (Photos courtesy of Everett Community College Library)

Robert H. Hanford with friends in an early (Premanes of Blume and Vandant)

reservations about the class struggle being a necessity for true revolution. In Everett, the debate about the value of political action to Socialists was especially heated, and the relative positions of radicals and moderates in this regard were not nearly so clear as they were in regard to the class struggle. Though some waved their red IWW cards proudly and condemned political action as a middle-class fraud, other local radicals, like the popular Jay Olinger, were at least willing to hope that they could achieve power at the polls.

Encouraged by the rising mood of reform in national life, and eager for some local action, the political militants were delighted when in 1911 Roland Hartley announced that upon the advice of his physician he was retiring from city politics (the advice of his poll-takers, said the *Labor Journal*). Hartley's withdrawal left the industrialists with no candidate. When both the Democratic and Republican nominees then called themselves reformers, it seemed sure that the old guard had lost its authority, and the Socialists presented a full slate for all city offices.

Their candidate for mayor was James M. Salter, a devout young Marxist who had distinguished himself in doctrinal purity and party loyalty. Whenever Salter spoke, he made it defiantly clear that he would remain a servant of the revolution. If it pleased the people of Everett to influence him in any matter, he said, they could do so through the councils of the Socialist party. His comrade-candidates for the city council shared this same righteous intransigence. In the fifth ward, there was Hans Solie, who, when asked at a public meeting to discuss local option and a proposed commission form of city government, told the crowd that if he could not talk about socialism he would not talk at all. After this singular statement, a burst of laughter and ridicule from the audience shattered Solie and left him completely inarticulate. The meeting ended when Jay Olinger took the platform and defended Solie, saying that he was an honest man who worked with his hands, not his mouth, and when elected he would be a true representative of the working class of Everett and the United States.

Solie did not have to be a fluent speaker. He won easily in his own ward, which was safely Socialist, and he drew a higher total of votes than any other candidate in any of the city's seven wards. The new council included Solie, two other Socialists, three Republicans, and one Democrat. The new mayor was R. B. Hassell, a reforming Republican who called himself an "insurgent" and who beat the Socialist James Slater by only four hundred votes of the sixty-five hundred cast.

Hassell had been a minister, a Populist, and an attorney. He had left the pulpit of Everett's First Congregational Church, he said, so that he could dedicate himself to the solution of social problems. He admired Robert LaFollette because LaFollette protested special privilege; he wanted the federal government to own and operate the railroads and the utilities; he urged the morality of the closed town. An outspoken critic of Stone and Webster utility company and of saloon excesses, Hassell impressed both conservative Republicans and radical labor leaders as a sort of middle-class and middle-aged Socialist who was confused enough to be really dangerous.

In his inaugural address—or sermon—which was the longest in the city's history, Hassell detailed the coming triumph of morality over greed and announced the advent of a new era. He promised harsh treatment of prostitutes, gamblers, and bootleggers. While he intended to lead the city gradually toward municipal ownership of all the utilities, he called immediately for a heavy tax on the private utility companies. He would also tax each and every corporation. As soon as possible, he wanted Everett to have a commission form of government and a single-tax system. The city should also do those things which ought to be done, he said, and do them "without regard for money." "Human rights," he emphasized, "are paramount. Property rights are secondary." Among Hassell's first acts as mayor were to order the fire whistles to blow an eight o'clock curfew for teenagers and to hire two private detectives to expose vice in the city.

As the new order unfolded, there were men like Charles Golden, who had just spent ten thousand dollars to build a new brick whorehouse, who waited in sullen silence. And there were men like Roland Hartley, who would not. Hartley had publicly bragged about his leaving the city treasury in good health, and he was deeply offended when Hassell asked for a stiff corporation tax to cover the city's burden of unpaid bills. When Hassell refused to sign payment for a fleet of fire trucks Hartley had ordered before leaving office, the former mayor became profanely indignant. Roaring through city hall, he shouted that he represented mills employing over four hundred men, and if these mills were to burn down, Hassell would be to blame. By the spring of 1912, Hartley's fury assumed crusading proportions when he convinced himself that Mayor Hassell was soft on the IWW. In April Wobblies talked twenty-four of Joe Irving's men into sabotaging one of his logging camps by walking off the job. When police reported that Wobblies in the hobo jungles were planning a May Day demonstration, Hartley and other millowners threatened to close down all the mills until the city took measures to keep the IWW out of Everett.

The city did nothing, and the IWW did not demonstrate. Hartley, however, was still disturbed, and with some reason. Earlier that spring he had with considerable pride induced the veterans of the Spanish-American War to hold a reunion in Everett during May. The veterans planned, of course, to parade, and they intended to carry an American flag which some of their patriots had taken from the Wobbies after a violent scuffle during a May Day demonstration in Seattle. When Mayor Hassell learned of these plans, he announced— to the delight of the Socialists—that in the interest of law and order the veterans would not be allowed to display the captured flag. "Colonel" Hartley tightened his lips, and when he delivered his address to the assembled veterans, his anger inspired him to a level of oratory that for the first time suggested the future governor. He moved from an emotional attack on Mayor Hassell to a frightful view of America in the grips of do-gooders whose actions pollute the moral purity of youth and country. "Where are we drifting when we have public officials like this?" he asked in his peroration. "It is not more men we need in this country, but more manhood!"

Although no more than a few people worried about the new administration's manhood, several people were increasingly alarmed by its dogmatic tone. Industrialists were concerned when the city council defeated Hassell's corporation tax by only one vote. Businessmen resented the dull week ends in Hassell's closed town. Others felt that the Socialists' consistently doctrinaire remarks about the Northern Pacific franchise might even endanger prosperity. And many more were frustrated by the council's refusal to heed any advice or persuasion.

The votes of Solie and his fellow Marxists, most people knew, were determined in lengthy private sessions at which a committee of ideologues debated the doctrinal dimensions of every issue. Each vote had to be measured rigorously by its implications for furthering the class struggle. It was painfully clear that the Socialists wanted only struggle, not unity. It was even more clear that in their minds the city of Everett was subordinate to the glory of the class struggle, and that the Socialists were philosophers of conflict who had no specifically relevant programs or goals for the people of Everett.

In a manner particularly offensive to a majority of citizens, the Socialists tried in every way to obstruct the movement toward a new city charter and a commission form of city government. Mayor Hassell himself was a leader in the city commission movement which, in this age of reform, promised to bring clean efficiency and professional specialization to the problems of urban society. Hassell believed that a commission could drive out the ward bosses, destroy saloon politics, and block special-interest legislation. He and Albert Brodeck of the

Businessmen's Association had drawn up the proposed new charter and had scheduled a referendum on it for April, 1912.

The Socialists quickly determined that ward politics was class politics and should be Socialist politics. The city ward was the base of their power, and none of the Socialists would have won their council seats if they had run at-large for seats on a city commission. In the proposed at-large elections, they could see yet another middle-class conspiracy to strip the workingman of political power and deny minorities a voice in political decisions. They set themselves to resist the new charter by every means open to them. With the help of the Democrat on the council, they delayed the election for as long as possible. They refused to follow legal procedure regarding the publication of the new charter until they were ordered to do so by the superior court. This tactic, however, brought them no advantage, for it appeared to most people as a foolish and even arrogant frustration of popular will as well as a violation of state law. When the people approved the new charter, their vote was generally seen as a repudiation of the Socialists.

As the city prepared for another election at which it would select commissioners for the new government, the Socialists presented their strongest candidates, Hans Solie and Jay Olinger. The shingle weavers were working openly for them in every precinct. Ernest Marsh announced the *Labor Journal*'s support of the two union men because this was, in a sense, a crisis of community confidence in labor leadership as well as a test of labor's ability to pursue its goals through politics. But at the end of an emotional contest, even Marsh could not persuade the city to vote Socialist. After less than a year in public office, Solie, Olinger, and Hassell—who campaigned not as a partisan but as the author of the new charter—lost by margins of about three to two.[4]

The new commissioners in 1912 were all businessmen: Albert A. Brodeck, a clothier, Alexander Thompson, a building contractor, and Christian Christenson, a real estate speculator and salesman. In a remarkable development, none was in any way identified with the industrialists. Brodeck had campaigned with his "union-made" dry goods and his friendship to unions, his help to "hundreds of widows and orphans," and his stand against the Everett Improvement Company. Thompson, prominent in the Masons and Elks, asserted proudly that as an employer he had never been at odds with the Trades Council. Christenson, who had been a street peddler in Minneapolis before coming to Everett, so well personified cooperation and harmony that his fellow commissioners selected him as mayor. All three were men in their forties, about ten years older than the Socialists they had driven from office. The Everett *Morning Tribune*, in 1912 dedicated to Theodore Roosevelt, was highly pleased with the new commissioners. The people of Everett, the editor wrote, had "declared emphatically that they do not want a socialist or near-socialist in office in Everett . . . the issue here was simply socialism."

Perhaps what the people feared most from the Socialists was that their political, economic, and moral rigidity would stand in the way of industrial growth. In 1912 there were exciting signs of economic revival. The mills had opened to full production in the spring without the usual gloomy talk of cutbacks or slowdowns. But by far the greatest promise was in the future opening of the Panama Canal, which would bring the world closer to Everett and its stores of timber. If San Francisco had produced security for many and riches for a few, the markets of Europe could raise eyes again to the wealth of Monte Cristo. By 1912 the canal seemed a certainty, and it was impossible to deny that it would bring unparalleled prosperity to the Pacific Northwest; United States Senator Wesley Jones said that the opening of the canal would move Everett into "the greatest period of development it has ever known." The Weyerhaeuser Company had already made its own unemotional calculations and was preparing to build its Mill B in Everett, an all-electric sawmill which would turn out four hundred thousand feet of lumber in eight hours, a capacity so huge that it would open a new epoch for the entire timber industry.

In the face of such confidence, it seemed only good sense to a majority of voters to turn the city government over to men with experience in business who shared a glowing faith in the capitalist system. Everett's new commissioners gave every indication that they would be hospitable to good fortune. They eagerly accepted their specializations—finance, public works, public safety—and seemed to act with the easy authority of experts. They abandoned the old radical idea of taking over the EIC water company for the city, and instead began to negotiate with the federal government for the acquisition of the Sultan River as a more permanent and abundant source of water. This would allow them to build a municipal system capable of supplying the future residential and industrial needs of a major metropolitan center. They began the systematic improvement of the fire department, ordering modern hook-and-ladder and pumping equipment that would form a versatile and efficient system for a large city of homes and mills. They prepared a single-tax measure for the November ballot that would gradually shift the tax burden from improvements to land. In all of these progressive steps, they had gracefully enlisted the support of labor and of the industrialists. Roland Hartley himself was serving on their civil service commission.

But perhaps the greatest expression of community confidence was the merger in 1912 of the Businessmen's Association and the Chamber of Commerce, which had for years been the lair of the founding capitalists. The new organization, initiated and engineered by Albert Brodeck, was the Everett Commercial Club. More broadly based than either of the former groups, the Commercial Club was to be an instrument of growth and harmony. Almost immediately it enrolled five hundred members: businessmen, industrialists, union representatives, physicians, lawyers, clergymen, and school officials. With all the energy released by visions of the Panama Canal, the Commercial Club sponsored industrial exhibitions, printed industrial prospectuses, and sent speakers across the country to extol the glories of Everett and its fantastic potential.

In these strong currents of optimism, the shingle weavers, under Marsh and their new president J. G. Brown, requested "trade agreements" with the Everett mills. Almost incredibly, they found the capitalists interested. After a period of negotiations which *The Shingle Weaver* reported was made possible by the "cordial approval" of the Clough-Hartley people, the wage earners accepted their first real contract with the industry. While tactfully silent on the matters of union recognition and the closed shop, the millowners, in return for a no-strike pledge, did bind themselves to a fixed schedule of wages and hours until 1914. Though radicals protested that the "agreements" would shackle the union during a time of rising profits for the millowners and would emphasize craft over industrial unionism, Marsh and Brown signed anyway, delighted that they had broken an industrial and social barrier, and convinced that they had saved the mills for the American Federation of Labor. Not for twenty years had Everett vibrated with so many reports and rumors of glorious change, and the future seemed even more tangible than it had to the men of 1892.

This optimism surged through the progressive spirit in Everett, blending the reform inpulse with a confident anticipation that the best times were just around the corner. It was elevated to the level of religious passion with the approach of the November elections. The state was ready to embrace Theodore Roosevelt and the Progressive party politics of his local disciples. Women would be voting for the first time. The people would accept or reject the constitutional reforms for the initiative and referendum. The city commissioners' proposal for a single tax would be on the ballot. And Everett would have to face again the battle over whether or not to license saloons.

With so much to gain from harmony, no one wanted to reignite the bitterness which had inflamed the community two years earlier. In the shift of positions, anti-saloon crusaders were on the defensive in 1912, and defending the absence of saloons was no easy matter. Most people in Everett were convinced that the no-license vote of 1910 had caused a severe financial crisis for the city, and it also seemed more than coincidental that the two dry years had also been years of industrial blight. Even more, as a dry city in a wet state, Everett not only had lost its attraction to many loggers, but had also been afflicted with an unseemly growth of "blind pigs," or speakeasies, which offered an illicit haven for illicit pleasures which, being underground anyway, were entirely beyond any regulation or taxation.

These were major irritations, and they caused H. B. La-Monte, who had led the Local Option League in 1910, to call for the return of the saloon. Though he favored national prohibition, he said, he was "opposed to local option and state-wide movements because of the ineffectiveness of the laws." The *Daily Herald*, formerly dry, took no firm position in 1912. Both the *Labor Journal* and the *Morning Tribune* endorsed an impressive list of business, professional, and industrial leaders who wanted license. The new city commissioners, in an impassioned letter to the citizens of Everett, said that "from any standpoint, moral or business, we prefer the license system of dealing with the liquor question."

Even with women eligible to vote on the issue, the churches and neighborhood temperance clubs were comparatively lethargic. The evangelist William John Minges came to town to beat the drum for Billy Sunday, but in 1912 he could evoke no terror that Everett was bound for hell. When the First Presbyterian Church, as it had done two years before, tolled its bells every hour through election day, many citizens were openly critical. Mayor Christenson threatened to quit that church if it could not stay out of politics.

The vote on the saloon in 1912 was predictably almost

twice what it had been two years before, and it was for restoration. Quite simply, enough people (4,308–3,636) had changed their minds to make a difference. The new Commercial Club assured everyone that it wanted no indecencies. Saloons, its spokesmen said, should be restricted to a narrow area downtown, and the new saloons should have no chairs, seats, or back rooms to encourage anything but honest refreshment. The city commissioners agreed at once and promised that if "any husband, wife, father, mother, son, or daughter" should object in writing to the sale of liquor to any member of the family, the city police would enforce the request.

In all but this saloon vote, the results of 1912 were a sweeping expression of reform sentiment. There were easy majorities to the constitutional amendments for direct legislation and for the local single tax. And though more of them voted for Socialists than for Democrats or Republicans, the people of Everett and Snohomish County gave their plurality to the party of Theodore Roosevelt.

In the mirror of its newspapers in 1912, the city seemed to be momentarily becalmed. It had ridden out the tumult of religious strife and class-consciousness and seemed poised on the promises of growth and progressive reform. A new group of leaders was using the city government to compromise, to buffer, to promote peace and progress. The Commercial Club, an integration of once frightful diversities, was ready to seek new opportunities. "Corporation politics" seemed forgotten, and women's suffrage, the single tax, direct legislation, and a municipal water system seemed consistent with progressive business leadership, stability, and vigorous growth.

The *Labor Journal* again had sweet words for progress and community. On Labor Day, 1912, the city saw the longest parade in its history, and the "unfair" list was the shortest since the *Journal* had started publication. Ernest Marsh was happy with the state reforms and with his immediate prospects.

Elated by the trade agreements, he was leading the shingle weavers in plans to extend their jurisdiction vertically throughout the timber industry and destroy the IWW before the opening of the Panama Canal.

Even the industrialists could for a while relish the future. The local Progressives—Sheriff Donald McRae, Prosecutor Robert Faussett—seemed to be reasonable men. Roland Hartley himself admired Theodore Roosevelt. Even more hopefully, the West Coast Lumber Manufacturers Association had come to life again after the rampant price wars and cutthroat competition of 1911. It was effective in obtaining favorable tariff legislation, in passing an industrial insurance law that circumvented a plague of accident litigation, and in turning the conservation movement—which in the curtailment of logging meant consequent higher prices—to the advantage of the larger companies. The state Railroad Commission was working for the manufacturers. As they looked forward to the opening of canal markets, it seemed to many millowners that the search for order across a turbulent decade was approaching a reasonable conclusion.[5]

VII

The Raised Fist

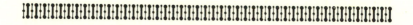

WITH the spirit that had moved Henry Hewitt, men of
the Commercial Club marked the new year as a time
to broadcast the glories of Everett across the land. But to their
unrelieved sadness, the new year seemed everywhere to begin
with panics over wages and prices as the country again slipped
into a murky period of stagnation and depression. If they
visited New York in 1913, Commercial Club speakers could
find bread lines feeding thousands of unemployed men and
women. On the Boston Common, they could hear angry
members of the Industrial Workers of the World resolve
that the unemployed wage slave must "preserve life by his
own efforts; that he must therefore take food, clothing, and
shelter where he can, regardless of the social edicts against
doing so." In Los Angeles, they might see police drive back
demonstrators who were protesting the unemployment that

meant "starvation amid plenty." In San Francisco, they would learn that the jobless were demanding work from the state government. In Portland, they would read that the city council had voted to give blankets to unemployed indigents who were sleeping on the cold floors of a public hall. Wherever they took their business evangelism after 1912, the men of Everett found that thoughtful citizens were considering the prospects of a deep social convulsion.

However certain the economic promises of 1912 had appeared to them, the reality of 1913 was that another period of vigorous but undisciplined expansion had come to an end. The railroads had been built, even to excess, and they had lost their appetites for steel and coal and wood and men. The towns and the cities that fed the railroads had, for the most part, also grown beyond their real needs, and the industries of construction were choking on their own products and turning more thousands of unemployed into the streets. When war began in Europe in the summer of 1914, the immediate disruption of world marketing patterns—the canceled orders, the stockpiles of goods that could not be delivered—meant more unemployment and at the same time a distressing rise in the cost of living. In the American West, particularly, the approach of winter brought a rush of grim incongruities: new streets where men stood in line to wait for the indignity of free bread; new railroad cars swarming with hoboes who rode new rails to the idle factories in new cities.

In the Pacific Northwest lumber towns, the promised opening of the Panama Canal had been the only shield against despair. Even the Weyerhaeuser Company found in 1913 and 1914 that the cost of producing lumber exceeded the market value of the product. But those who could do so kept their mills open in the increasingly desperate belief that the canal would justify their apparent folly. When the canal did finally open in the summer of 1914, there was for a brilliant moment the hope that the timber industry's capacity for excess production was not the design for madness. Douglas fir lumber and red cedar shingles could be carried by water to the cities of the world. But when war came in August, a government order closed the canal to civilian shipping. The years of waiting had yielded only more dismal years of waiting. In 1915, no lumber found the fabled markets. The railroads did not buy, and their rates helped to keep western products away from those who did buy. The growing preference of builders for concrete and composition shingles diminished a meager cargo year in California. Many millowners in Washington could wait no longer. Of the 1,143 mills in the state in 1909, 389 remained in 1915, and the loss only infrequently resulted from combinations or mergers. In 1915 the industrial work year was only 129 days.[1]

These figures meant cruel pressures on the progressive spirit. In Everett, there were so few payrolls that the saloons were overwhelmed by full houses of destitute men. Each month, in fact, hundreds of the unemployed lodged themselves in the city jail for simple food and shelter. In their anxiety over the health of the business establishment, the city's efficient commissioners soon abandoned whatever commitments they had made to moral reform. Following the vote in 1912, they had licensed twenty-seven saloons, confident that middle-class morality and business profits need not be inconsistent. When the loggers returned to town, it was true that at least some of their money was spent on dry goods. But when the mills and camps began to close in 1913, saloon competition for what few dollars a transient might hide in his pockets again encouraged the slot machines, card tables, cock fights, prize fights, and prostitution. This competition was again accelerated by events in Seattle, where, to the astonishment of business interests, the reformer George Cotterill had been elected mayor. Cotterill's rigid prejudices had brought a season of instability to the historically favored fleshpots and encouraged a worried underworld to make the easy move north to Everett.

By February, 1913, Everett was a depressed city and an

open city. The "restricted district," wrote one observer, was "restricted only to the city limits," and decent women, he said, were no longer safe on the streets. The new county prosecutor, Robert J. Faussett, appeared before the city commissioners to advise them that the city had gone to hell and that they should join him in an attack upon prostitution, gambling, and illegal saloons. When the commissioners indicated no enthusiasm for such a crusade, Faussett, with his own money, hired Burns detectives to uncover evidence he might use to arouse the community.

The prosecutor was a man of small stature, large eyes, a full Teddy Roosevelt mustache, and enormous energy. A leader of the local Progressive party, he was, like the commissioners, a man in his forties. As he argued with these officials, he was speaking for those in the city who were gripped by what has been called the national "white-slave panic." He was determined, in his way, not only to abolish corruption but to make Everett safe for chastity. Among the many social and legal inequities that disturbed Faussett was the fact that the Mann Act did not cover intrastate assignations. "Under our statute," he wrote to the governor in 1914, "it is a felony to steal a horse and a gross misdemeanor to steal a girl's virtue. It would seem," he continued with more emotion than grammar, "that justice and society should at least value the girlhood of our land greater than the stealing of a horse, although noble as that animal is, and enact a law or strengthen the present one so that those who engage in debauching a virtuous girl should pay a penalty that will teach others that such cannot be tolerated in the State of Washington."

Faussett's annual reports to the governor are indeed noteworthy in the number of sexual relationships that he brought to the attention of the state courts. Until he took office there had been no more than a dozen before the bar in the history of the county, but during his first year alone Faussett filed thirteen charges of adultery, five of rape, three of sodomy, nine of contributing to the delinquency of a minor, two for lewdness, and ninety-one for vagrancy which, in that year, meant prostitution. When his detectives reported to him their adventures among vagrants in the spring of 1913, Faussett was electrified with the kind of generous indignation that characterized many followers of Theodore Roosevelt. He revealed his findings to a mass meeting of uneasy citizens, telling them that Everett was infested with whores who were bribing police officials for protection and for information about any perfunctory raids. "By the gods!" he shouted that evening, he would not "tolerate such evil." If necessary, he promised, he would "call upon the governor" for troops to police the city and enforce the state's new "red light" law. He concluded with an earnest pledge to drive prostitution from the city and county even if doing so should cost him his life.

When he later presented his evidence to the three city commissioners, he learned that they found such public heroism extremely distasteful. After having been told on several occasions to mind his own business, Faussett became convinced— and he so announced—that many of the new saloon licenses had been obtained through bribery in high places. Turning then to fellow Progressives in county offices, he found the same turgid indifference. When he presented Sheriff Donald McRae with warrants for thirty prostitutes at Charles Golden's elegant "resort," the sheriff declined to serve them. McRae said that he could not circumvent city officials by going over the head of the chief of police, who had already assured him in deep confidence that there were no whores at Goldy's. When Faussett complained in public about the sheriff's refusal to become concerned, he talked himself into a fist fight with a deputy sheriff on the steps of the county courthouse.

Though he was punched in the nose, Faussett was not intimidated. In January, 1914, federal agents arrived in Everett, and after several days with Faussett, they took into their custody one man and four women identified in the newspapers as "French women" charged under the Mann Act. This event stirred the city police to arrest the notorious Mr. and Mrs.

Golden and their "girls." Faussett had the satisfaction of seeing Golden convicted in court and having a judge sign an order for the sale of his formerly plush resort at a public auction.

But Faussett had not forgotten the indifference of city and county officials, and his next step was to call for a grand jury to investigate prostitution in the county and the performance of those officials whose duty was to prevent it. But here he was again tripped by members of his own Progressive party. The county commissioners, claiming that their treasury could not support it, refused to grant funds for such an investigation. By this time, though, the wake of the Golden scandal had tumbled the city commissioners into a quarrel over the moral health of the city. Mayor Christenson was calling for "moral rejuvenation" while Commissioner Brodeck was resisting scattered pressures to engage the police force in a new crusade. For several reasons this was a propitious time for Faussett to begin a recall movement against the city leaders.

Recall was the reformers' ultimate weapon, and in 1914 Faussett could load it with the power of the white-slave panic on the one side and a growing hysteria over law and order on the other. It had become terribly clear that as the lumber market deteriorated, the urban environment as well as the surrounding area of stump farms and logging camps suffered from a kind of social rot that threatened life and property. Throughout 1913, to the dismay of businessmen, teams of safeblowers had worked their way through the more prominent mercantile houses. And hardly a night passed without a burglary and several holdups to alarm citizens everywhere. During a single evening in February, there were six holdups on the sidewalks downtown. Into 1914, hardly a month went by without a frightful number of lootings, rapes, knife fights, and murders. Bandits robbed the interurban to Seattle with cruel regularity, terrorizing passengers and on special occasions shooting a few. In January of 1914, four men identified only as "Italians" hit a bank at Granite Falls, a logging town

near Everett, holding the entire neighborhood under cover
by firing more than a hundred shots. (At the time all the
sheriffs in the state were meeting in convention in Everett.
Donald McRae invited the delegates to leap into automobiles
and chase through the countryside with him, but the robbers
disappeared in the woods.) In February, a Great Northern
mainliner was robbed by men who killed three passengers. In
March, garroters robbed men in the downtown alleys, and
there were several gunfights in the city streets. By that time,
twice as many suspects had been arrested in the city and
county as had been arrested a year before. Albert Brodeck,
as commissioner of public safety, and Donald McRae, as
sheriff, were being harassed by impossible demands on their
resources.

By that time, also, men from the logging camps, driven into
the city by unemployment, were bringing with them the
bitter slogans of the Industrial Workers of the World. During the winter of 1913, the Wobblies had marched through
town in a morose protest against the low wages of Great
Northern snow-shovelers in the mountains, and in the weeks
following, scores of these workers left their shovels in the
passes and came down to join their friends in Everett. They
formed a responsive audience for the national leader, Big Bill
Haywood, whose huge shoulders and blinded eye gave him a
natural rapport in Everett, when he appeared to address a
crowd of four hundred and tell wage slaves to fight a poor
day's pay with a poor day's work. "The IWW is . . . without morals," he roared. "To hell with reform! We want revolution!" Later that winter in Seattle, the Wobbly organizer
James P. Thompson declared before the United States Commission on Industrial Relations that the plight of workers
in the Pacific Northwest justified violence. The governments
of every state, he predicted, would soon collapse under the
strain of a nationwide general strike.

With such rhetoric in the air, Sheriff McRae took on the
additional burden of keeping Wobblies away from the few

operating logging camps. In the city, Brodeck enforced a hastily passed ordinance against using the streets for public meetings. The first victims of his edict were not Wobblies, but members of the Salvation Army, who subsequently accused Brodeck of not believing in God. When police did break up Wobbly meetings, the men they arrested said they welcomed the city's hospitality and the warm security of the city jail.

Thus the progressive leaders of Everett found that the period of their leadership was congruent with a period of appalling social disorder. In fifteen months, the people of the city had been variously distressed by an invasion of the unwashed and unemployed, by the apparent collapse of law and order, and by the flagrant expansion of prostitution. The depression had eroded just about everyone's tolerance and patience. Faussett's recall movement provided a safety-valve for a kettle bubbling with explosive social forces.

Of those to be burned, it was Albert Brodeck who had most disappointed the expectations of his fellow citizens. It was he who, in the Commercial Club, had united the diverse interests of businessmen, industrialists, labor leaders, and clergymen with promises of a new era. Brodeck had drafted the new city charter, a document of peace and progress, and convinced people that it was necessary for a prosperous future. But it was also Brodeck, for whatever motives, who had most heatedly opposed Faussett and resisted moral renewal. It was his police who seemed unable or unwilling to guarantee public safety.

And then, at the very time when his personal integrity was a matter of grave public concern, Brodeck was exposed in a spectacle of moral nudity that temporarily destroyed him as a community leader. Even while the recall petitions were being prepared, Brodeck's wife caused the delighted prosecutor to indict the Commissioner for adultery. In a sort of comic festival of righteousness, prominent citizens crowded the hall of the superior court to hear testimony in the case of the State of Washington versus A. A. Brodeck and Mrs. Freya Fredlund. Witnesses swore to having seen Brodeck enter Mrs. Fredlund's apartment on the night of the alleged crime, but Brodeck's friends, including Joe Irving, swore with equal fervor that Brodeck had spent that night with them in the sanitary rooms of the Commercial Club. Though he was acquitted in court, a nasty divorce suit followed that separated Brodeck from his wife, his clothing store, and his prestige in the community.

While Brodeck's tribulations still echoed in rumor, Faussett and former mayor Jacob Hunsaker revived some of the antisaloon groups and began circulating petitions which demanded the recall of the three commissioners. They charged that Brodeck, as commissioner of public safety, had not kept the public trust, and that Christenson and Thompson, the other two officials, had not compelled Brodeck to do what he should. Though these charges were legally vague, Faussett was not at all concerned. Under the recall law, he did not have to prove anything; enough signatures on the petitions would authorize a special election. The movement was opposed by the *Tribune* and by an organization of four hundred industrialists and businessmen who warned, with singular insensitivity, that a recall election would disturb business conditions.

Brodeck resigned immediately, and his enemies dropped the case against him. Had Alexander Thompson and Christian Christenson then sought the confidence of the entire community as they made their selection of a new commissioner of public safety, they could perhaps have put an end to the recall movement. But instead of trying to unify the city, they consulted only a few millowners before they chose Thomas J. Kelly, a former saloonkeeper and policeman who had gone into real estate and was a close associate of Commissioner Christenson.

This sudden appointment outraged the editors of the *Herald* and the *Labor Journal*, and these newspapers joined the de-

termined effort to recall Thompson and Christenson. With
this support, the Citizens' League for Recall combed each
precinct to register voters and validate petitions. When they
had achieved the required number of signatures to assure a
special—or recall—election for the commissioners' offices,
Christenson resigned. Thompson refused to give up his office,
but he also refused to work at it. He in effect turned the city
government over to Thomas Kelly. Thus the commission form
of government, embraced only two years earlier as a major
step toward a more perfect democracy, fell into the hands of
a former saloonkeeper who had never stood for election.

While Kelly held the municipality together as the one
remaining commissioner, twenty-two candidates filed for the
two open positions. To the consternation of many, these included both Christian Christenson and Alexander Thompson,
who saw an opportunity in a field so widely split. Besides the
recallers, their most heated opponents were the Socialists, who
were rallying everywhere in the city to regain their former
power and influence. James M. Salter, the school teacher and
editor, rushed back to politics, and with him came Frans
Bostrom, who for years had operated a Marxist bookstore
and had been the organizer and secretary for the state party.

The campaign incited more personal animosities than any
since the earlier public outrages over local option. Businessmen were angered by the cynicism of Thompson and Christenson, but they were enraged by the thought that they might
again have to endure the Socialists. On the other hand, the
Socialists had their own grievances and were determined to
take the local government away from businessmen. Their
men Salter and Bostrom did emerge triumphantly from the
primaries. The Socialist vote had been about 20 percent, which
was probably a good measure of their numbers in the city's
population. Salter faced Thompson in the final contest for
commissioner of public works; for commissioner of public
finance, Bostrom ran against W. H. Clay, who was a leader
and the favored candidate of the Citizens' League. While

city politics again brought men into the streets shaking their fists, the league supported Clay, of course, and it was morally bound to endorse James Salter rather than the discredited Thompson. Ernest Marsh ran an unusual front-page editorial in the *Labor Journal*, accusing Bostrom of not paying his union dues and of using the union to get a soft job in the Socialist party. The *Herald*, which had given the recall movement its greatest strength, was infuriated because its efforts had opened the possibility that the Socialists would come to power again. The voters made Clay, the recaller, and Salter, the Socialist, the new commissioners of the city.[2]

James M. Salter was then forty-one years old. He had grown up on a farm in the Midwest, where he early found himself among those of his generation for whom the drudgeries of agriculture offered few satisfactions. Like many of his contemporaries, he had sought an escape through a normal-school education. But his studies—as he said later—ruined his eyes, and he was thus forced to abandon his proposed career in teaching. Rather than return to the farm, however, he took up well-digging, and it was perhaps at the bottom of a well that he enjoyed his first hours in serious thought about social problems and the beauties of Marxism. He was soon attracted to more stimulating urban environments, and in 1907 he brought his wife and two children to Everett. Working up from the bottom of the depression, he found jobs as a millhand, a carpenter, a piledriver, a camp cook, and a tugboat skipper. Somehow in the course of these varied experiences he recovered the good use of his eyes, and he again took up the study and the teaching of American history. In 1914, the year of his election to the city commission, he was a teacher and the principal of a small rural school where his duties left him time to edit the Socialist paper, *The Commonwealth*.

As an editor and a teacher, Salter felt obligated in conscience to "insist on historical truth" and to prepare the city, county, and state for revolution. Following his defeat in 1912, he had convinced the local Socialists that their most promising approach to power and influence was through the schools. Under his guidance, they had found no difficulty in electing a number of Socialist school boards in small logging and farming towns around Everett—in Arlington, Silverton, Fortson, and Silvana. These triumphs were so impressive that the editors of the *Herald* were soon apprehensive, and they became hysterical when Salter as head of a Socialist Parent-Teacher Bureau published a manifesto that declared his broad intentions: "My brutal capitalist neighbor," he wrote, "we are after everything you have filched from the toiling masses of the world; but firstly and eternally, we are after YOUR SCHOOLS wherein you compel intellectual serfs to teach . . . the monstrous lie that the system you stand for is just."

The *Herald* began a persistent effort to eliminate Socialist teachers from the county. The first real confrontation with Salter came in 1913 when a Socialist board in Arlington appointed Salter's friend and comrade J. E. Sinclair as principal of a local school. Sinclair's administration began with a letter from him to the children of Arlington urging them to resist the capitalist requirement that they open school each morning by saluting the flag. The *Herald* aroused the few businessmen in Arlington, who caused the county superintendent of schools to revoke Sinclair's teaching certificate. Salter, through *The Commonwealth*, demanded that Sinclair be reinstated, and he added for the benefit of the *Herald* that the real threat to the children of Arlington was not a Socialist teacher but the whorehouses "known to all school girls" where "the filth that accompanies perpetual drunkenness makes these places cesspools of loathsome sores that fester down to the fourth generation." If the editors of the *Herald* did not understand this, the Socialist members of the school board did, and they fired the superintendent who had refused to allow Sinclair to teach without a certificate.

The *Herald* was in a frenzy. James Salter, an editorial said, was convinced that the United States was on the verge of revolution and wanted the honor of starting it. He led the county's Socialist teachers, who referred to the heroes of American history as "bums" or "blood-thirsty guys." This so agitated a group of people at Fortson that they locked out their Socialist teacher, who conducted his dwindling classes on a public highway. In Silverton, parents kept their children at home. The Socialist teacher there fulfilled his contracted duties by opening school on time each morning and then reading aloud all day from Socialist literature to an empty classroom. In 1914, the *Herald* editors fretted over Salter's victory in the primaries and were horrified when he won a seat on the city commission. Too many Socialists, the editors grieved, were IWW, and a Socialist commissioner could turn the city over to terrorists. Salter immediately probed the editor's deepest fears when, a week after his election as commissioner of public works, he announced that "other things being equal, red-card members of the party will be given preference" in city employment.

This was an open invitation to the proletarian radicals in the party and a clear indication that the party was still afflicted by deep schisms. In 1914 most Everett Socialists probably believed they should be politically active—that they should work to elect Hans Solie, James Salter, Eugene Debs —and probably most still believed that socialist education would bring about the proper socialist state. But these were the older men, the family men, those who owned their homes, went to church, and found in socialism as much fraternity as they did economic insight. They believed in union militancy because they knew low wages, the insecurity of employment, and the ten-hour day. Few of them felt any inconsistency in the doctrines of class struggle and political action, and fewer still understood the precarious nature of the lumber and shingle economy. They held a simple faith that collective ownership meant individual security and that most people would share this faith if they looked hard and honestly at the failures of capitalism.

But by 1914 these men were being relentlessly beset by younger radicals who had been uprooted by the depression. As they roamed from town to town and mill to mill, disfranchised by their mobility, they ridiculed Socialist politicians who had no power to help them and jeered at Socialist educators who offered only the securities of a dream. They had no respect for the capitalist system and no use for the attitudes of compromise or tolerance. In their sometimes explosive anger, they were eager to strike any kind of blow. The older men extended them sympathy, and, to hold the union together, made considerable efforts to accommodate their militancy. Since union and party in Everett were often almost the same, the Socialist party, the IWW, and the shingle weavers sometimes supported the same halls and sponsored the same meetings. It was not uncommon for a shingle weaver to carry his union card, his Socialist card, and his IWW card in the same pocket.

As the depression encouraged a rising tenor of militancy, party leaders brought in a young radical named Maynard Shipley to edit *The Commonwealth* after James Salter left the paper to join the city commission. Then in his early twenties, Maynard Shipley had attended Stanford University before becoming a professional Socialist. A nomadic lecturer and debater of real brilliance, he may have been the best editor the Socialists had anywhere at that time. Shipley was a writer of significant talent and enormous energy, which he consumed in a Faustian passion to know everything. He had dedicated himself variously to literature, science, politics, and religion, all of which had enlarged his capacity for social protest. He had written reams of poetry, and he directed his own play, *The Call of Conscience (A Socialist Drama in Three Acts)*, in Everett in 1914.

Maynard Shipley had come to Everett in emotional distress,

suffering the agony of a broken marriage, and he was even then the Byronic rebel, erupting in pride and anger, possessed alternately by alcohol, physical illness, and empathy for the masses. Living alone, he brooded in the rain and fog, and he was often shattered by loneliness and despair. But when he pulled himself together he was a driving charge of energy. He lectured, debated, wrote, edited, organized, planned, fought, and reasoned, and he tried seriously to unify the divergent and often hostile camps of the local Socialists. Both elegant and militant, Shipley could condemn capitalism, preach the necessity of industrial unionism, and bring crowds to feel the power of "the raised fist." Yet he defended political action and education. He held an unqualified admiration for Eugene Debs.

With his enormous output of social and political rhetoric, Shipley made *The Commonwealth* a going concern. He changed its name to *Washington Socialist* and spoke more for the state organization than for Everett, though the leaders were often the same. And they were pleased with Maynard Shipley. When a radical complained that he was middle-class because he did not belong to a union, Shipley was quickly adopted by the electrical workers—among the most radical of the AFL affiliates—who made him an apprentice lineman. He appreciated the brotherhood more than the affiliation, for Shipley hated the American Federation of Labor with a predictable passion. Sam Gompers, he said, presided over a simple labor trust, as corrupt and as harmful as any other capitalist combination. There was no inconsistency, he reasoned, in a man being both IWW and Socialist because both organizations were working for the overthrow of a rotten system.[3]

To the AFL unions, this was a dangerous rationalization. Maynard Shipley came to Everett just as Ernest Marsh and the shingle weavers had demanded and received from the American Federation of Labor full jurisdiction over all workers in the timber industry. They at first called the new union the International Union of Shingle Weavers, Sawmill Work-

ers, and Woodsmen, and later changed it to the less burden-
some International Timber Workers. J. G. Brown of Seattle
was president, while Ernest Marsh became president of the
Washington State Federation of Labor as it entered a new period of organization and challenge. Marsh had already accomplished much for the state federation, and he was the leading
spokesman for the idea that industrial and craft unionism
could be integrated. The Timber Workers Union was, openly,
an effort to stop the IWW in the Pacific Northwest, and
Marsh and Brown were working in the lumber mills, the shingle mills, and the logging camps to organize the industry before the Panama Canal opened a new boom.

Most significantly for Everett, this new AFL union drew
its initial strength from the shingle weavers, and the city was
the natural center of its activity. Marsh kept his residence
there, and he continued to edit the *Labor Journal*. Though
some industrialists had threatened to fire any man who joined
the Timber Workers, Marsh and Brown had issued nearly a
thousand cards in Everett alone by 1914, and the union was
the strongest the city had ever known.

This burst of unity drew in part from a general anxiety
over the expiration of the trade agreements which the shingle
weavers had accepted in 1912. Though Ernest Marsh regarded
these agreements as the greatest achievement of the state
federation at that time, neither the wage earners nor the industrialists cared to renew them. The younger workers—especially the Socialists—sneered at contracts that favored craft
unionism, and they were sure that the canal would open a
period of growth and inflation during which they did not want
to be bound to any agreements written before the growth
began. David Clough, who usually spoke for the millowners,
was in no mood to negotiate with any union, and this mood
was hardening into a rock-like determination. In this climate
of opinion—and in February of 1914, when most people in the
city were feeling threatened by unemployment, radicalism,
crimes of violence, prostitution, political corruption, and the

personal animosities of the recall movement—the timber workers announced that on the first day of May, without contracts, they would open a new era of the eight-hour day. Fail-
ing this, they said, they would strike the entire wood-working
industry.

Within a week, twenty-five sawmill workers who had recently joined the union were fired from the Robinson Mill.
When the other two hundred men at Robinson's walked out,
all the mills in the city closed down, locking out their employees. David Clough, representing the industrialists, including
even Weyerhaeuser, then presented an inflexible ultimatum.
The mills of Everett, he indicated, would stay closed for at
least a week. When they opened again, it would be with the
understanding that the owners would under no circumstances
discuss wages or hours with anyone. Furthermore, there would
be no union buttons in the mills and no union activity. The
industrialists, Clough said, had decided that they would "permit no outside interests to interfere in their business," and he
hoped that the workers would see where their best interests
lay. "We can show the working men," he said, "that we are
better friends to them than any labor agitator or union can
possibly be."

Almost immediately, about five thousand workingmen assembled at the Labor Temple and marched in protest to Clark
Park. The crowd soon grew to nearly eight thousand and
Albert Brodeck, who had already decided to resign his city
commission, told them that they could meet any time or anywhere on the streets of Everett. Then Jay Olinger, the Socialist leader of the electrical workers and a new power on the
Trades Council, said that all of the unions of Everett would
demand that a man be allowed to join the Timber Workers
without fear of losing his job. This, he said, was the only issue.
Unless it could be resolved quickly, he added with heated
defiance, Everett would learn the terror and the glory of a
general strike.

In the meetings that followed, Marsh and Brown knew that

to save the Timber Workers Union they had to contend with
radicals and industrialists alike. Unless Robinson took back
the men he had fired, the radicals would call a general strike,
and this, they believed, would destroy the union. But the mill
men stood unanimously behind Clough in his insistence that
no mill open at all until it was clear that there would be no
negotiations, no agreements, and no strike on May 1. The
radicals might give up other considerations, but they would
sacrifice neither their men nor the battle for the eight-hour
day. To avert what he saw as disaster, Marsh abandoned his
hope that at least the principle of the trade agreements might
endure. In a long speech before union delegates, he reminded
the moderates who wanted agreements that they had not been
able to discipline the radicals within their own locals. They
had allowed the conservative men of the Federation to be
criticized and ridiculed until the leaders were widely accused
of "being little better than dupes of the employing class."
The rank and file, he noted sadly, had rejected the idea of
compromise and reason and were following those who cried
the necessity of accelerating the class struggle. The trade
agreements, he said, could not be extended.

This compromise was difficult enough for Marsh, but he
did it to get the fired men back to work. Much more difficult would be to turn the radicals away from the May Day
strike. In a remarkable triumph of persuasion, he evoked the
last dying glow of the progressive spirit. Why, he asked,
must they risk humiliation and the future of the union itself
to strike impoverished mills when their owners might not
even want to operate? Why risk all this when the issue might
be more reasonably and easily won by education and political
activity? Only Marsh's sincerity and prestige could have carried this question without drawing hoots and jeers. In what
was probably his most eloquent urging of the progressive
faith, he called for an "appeal to the reasoning faculty of men
and women" across the state who would surely grant to labor
it dignity. If the union would not strike, he said, he would

make two solemn promises: first, that he would work up an initiative measure requiring all industry in the state to grant the eight-hour day and have this before the voters in November; second, and more militantly, that, "come what may," union leadership would "fight all reduction in wages." In a high tribute to the man and to the cause he represented—and in an impressive affirmation of the progressive temper among union delegates in 1914—the federation accepted his resolutions and again gave its confidence to Ernest P. Marsh.

The history of the State Federation of Labor before Marsh's leadership had been a mosaic of crises—strikes, lockouts, threats, explosions of personal bitterness, and desperate violence. But Marsh had made it an integral part of the progressive movement, politically alert and flexible, vigorously working for legislation that defined the social goals of the middle-class reformers. Marsh had encouraged the unions to see a reform achievement in the State Bureau of Labor with its several commissions for factory safety and industrial health. If the commissioners were sometimes negligent or grossly biased in their recommendations—or if the safety devices and other recommended changes never seemed to appear—Marsh still spoke well of the commission ideal as a step toward reason and as evidence of the progress of wage earners toward full citizenship. He had persuaded the unions to see a signal triumph in a workmen's compensation law that provided a rather meager schedule of accident insurance for wage earners while it relieved industrialists of an onerous and expensive burden of accident litigation. But at the least, Marsh said, the law represented a revolution in attitudes. It made society responsible for the crushing and tearing of flesh across the industrial base of the state, and the state of Washington was among the first to accept such responsibility. If he appeared at times as a "dupe of the employing class," no one questioned his integrity or his dedication to the union movement or the sincerity of his contagious belief that the unions could create a better world.

In November of 1914, his credibility would be on the line. The European war had further weakened an already miserable timber market and abruptly destroyed the promise of the canal. The new International Timber Workers, in numbers strongest by far among the unions and central to any labor power, was balanced dangerously between the evangelism of industrial unionism and a traditional allegiance to the American Federation of Labor. It could explode at any time in a red wave of radicalism and violence.

In his pledge to achieve the eight-hour day without a strike, Marsh had staked the future of the federation on his faith in direct legislation, which was constitutionally possible in the state of Washington for the first time in 1914. Those most eager to use it were, in fact, the Unions and the antisaloon groups. Marsh had to draft his proposed law, direct the circulation of initiative petitions throughout the state, and see to the validation of these petitions, all the while writing and speaking to urge voters to sign the petitions and vote for the law. He and his friends worked at a killing pace throughout the summer and fall, learning a political process that was as new and unfamiliar to them as it was to the voters. They worked against the opposition of employer groups that were quite willing to drown the initiative measure with their money, and against the opposition of almost all the important newspapers in the state.

Besides working for the eight-hour bill, Marsh had to fight the prohibition initiative that would push saloonkeepers, saloon musicians, brewery workers, and distillery workers into the embittered aggregate of the unemployed. And beyond the initiative measures, there were the candidates with whom Marsh had to be concerned. In Everett, Roland Hartley was running for a seat in the legislature, and his speeches were stridently antilabor. In addition to Hartley, Marsh identified a corps of undesirables, "as fine a bunch of stand-pat, corporation-hitched, reactionary men . . . as you ever glanced an eye over." The friendly candidates he could find were almost all on the Progressive ticket, which that year stood little chance of any achievement.

Though he worked with the energy demanded by this most crucial test, Marsh lost everything in November. The eight-hour initiative failed, even in his own county, where the major newspapers had apparently convinced most voters that the law would bring ruin to many mills and mean more unemployment rather than less. The prohibition initiative passed, even in Everett, where large numbers of union voters again accepted the vision of a sober and rational society. Hartley went to the legislature, and the Progressives almost everywhere collapsed. A week after the election Marsh wrote that labor had indeed lost everything "but our hope in a hereafter."

Within the ranks of the timber workers, the moderates had clearly seen their day. November, for the radicals, had exposed the polite dream of education and political action as a fraud, a dirty trick on the patience and humanity of the wage slave. They said that political action would never bring anything to the workers because the barons would never allow newspapers to tell the truth. There would be no eight-hour day until the wage slaves closed the mills that worked more than eight hours. They said that direct action was the only "reasonable" tool: threaten the industrialists with the same robbery to which they subjected the workers, and perhaps then they would respond. Such grumbling supported the more extended radical dialectic that soon dominated most local meetings. Among the shingle weavers, the older and more moderate men lost their positions, and they cried in despair when a group of radicals organized a frankly military auxiliary and began to study and drill in the tactics of industrial violence.

The persuasion of anger overtook the Everett Trades Council at about the same time. Between January and April, 1915, the president and three of the five council members lost their

David M. Clough (Photo courtesy of Edward Hartley)

William C. Butler (Photo courtesy of Everett Community College Library)

Donald McRae (1912 photo courtesy of *Labor Journal*)

Jay Olinger (1912 photo courtesy of *Labor Journal*)

Ernest P. Marsh (1912 photo courtesy of *Labor Journal*)

Albert A. Brodeck (1912 photo courtesy of *Labor Journal*)

offices. A new council created a board of control to determine union strategy, naming Jay Olinger as chairman. Among the board's first decisions was to take the *Labor Journal* away from Ernest Marsh and give the editorship to Maynard Shipley, the Socialist firebrand who hated Sam Gompers and the American Federation of Labor. Shipley quickly converted the *Journal* from a newspaper into a weekly digest of national Socialist propaganda and an adjunct to his *Washington Socialist*. The *Journal* was seldom thereafter directly relevant to the daily affairs of Everett.

Concurrently, a steady drop in the prices of timber products made the winter of 1914–15 the dreariest since 1907. Clear shingles fell from $2.87 a "square" (a bale large enough to roof one hundred square feet) in March to $1.61 in November, and this low carried through the next months. In February the shingle-mill owners, acting in concert behind David Clough, posted a 20 percent reduction in wages that was coupled with a stern open-shop declaration: "We will employ only such men as we please, organized or unorganized, and will discharge anyone when in our judgment it is necessary."

As the timber workers gathered to protest, Marsh tried to reason that conditions in the shingle economy might have forced the reduction, but the men were furious. The cost of living had been rising about 6 percent annually since 1909. They knew what had happened to the price of wholesale shingles, but they knew also that there had been no reduction in the retail price. Somebody was getting the money, and they would not be cheated by more appeals to reason. In a vote of 274 to 7, they rejected the wage cut, without, Marsh said, "the formality of argument." Jay Olinger again gave testimony against the capitalists and threatened a general strike.

When news of the meeting reached Clough, he made no official reply. The industrialists quietly closed their mills without indicating when they might be opened again. After a few days, Clough did consent to speak to the newspapers, and he explained that the Everett mills must conform with wages and working conditions prevailing in other parts of the industry. Mills in Oregon, other parts of Washington, and British Columbia, he said, were operating on the wage scale recently posted in Everett. Everyone knew, he said, that Everett for years had enjoyed the highest wage scale in the industry. But, he noted gravely, whatever justification there had been for this scale did not exist at the present.

On this point Clough seemed sincere: Everett shingles were not what they had once been. In fact—and everyone knew it was fact—the quality of shingles from British Columbia gave the Canadian mills a substantial competitive advantage. The fact was, Clough said sadly, that Everett produced an inferior product. Poor workmanship—and not the millowners —was ruining Everett, he implied, and to save the city the operators would have to demand better work. Thus the open shop.

The old man went on with growing intensity to tell how he had suffered from the trade agreements of 1912. The competition had forced him to beg the sawyers for more quality, he said, and while paying a union scale he had offered still more for better shingles. But for all his pleading, he got nothing but radical slogans and threats. Now his mind was set. He would produce without a union or he would not produce at all. He would, he said, "pay what the market permits," and he would hire good workmen and fire poor ones. He did say that wages would rise again when market conditions allowed, but that was all he would promise. For the present, he concluded, "there is nothing to arbitrate."

Most people in Everett knew that this impassioned defense was at least in part accurate. They might remember that Marsh in 1912 had emphasized how "cordial" Clough had been in leading the industrialists toward negotiations. They knew that Everett wages had been better than most. They had heard enough of rumor and substance to know that shingle weavers in their fierce fraternity usually gave more loyalty to their crews than to their employers, and that even a reprimand to a sawyer, no matter how sloppy his work, could ignite a local crisis. They knew also—and this was particularly dispiriting—that while Canadian shingle makers were grabbing Everett's lean markets, the manufacture of composition shingles was raising a black shadow over every part of the cedar industry. There was the obvious but almost incredible fact that some of the newer and more marginal cedar mills in Everett were roofed with composition shingles.

Most people knew too that whatever the relevance of these factors, David Clough and his associates had determined in this hard winter to use bad times as a club to smash the union. In the Labor Temple, the radicals seemed momentarily unnerved by Clough's iron will. Ernest Marsh went to work again, even in the face of doom. He spoke to the newspapers, and he talked of the dignity and decency of shingle weavers, most of them with families, who hoped to build a better life and a better city. The union's contribution to what had once been Everett's sense of community was much on his mind, and he said that the union, as much as the millowners, had its integrity. He wondered why Clough refused to talk with him. He was not, he noted, economically illiterate. Furthermore, it seemed to him that the mills in Aberdeen, Washington, paid the same price for logs as the mills of Everett did, yet Aberdeen paid union scale. If Clough would only show him the facts of production, he could in turn explain things and reason with the union men.

But Clough, Hartley, Stuchell, and the others would no more open their books to the union than they would their bedrooms. The very suggestion brought them to a spasm of moral outrage. They were set: there was nothing to arbitrate, and the mills stayed closed. For two months the only shingle mill in Everett to operate was J. E. Nelson's, and Nelson had independently sworn to "fight them to the finish" after several union men had beaten him in a fist fight on the city dock, where he was welcoming strikebreakers from Seattle. When his strikebreakers crashed the picket lines and there was more fighting, he obtained an injunction against the union's interfering in any way with the operation of his mill. Strikers then claimed that Nelson had imported professional thugs to provoke violence so that the court could move against the union. On May 4, over two hundred men were tangled in a brawl along the waterfront, and the police arrested thirty pickets.

When it was clear that the strikers might all go to jail, the last hopes of the union crumpled. The Commercial Club forgot its unity and endorsed the open shop; in another resolution it even urged the union to accept the wage reduction. When Commissioner James Salter resisted efforts to have the city police arrest pickets, Sheriff Donald McRae told the industrialists that he knew who the "troublemakers" were and would gladly run them out of the county. McRae's participation was a profound shock to union leadership, for the sheriff was himself a former shingle weaver, a dues-paying member of the Timber Workers, and he had twice been elected as a Progressive with unanimous labor support. The *Journal* asked plaintively what had happened to Brother McRae, and there seemed to be no answer.

By May, Clough and Hartley had built "scab pens," protected with searchlights and armed guards, within the Clough-Hartley complex. They offered five dollars for a ten-hour day to any sawyer whom they had not seen on the picket lines. Everett was a city of smoke again, but it was also a city of terror. Desperate for work, the men began to abandon the union. More than half had stopped paying dues by May. Many of those who were refused work took out IWW cards, cursed the union as a fraud, and talked dynamite. Marsh and Brown tried to get union carpenters to boycott scab shingles, but the carpenters, in common with the other more conservative unionists upon whom Marsh had always depended, had more than enough of their own problems born of the depression. Brown exhausted himself trying to organize coop-

erative shingle mills for the men who were blackballed, but
these mills all failed in a few weeks or months. In these last
moves, the two leaders had fought a destructive retreat, for
they left the federation in financial shambles. Finally toward
the end of May, Brown announced that the strike in Everett
was lost. But he and Marsh had lost much more.

It was perhaps Ernest Marsh who suffered the greatest
anguish of defeat as he surveyed the wreckage of the state
federation. For fifteen years he had spread his faith, pushing
it along with a smile, a joke, a pat on the back, a loan, a
speech, an article, a warm handshake. He had come to per-
sonify the ideal that the industrial exploitation of natural
resources could be humanized and that industrialization itself
could add dignity to labor. In trying to realize the ideal, he
had accepted the tools of the progressives, and these tools
had failed him sadly. Cooperation and compromise were
words that no one in the timber industry could use with
a straight face in 1914. Universal suffrage had apparently
hurried Roland Hartley toward what Marsh called "the most
reactionary legislature ever convened in the state capital,"
where Hartley would do his part to see that progressive ideas
were "slaughtered." Direct legislation, which Marsh had in a
moment of elation called "the scourge of defiant legislatures,
the instrument of popular control," had destroyed the movement to achieve an eight-hour day. It had further crippled
the federation by carrying in the prohibition initiative which
abolished many unions and upset the balance of conserva-
tives and radicals. Reforming legislators had written laws to
create commissions and bureaus, but the commissioners and
the bureaucrats brought about no significant reforms.

In Everett, it seemed that the community which unions
had helped to build was deserting labor in its most trying
hour. There was no reason for Marsh to believe that the
sense of community he had once with so much pride seen
growing in Everett could ever survive in the industrial age.
Yet he did believe it. Even when union meetings brought out

only the old men and when the offices in the Labor Temple were tended by the unemployed, Marsh continued to write and to speak, to assure five men or fifty that conditions would soon be better and that they could surely rebuild what had been so wantonly destroyed.[4]

VIII

Phlebas, the Phoenician

THROUGH the summer of 1915, Everett was a smokeless city, tight with silence. There were no crowds of immigrants bustling through the Great Northern depot as there once had been, no clusters of men and women eager with their quick talk, excitement, and cresting anticipations. Nor were there newcomers for the older residents to impress with the water and mountains and with the sounds of a growing community. There were no battalions of carpenters hammering out a future, nor was there any of the humor and security that had once glowed around the men with lunch pails who followed the mill whistles into a long summer day or across the northern twilight.

Yet in the mood of 1915 there was more suspense than despondency, for most people could not entirely dismiss the hopeful projections of 1912. Every indicator or analysis showed a world that should be reaching out for timber products, but, by some insane logic, was not. Some providential stupidity, some incredibly mad or capricious convergence of circumstance had numbed the fundamental attractions of supply and demand. Depressed markets should revive, but they did not. Trade routes should open, but they did not. The war was everywhere creating and destroying, extending and denying. The war was so meaningless that it explained everything from sense and nonsense to good and evil.

Or it explained nothing, promised nothing. In the fall when salmon leaped in silver splashes of green and blue, men watched idly and talked of the madness in Europe. Across the bay there were no schooners, no steamships rigged for the cargo trade. Prices were as low as they had ever been since the panic year, 1893. The approach of winter promised only rain and darker days.

Of those in Everett who suffered least from the depression, perhaps the most imperturbable was William C. Butler. Whatever his personal hungers, he did not lack money to feed them, and this trial by endurance may have held for him certain gray satisfactions. The crisis would surely shake out the petty operators. It would leave labor more docile; it would allow serious and responsible men to restore order and reason. It would soon end, of course, and he would be stronger than ever before. The demands of war would soon be clear: if the destruction of San Francisco had made princes of the Everett capitalists, the destruction of Europe would make William C. Butler a king.

When Maynard Shipley wrote in 1915 that the Everett millowners did only what Butler wanted them to do, he wrote as much from fact as from Socialist prejudice. Outside the Weyerhaeuser complex, Butler's Everett First National Bank and his Everett Trust and Savings Bank stood like the

posts and beams under a vaulted ceiling to square the structure of a sawdust economy. Throughout the city and county
there were at least sixty-five mills and logging companies in
which he held a compelling interest. Butler's money had built
mills and bought machines, financed businesses and services,
and sustained wage earners in their aspirations to own their
homes. And this was money that integrated the communal
identities of purpose and direction, for the notes of demand
Butler held in his files represented a vast potential for confidence or despair. In manipulating this potential, Butler enriched himself by perhaps a million dollars a year. There was
more than enough truth in the saying that Everett rested on
Jim Hill's land and Butler's gold.

But few people, and certainly not the young radical, Maynard Shipley, knew the full dimensions of Butler's logging,
milling, and commercial investments around Everett, and none
of these few realized the extent of his holdings in rail and
utility stock and in the banks of New York. Those who
could understand his national political influence were not in
position to see how he supervised the Republican party in
the state of Washington. The broad scope of his economic
and political power was, in fact, not open to any scrutiny,
for of all the Everett elite, Butler concealed himself with the
most skill and determination. Perhaps he needed to be feared
and knew how fear can feed on mystery. Or perhaps he
only wanted to hide from historians. Whatever his motives,
he drew between himself and the world a curtain so fine
that he could not be known even by his contemporaries. As
some men seek fame to herald or to enhance their power,
Butler resolutely sought obscurity, and, as was his custom
in life, he achieved most of what he wanted.

But this much we know: in 1915, Butler stood aloof and
alone among the Everett barons, a link between the past and
the present, as hard and as cold as the first bar of silver he
had carried more than twenty years before from the smelter
he managed for John D. Rockefeller. Pre-eminently graced

with intelligence, wealth, education, and familial prestige, he had reached his maturity with unshakable confidence. His speech, his demeanor, the cut of his clothes, the thin line of graying hair, the silver-rimmed spectacles, the slight physical frame, the soft face, clean-shaved except for a carefully clipped, even severe, mustache—there are men who still remember these things about Butler which suggested a thousand other men cut from the same culture at the same time who looked like Elihu Root or Woodrow Wilson. They suggested also the distinctive and distinguished aura of established riches and traditions, of New York Butlers and Rockefellers, of the deep reservoirs of calm dignity and endless vigor. He was Everett's most brilliant intellect, most influential political force, most sophisticated gentleman. He was Everett's evidence that the city was more than a shop and trading post for backwoods entrepreneurs. In an age when capital was power and the manipulation of it was strength, Butler glittered when he walked.

In the years following the San Francisco prosperity, Butler had built his colonial mansion in the northern reach of the city, near the edge of the bluff above the bayfront mills. This beautiful stretch of land and woods rose abruptly from the beach where Captain George Vancouver had first claimed Port Gardner Bay. It gave Butler an imperial view of the city's industrial organs, and beyond them, of the water, the timbered islands, the Olympic mountains and wilderness. The house itself was sumptuously spacious, yet of conventional grace, a studied acceptance of luxury without ostentation. It would have pleased Elihu Root or Woodrow Wilson.

It may have pleased William C. Butler. Yet he customarily left the house for three months of each year, joining his brother and a small group of friends in California or Hawaii for golf each day and for their deep soundings in the drifts of money, politics, and power. He left no indication of what the house meant to him or what Everett meant to him. There is nothing to indicate that he ever enjoyed a day on the bluff or that his blood ever rushed to the fall of rain, the movement of boats, the cry of a gull, or the deep swell of the sea.

This we do know: newspapers from the early 1900s show that the presence of Mr. and Mrs. William C. Butler quickened the tone of many a yacht rendezvous, dinner party, musical evening, and holiday extravagance. But even then, one senses, he was somewhat insulated from the pulse of community by his college degrees, his library, his verbal elegance, his impenetrable reserve. Though his only child, a boy, attended the public schools and roamed the river banks and the woods with the young Hartleys and Cloughs, Butler himself never accepted any intimacy with the industrialists. Then in 1911, at a time very nearly concurrent with his opening the new home, Butler's son died. Local lore held that a shattering grief pressed the parents into an enduring seclusion. We do know that in the house that would have accommodated a family of twelve, servants hardly ever opened a door to a visitor.

Butler was awake at five, dressed and reading before six, seated for breakfast at seven. His morning reading was the newspapers: the Everett *Daily Herald*, of which he approved because among the local dailies it carried the most national and international news and because it faithfully reflected his views and stood with the regular Republican party. For more local news, he scanned the Everett *Tribune*, gone soft on progressivism, but in 1915—very likely with his explicit encouragement—finding stability again. It was also a matter of some interest to him to see with what fidelity the editors of both papers complied with his wish that they carry no news whatsoever about William C. Butler. Besides the Everett papers, he must have found it necessary to sharpen his political intelligence on the Seattle dailies. And for matters of more substance, he read the New York papers as thoroughly as did any resident of the larger financial and political establishment to whom a mastery of current detail was a formidable weapon.

A few minutes before nine, he stepped to the porte-cochere where his limousine was waiting. Butler had developed an early enthusiasm for motoring, and his machines were among the first and the finest in the city. By 1915 there were maybe a hundred or so automobiles around the streets, and the police, the sheriff, and the fire department had motor vehicles. Many of the leading citizens were driving closed sedans, but none was more distinctive than Butler's, with its chauffeur, and with the flawless and sober formality of the banker's suit, coat, hat, and cane. The appearance was enough to inspire the stories that Butler personally checked the grocery lists of those who borrowed his money, searching for any unseemly personal extravagance, or that he frightened businessmen into opening their stores before nine o'clock so that he could never see them closed.

At precisely nine o'clock, he stepped through the doors of the First National Bank. After a minimum of pleasantries, he sought the absolute security of his private office and the confidence of his male secretary, who served also as his administrative assistant. It was through this agent that Butler conducted most of his business and investments, and supported most of his charities. The Butler name could appear in formal context as an officer of his banks, or, less often, as secretary-treasurer of the companies he established, or as a board member of the Everett General Hospital, which he had sponsored. But even in these matters he was reluctant to be identified. Beyond these instances he never allowed his own name to appear on the stocks, securities, deeds, and sales that were the substance of his empire.

During the morning he might spend his freshest hours in correspondence with politicians, financiers, brokers, millowners, or with his brother, Nicholas Murray Butler, then president of Columbia University in New York. Writing was a severely demanding performance, not because he lacked fluency, but because he wanted to be perfectly understood. W. C. Butler was an engineer of syntax and grammar, and he might spend an hour balancing one sentence. This effort was no idle conceit, for it pleased him to know that his letters to his brother were not infrequently read aloud to men of predominant financial and political power, including, sometimes, the President of the United States. By 1915, however, he was using the telephone with considerable versatility, and this allowed him to write only when he wanted his views and opinions raised at the highest levels. During these years, letters to his brother show his increasing reluctance to commit the details of his life or work to paper. When his secretaries could get "NMB" on the line in New York almost as easily as they could Clough in Everett, he mastered yet another step into obscurity.

At one o'clock—and again with precision—his limousine stood waiting. He left his offices and was delivered to the rooms of the Cascade Club, where he took lunch for an hour. The afternoon there and at the bank was for conferences to which the principals of the "Butler interests" came singly or in groups to inform him of their wishes and to hear his conclusions. This elite group included, often enough, David Clough, generally referred to as "the governor." With his youth as well as several fortunes behind him, Clough wanted still one more bonanza before he died. As vigorous as he was imperious, he had the impatience of an old soldier waiting to be touched again with the keen exhilaration of decision, command, and triumph. Gruff and patriarchal in his bearing, Clough was not a man to accept advice, and whatever harmony there was between him and the banker must have been based on Butler's respect for the old man's character and the rigidity of his convictions. He was unlettered but baronial, perhaps the last of the nearly great semiliterates, insensitive to the affairs of the larger world but a master in his own domain.

Usually with Clough came the son-in-law, "the colonel," Roland Hartley, who in age and interests was somewhat closer to Butler. Hartley's sons were then at Yale, and middle age had stirred in him swirls of ambition and restlessness which money and Everett alone could not satiate. Carefully mustached, but as short as Napoleon I, his fastidious appearance and mercurial temper might easily incite ridicule from the irreverent. But the pickets who jeered him as "two-by-four Hartley" only encouraged him to be more garrulous and impetuous. His belligerence and loud-mouthed virility had not always served him well as a businessman. He was never the industrialist that his father-in-law was, and he apparently did not care to be, except, perhaps, to make the old man and the world admit that he had the capacity. But unlike Clough, Hartley could display great personal charm. He was lively, outspoken, energetic, courageous, often cynical, and frequently witty. He was a man of intensely strong convictions and of intensely loyal friends and enemies. He was the soul of gregariousness, ever prominent in the Masons, the Eagles, the Elks, the Woodsmen of the World, and in a fraternal order of lumbermen who took a curious glee in calling themselves the Hoo Hoos.

Everyone knew that Roland Hartley was warmly stimulated by crowds and acclaim, and that he was moving inevitably toward political power. He liked to travel. He liked to meet strangers and startle them with clichés which defined his serious philosophy of life. The right words came easily for him, and he could speak without notes literally for hours, villifying labor unions, cursing socialism, or praising economic individuality and industrial freedom. There was little about progress and nothing about the Progressive Age which he could not hold up to wrath and condemnation. He detested prohibitionists, social workers, suffragettes, direct primaries, and direct legislation. He hated radicals, agitators, internationalists, pacifists, unions, taxes, and progressive education. He was proud that as a legislator he had introduced laws against picketing and against the teaching of social science. He had voted against an eight-hour law for women. Though Hartley sometimes worked himself into uncontrollable passages of vulgarity and profanity, Butler had more in

common with him than with David Clough. Butler had the
money, the knowledge of men, and the sources of power that
could and would become the instruments of Hartley's inde-
pedence from his father-in-law and of his ultimate value to
Butler. Already in 1915, Roland Hartley—undoubtedly with
Butler's concurrence—had decided that he would become
governor of the state.

However well these men furthered Butler's ambitions, it
was Joe Irving who best served him in the daily challenges
of making money in mills, land, and logs. In 1915 Irving was
still a huge and powerful man, still a swaggering folk tale
of physical strength, whisky, women, the fist, the oath, and
the command. Butler tolerated and even validated the legend
by keeping in his private office a case of whisky and a box
of cigars, neither of which Butler himself would ever touch
or offer to anyone but Joe Irving. As the overseer of the
Butler interests in the woods, Irving enjoyed an access into
the inner offices—one of the few personal privileges that
Butler ever granted to any man. In their smoky conferences,
Irving brought to Butler the insights that the banker could
turn into millions of dollars, for Irving knew land, leases, and
logging, and he knew how to work machinery and men.

At precisely six o'clock, the sedan appeared again, and
Butler rode directly to his Grand Avenue home. At dinner he
saw only his wife, Eleanor, and the servants, for the Butlers
did not entertain. Though his brother may have visited him
once or twice, and though he may have spent a rare evening
with Jim Hill's men—McChesney in Everett and Judge
Thomas Burke in Seattle—after their son's death the Butlers
had fashioned their lives in a way that excluded their being
either hosts or guests. Thus night after night, year after year,
sun, moon, stars, rain, the Butlers faced each other across a
polished room where sorrow ran so deep or pride so high
that apparently no other mortals could share their silence.
This much we know: it was said in Everett that Butler spent
each evening at a desk, working or reading, always fully

dressed with his coat, tie, and high collar, pondering always the profit and the loss. At the hour of nine, again with inexorable regularity, servants locked the doors and extinguished the lights, and Butler retired with his wife to the darkness of their unspoken griefs or exultations.

Who was William Butler? Like those who so bitterly hated him, he found his identity not in where he lived or where he came from, but in his own accomplishments. He was a banker. He manipulated capital. He bought and sold. He organized and disorganized companies. He invested, collected, leased, loaned, and controlled. And he did these things better than most men of his time.

He was a conservative. He fought against municipal ownership, against every new scheme of taxation, every reform, every wave of change. He frustrated compromise, directed the opinions of newspapers, and shaped candidates. He hoped to make Hartley governor of Washington. He hoped to make his brother President of the United States. He hoped to break Hiram Johnson, the California insurgent, and Robert La-Follette, the liberal from Wisconsin. He worked with money to defeat Democrats, Progressives, Socialists, labor organizers, and all varieties of social reformers. And in this, too, he was more successful than were most men.

He was an anonymous philanthropist. He quietly underwrote the future of the Everett General Hospital, for years balancing the budget with significant sums of his own money. As an officer of the hospital he wrote off the debts of individuals who could not pay their bills, for in this capacity he was never the stern judge of the loss or the profit. We know that he gave the hospital $250,000 to build a maternity ward, and that he and his wife left more than a million dollars in trust for "aid to charitable institutions for relief of the aged, indigent, sick and maimed, and for the support and education for orphans and indigent children."

Who was William C. Butler? He was what he did. He played golf in Santa Barbara, motored in Yosemite, plotted politics in Pasadena, bought, sold, loaned, and invested in Everett, collected dividends in New York. He also thought sometimes upon the poor and the sick and those who knew despair. He kept men at a distance while he tightened the curtain. He let no one inquire into the passions of his past or present, and he left no proud mark to suggest the longings of his firm and secret heart.[1]

IX

The Iron Law

||||||||||||||||||||||||||||||||||||||||||||||||||||||||||||||||||||||||

WHEN Butler closed his house in the fall of 1915, he could take certain satisfactions in the year nearly past. The Timber Workers' Union, which he saw as the chief danger to industrial peace and profit, was broken. The local Socialist, James Salter, was defeated. The state's Progressives had disappeared, and the legislature, with Hartley's participation, has reversed several of the most threatening Progressive achievements. But most encouraging of all recent developments were the billows of smoke and cinders that rose again from the Everett mills.

Economic gloom had dissipated in a few short weeks, and the causes were so simple that most timber men had not anticipated them. When American farmers had sold their wheat and corn that autumn, they had delighted in an in-

satiable market at war-bloated prices for everything they
offered. Money came easily, and they spent it on the lumber
they had not bought for years. At the same time European
markets also demanded lumber, especially pine for ammunition boxes and coffins, and every shipload of pine left a new
American demand for Douglas fir and red cedar. As late as
September, depressed manufacturers had noted two hundred
thousand idle freight cars across the nation, but in November
the mills were running two shifts, and there were not enough
freight cars to go around. Businessmen as well as industrialists
could smell a sweetness in the air that they had not known
since 1906.

These winds of optimism had brought misfortune to James
Salter when he stood for re-election as commissioner of
public works in November. He had been challenged by
Dennis D. Merrill, a real estate salesman, who told the people
that his business principles and experience offered more to
Everett for the good years to come than did schoolteaching
and Marxism. Though Salter's rhetorical intemperances had
not seemed disproportionate during lean times, they brought
him real embarrassments in 1915 when he felt the city rise
against him from both the right and the left.

On the one hand, the Socialists themselves opened a new
season of intraparty discord over doctrinal purity. During an
uproarious evening, Dr. Edwin Brown of Seattle, a dentist
and a prominent moderate whom the state's radicals had
excommunicated a few years before, came to Everett and
told a large audience about the "corruption" and "trickery"
of the "reds," including James Salter. Brown argued noisily
with the Everett hecklers, including Salter, and Salter himself moved to the stage to push Brown aside and shout down
his followers. In the balcony, Jay Olinger brought the reds
to their feet, while below on the floor Frans Bostrom defended Brown and the moderates. The principals were
cheered and encouraged by a crowd of men and women

who had not seen such a good show in years, but newspaper reporters wrote mostly about how some Socialists had accused others of pay-offs, kickbacks, and rigged elections.

Then the Spanish-American War veterans, led by Roland Hartley, hit Salter with a tensely humorless list of his alleged disloyalties. As a teacher, they accused, he had removed the pictures of George Washington in his schoolroom and replaced them with photographs of Eugene Debs. He had refused to stand in the presence of the American flag. He had referred to the Liberty Bell—then in Everett on a national patriotic tour—as "a bunch of junk." Salter was even more startled when on election day the city blossomed with American flags on homes and buildings, automobiles, wagons, and lapels. Merrill's workers paraded their flags several times during the polling hours, and Salter lost, 2,851 to 3,624, carrying a weak majority in only ten of forty precincts. Merrill became commissioner and, by a vote of the commission, the new mayor of the city.[1]

With the election of Dennis Merrill, what the *Labor Journal* called the "business crowd" was in control again, as solidly as it had been in 1912. The climate of opinion in 1916 was in fact similar to that of 1912, for to many people the most urgent civil goal was a city safe for prosperity. There were differences, however, in the spirit of this urgency. First was the fact that 1906 and 1912 had been years of great optimism, years of confidence in the manifest destiny of American industrial capitalism and western entrepreneurship. In 1916, few people were without doubts about the lumber industry and its afflictions, and few people believed that progress was as inevitable as it once had seemed. In 1916, those who controlled lumber resources—and those who worked them—were almost fiercely determined to get all the profit that war could turn to them before the system itself collapsed.

Another difference was that in 1916 Everett suffered from deep lacerations within its sense of community. The labor union movement was crushed. To many people, its ruin seemed to give the oratory of class struggle a sort of dark and vital poetry that clarified a basic conflict in American society. In breaking the union, and in what they said and did, the Everett industrialists, no less than the Socialists, had apparently accepted the reality of this conflict. And the Socialists, on their part, seemed ready to believe that the entire world was approaching the final confrontation of evil forces. To the more thoughtful, this confrontation among the imperial powers in Europe was the most significant development in all history. Thus Maynard Shipley, at the *Labor Journal*, generally ignored local news and printed instead dozens of columns against "preparedness" in the United States, warning the workingman to keep out of this world war from which he had nothing to gain and everything to lose. As the world did indeed seem to be crumbling around them, many citizens began to probe their deeper interests and confusions. A man who was uncertain about the implications of his national origins—German, Norwegian, English, or Italian—might find solace in waving the flag or in memorizing Karl Marx. Everett was a community of rising tensions.

Shortly after Dennis Merrill and the businessmen took over the city government again, they reorganized the Commercial Club in an effort to revive the civic consciousness which depression, strike, and anxiety had nearly extinguished. The new plan, brought up from California, was to get all "wide-awake" citizens involved in a "pull-together" movement to unify the community and open it to the opportunities of a "new era." A steering committee assigned the various activities of attracting business to Everett—such as advertising, transportation, and tax reform—to the several bureaus it formed among the members. The committee also revised the older patterns of membership by dropping the delicately representative system of including industrialists, businessmen, labor leaders, professional men, and the clergy; instead it issued blocks of stock to employers for distribution among their executives and employees. John McChesney, for example, took twenty-five shares, or memberships, for the Everett Improvement Company. The Weyerhaeuser Company took ten, the Clough-Hartley mills took five. Albert Brodeck, again active, hoped before the year was out to sell at least eight hundred shares for the committee.

The Trades Council took twenty shares and showed its cooperative spirit by encouraging the "buy at home" drive which the new club sponsored. For a while the *Labor Journal* even enjoyed a profusion of advertising from club members. Then in a striking change of attitudes at the Labor Temple, it was Ernest Marsh, still depressed by the failures of the Progressive Age, who became gloomy. He pointed out that labor's twenty shares would not be heard among eight hundred, and that among the new bureaus there was none for labor or industrial relations.

Certainly no one had more interest in prosperity than Marsh. When the price of "clears"—the highest grade of cedar shingles—rose to $1.71 a square in January 1916, not even David Clough watched the rise more intensely than he. Shortly thereafter Marsh took from the executive board of the Washington State Federation of Labor a mandate to subordinate all his other activities to the task of reorganizing the shingle weavers. In February he and J. G. Brown were again going through the mill towns seeking out their friends. They spoke candidly about what they saw as the sickness that had killed the old union and about what they wanted the new one to be—it must be moderate, but determined, responsible, and disciplined. In April, when clears stood at $1.83, they had once again organized Everett, as well as most of the Seattle and Aberdeen mills. Marsh then called thirty delegates from all over the state to meet in Seattle to ratify a new constitution, the third since 1900, for the International Shingle Weavers of America.

The structure and tone of the new union reflected Ernest Marsh's drift away from the smiling moderation of earlier years. It welcomed sawyers, packers, filers, engineers, and firemen working in the shingle mills, and was immediately more of an industrial union than a craft union. The preamble of the constitution pledged members "to promote working class solidarity." The constitution further bound them to the principles of trade agreements and of central union authority. Strikes, it read, could be called only by the executive committee of the international, which was Marsh and Brown. In return for such power, these leaders promised to move militantly toward the restoration of the 1914 wage scale. They themselves set a deadline: the symbolic First of May.

Well before the end of April, over half of the shingle mills in the state had adjusted their wages to the level that Marsh requested. Everett, however, stood alone and united as a fortress of intransigeancy. When Marsh and Brown asked the Everett industrialists to meet with them, they received a curt refusal. Everett, then, was to be the battleground, and there is no reason to suppose that Marsh regretted this development. He had tried to deal rationally with these men for a decade, and he knew them well. Perhaps he also knew himself better, and surely he knew his new union. To emphasize the importance of the coming battle to the city, to the state, and to the American Federation of Labor, Marsh himself took the chairmanship of the strike committee. He was where he most wanted to be, leading the shingle weavers, among men he had known all his life, once again praising the union men "of the sober, industrious variety, owning their own homes, maintaining the city's schools and churches. . . ." He moved with the conviction that it was David Clough who had now to be broken, and he was ready to pursue this course to the bitter end.[2]

On May 1, 1916, the shingle weavers in Everett were behind their machines when the morning whistles blew at seven o'clock. They stood quietly while the stewards at each mill entered the owners' offices to present their request for the restoration of the wage scale they had lost in 1914. Ernest Marsh had drilled the stewards to make their presentations with respect but without discussion, and to suggest in no way that the union was demanding a contract or even recognition. They did precisely this, some of them performing with such tight-lipped obedience that Fred Baker thought them surly and insolent. With a similarly exact discipline, each millowner ignored the request. The stewards left the offices, the men left the machines, and there was neither smoke nor cinders that day from the shingle mills in Everett. Nor were there picket lines, for every man who might work was with the union.

When reporters for the daily newspapers reached David Clough, he did not deny his promise in 1915 to restore the wage cut after prices rose again. He said simply that conditions did not yet justify any wage adjustments and that there would, consequently, be none in Everett. His own mills, he said, had not earned a dollar in two and a half years, and he made it clear that under present conditions the closure of the mills was not a matter of great concern to him. They would remain closed, he said, until he could find good men who would work for the wages he could afford to pay.

Marsh was ready to reply, but he found the newspapers curiously uninterested in what he had to say. Only the *Journal* carried his response to Clough, in which Marsh stated that clears, at $1.91, were at their highest price since March, 1914, and that the price was still rising without resistance. Many mills in the state, all of them presumably operating with the same factors of cost and expectations of profit as Clough's mills, were paying the 1914 scale. Marsh pointed out—and here he really hoped for wide publicity—that some Aberdeen millowners had indiscreetly made public the fact that the war had denied the roofing industry its metals, and that consequently shingle mills in 1916 were again like gold mines. Clough's statements about Everett, Marsh said, would not stand against this evidence. Furthermore, Clough and his associates adamantly refused to discuss anything with union leaders. If Clough had cost factors that were different from those of mills in other cities, Marsh challenged again, let him come forward and be reasonable. Within a week, the absentee owners of the Seaside and of a few smaller mills had agreed to the increase, and their plants were again deep in smoke and sawdust. But the hard core of the Everett barony —Clough-Hartley, Baker, Jamison, and the other major employers—had made no further comment. There was still no need for pickets, and the city lay suspended in a remarkable calm.

The daily papers carried little news of the strike. Even Maynard Shipley's *Labor Journal* gave scant coverage to local industrial conditions. Shipley was much more interested in Europe than he was in Everett, and the First of May had not moved him to change his focus. The break at Seaside, however, made current news absolutely necessary to the shingle weavers. As a result there was an upheaval on the board of control of the Trades Council, and perhaps coincidentally, perhaps not, Maynard Shipley resigned and left Everett to become a speech writer for and assistant to Eugene Debs. Thereafter the *Journal* was more responsive to the needs of the strikers. Marsh himself occasionally took a turn at the editorial chair, but no one seemed to be regularly in charge. The strike effort continued to suffer from a dearth of news and propaganda, and from an indulgence in socialist sermons.

Uptown, the news was carefully controlled with a strategy that suggests—as most people at the time suspected—the precision and power of William C. Butler. This was clear enough in the sequence of events following the early involvement of the Commercial Club in the strike. The president of the club that year was Fred Baker, owner of a struck mill, and late in May, Baker appointed a committee to investigate the strike. While Marsh and Brown waited for an invitation to appear before this committee, its members wrote a report which emphasized that the Everett mills could not operate if they increased wages. Wages in Everett were, in fact, adequate, the committee concluded. The strike, the report said, was the destructive work of "professional agitators."

Under Baker's gavel, the membership quickly accepted this report and resolved to blame the depression of 1914–15 on trade agreements in the lumber industry. They further resolved, in the interests of business and prosperity, to support the principle of the open shop. Despite the protests of union members and their friends—notably the former Progressive prosecutor, Robert Faussett—these resolutions passed by a margin of four to one. The *Herald* and the *Tribune* gave unusually full publicity to the club's resolutions and to Clough's pronouncements.

Though Marsh and Brown had taken care to keep the issue of the union shop out of the conflict, they could see that the industrialists wanted to use the strike in their own way to break the new union, and that Clough, Butler, and Baker could easily persuade the businessmen to help them. Hoping to reach at least some businessmen directly, Marsh and Brown called a mass meeting on a Sunday afternoon, and several hundred people turned out to hear Robert Faussett condemn the actions of the Commercial Club. Those who met that afternoon resolved to boycott businessmen who supported the club. Union men holding memberships in the club resigned, and they were followed by several merchants whose stores depended on union customers. By the middle of June, the Commercial Club had ceased to represent organized labor. By that time, too, the Clough-Hartley Mill was recruiting strikebreakers outside the city, and the union for the first time called out its pickets. There were probably some men in town who did not hide their feeling that the way to close Clough-Hartley was with dynamite, and the waterfront bristled again with barbed wire, bunkhouses, searchlights, guns, and hired guards.

In June, even though the scabs were being herded again, Marsh felt confident. The pickets were mature men who would not be provoked into courting their own destruction. Marsh had been able to use his influence to find jobs for most of the striking weavers, and these jobs would carry them through the summer. He had been sure that the city was aware of union solidarity, and he was pleased that more and more businessmen were leaving the Commercial Club—over a hundred during that one month. He and Brown had been planning, more carefully than in 1915, to have the union finance co-operative mills and to have the AFL carpenters, when necessary, boycott the scab shingles. But even these tactics, he reasoned, might not be necessary, for the millowners were hurting. With clears at two dollars, they were losing out in the war bonanza. Businessmen had almost exhausted their thin stores of patience since May 1, for the pressures upon them were aggravated by a longshoremen's strike up and down the coast that periodically closed the port of Everett. This strike was for a closed shop, and it was supported by the tugboat operators. As coordinator for all the unions, Marsh faced a complex and possibly ugly situation, but he felt that this time the power and militancy within the shingle weavers and the federation were in his favor.

It seemed to union men that Clough was throwing off any pretense of reason or benevolence and was resolutely creating the social and industrial conditions under which the iron law of wages would prevail. If the Everett millowners resisted the wage increase—and they seemed determined to do so, even with guns—the mills throughout the industry, in order to protect their own competitive positions, would be forced to follow Everett's leadership. Wages everywhere would move downward: such was the iron law. To Marsh and Brown, and to most of the membership, it seemed that the welfare of all shingle weavers, perhaps all workers in the timber industries, was at issue in Everett.

It was the sweep of events everywhere that favored the men who met in the cold dusty IWW office of Seattle. The depression of 1914–15 had collapsed the Wobbly movement, and in 1916 only a dozen or so of the faithful were at first aroused to take advantage of the new prosperity. A call to convention in July turned out about a hundred more—loggers, most of them—who were willing to pay up their memberships and join in dramatizing the class struggle. The leadership was by then informed of developments in Everett, which seemed to justify the attention of a first-rate agitator and organizer. After a brief search they located James Rowan, who had recently done well among the railroad "slaves" in Canada and who in July was spreading the gospel among the "timber beasts" of northern Idaho. To the joy of the Seattle office, Rowan agreed to explore the possibilities of making friends or enemies in Everett.

On July 31, Rowan was speaking at the corner of Hewitt Avenue and Wetmore Avenue where for years the city had tolerated almost nightly excesses of religious and political evangelism. When word spread that an IWW professional was in town, a friendly and curious crowd gathered for an evening's entertainment. Jake Michel, secretary of the Building Trades Council, was there, probably on assignment from the Everett Trades Council or the strike committee, and Sheriff McRae was sitting in an automobile parked near the speaker's stand. Rowan appreciated both these presences, and he threw himself into a spirited attack upon craft unionism. He pointed out that if the loggers would stop feeding the struck mills, then shingle weaving scabs would have no wood to work. The AFL promotes organized scabbery, he shouted, and the only way to freedom is the One Big Industrial Union.

Rowan knew very little about the Everett unions, and after

one of his more vigorous generalizations, Jake Michel interrupted to call him a liar. Just as a sharp argument between the
two began to warm the audience, Sheriff McRae forced
Rowan from his speaker's platform and led him to the county
jail. The sheriff warned Rowan that although Everett had never
cracked IWW heads in the past, the city would not allow
radicals and outsiders to play upon the tensions of the community this summer. With this, McRae released the Wobbly,
advising him to leave the city.

Rowan, deeply interested, returned immediately to Hewitt
and Wetmore to speak again until a policeman arrested him
for peddling literature without a license and locked him in the
city jail. When he learned the next morning that he could take
either a thirty-day sentence or a free ride out of the county,
Rowan took the interurban to Seattle.

Fellow workers in Seattle were impressed by these experiences, and they sent up their one-armed orator, Levi Remick,
to open an IWW office in Everett. Remick had an easy rapport
with shingle weavers and longshoremen, to whom he preached
industrial unionism by the hour, day by day, as he passed
around copies of the *Industrial Worker*. This Wobbly newspaper was increasingly popular in Everett because it reported
the shingle-weavers' strike in far more detail than any local
paper did and because it savagely attacked capitalists in general
and the lumber barons in particular. Though the Commercial
Club officers later claimed that the shingle weavers had invited
Remick, Ernest Marsh repeatedly and indignantly denied that
the union had in any way encouraged or discouraged the
IWW's attention to Everett.

For a while, though, both the union and the industrialists took
only indifferent notice of Remick and the IWW. The sensitive
areas of the city were not around the Wobbly office but
around mills where pickets went about the daily chore of
demoralizing strikebreakers. As the weeks passed, time and the
dreary nature of the task eroded patience, and the persuasion
became more and more vituperative. In July, some of the more

imaginative pickets reasoned that while city and county officials seemed eager for some excuse to stop the picketing— police and deputies patrolled the waterfront night and day— most of the mills were built at least in part over water, which was a federal jurisdiction. On otherwise dull days, a few pickets began rowing boats alongside the windows of the mills and shouting unrecorded obscenities to the men working inside. This daily chorus finally unnerved Neil Jamison, who acted independently of the other millowners and hired a dozen thugs to keep the pickets away from his mill.

On the morning of August 19, two groups of guards and strikebreakers, urged on by Neil Jamison himself, surrounded ten pickets and lay on them mercilessly with fists and clubs. Jamison, perhaps more than his hired goons, was caught up in an irrational fury. When he identified Robert Mills, the business agent for the union, he shouted "Get Mills, the son-of-a-bitch!" and directed his men in a particularly bloody beating of this one individual. All the while, city policemen looked on from across the invisible line along the beach that divided the city's responsibility from the county's, and they made no effort to stop Jamison's brutality. That evening when the shift ended, the pickets who could still walk returned with clubs of their own and the support of about 150 furious union men. As they approached the strikebreakers, police discovered that the dispute had crossed the invisible line. Shots were fired and one striker was wounded as the police drove the strikers away from the waterfront.

When Robert Mills and others took their story before the Everett Trades Council, the Labor Temple seethed with grievances against the millowners, the police, and the sheriff. The unions had not expected help from the police, but the men were particularly bitter toward Sheriff McRae, who was a union member and who could, they believed, have prevented the violence if he had chosen to do so. More and more vexed by the antiunion bias of the daily news stories, the Trades

Council again held a mass meeting so that union leaders could "lay the facts before the citizens of Everett."

All of this stimulated the Seattle IWW to give Everett its very best efforts. Soon after the Trades Council's public meeting, Wobblies spread the word that James P. Thompson would speak at Hewitt and Wetmore. To the worried city commissioners, Thompson's name meant much more than did Rowan's or Remick's. His reputation as an agitator was, in fact, colorful enough to bring them a sharp sense of anxiety, for it was Thompson who had led the Wobblies in what they called their "free speech fight" in Spokane. This had been their classic triumph in passive resistance. When the Spokane police had arrested speakers in 1909 for violating an ordinance against street meetings, there seemed to be Wobblies everywhere willing to take to the soapbox and then be hustled off to jail. The unwashed, the profane, the irreverent—in their own phrase, the "soldiers of discontent"—came pouring out of the woods and the harvest fields to teach Spokane a lesson. Soon the jails were full, and under Thompson's direction more and more Wobblies came and spoke until the police had no time or facilities for real criminals. Before the Spokane City Council finally admitted defeat by repealing the ordinance against street meetings that had invited the invasion, it had spent a quarter of a million dollars jailing over twelve hundred Wobblies who came impishly from everywhere to speak, to sing, and to jeer. But the lesson Spokane learned from Thompson and passed on to other cities of the Northwest was not about the sanctity of free speech. It was about the terror the middle class can feel from a siege by a class-conscious, leering, jeering army of vagrants and bums.

Everett's own street-meeting ordinance had been written by the Socialists and was a model of liberal intent. Speakers could use the cross streets along Hewitt Avenue if they stayed fifty feet back from the thoroughfare, a restriction necessary to facilitate the flow of traffic from riverside to bayside. No one had ever objected to this restriction, and the Wobblies had always measured off exactly fifty feet before raising their platforms. They had planned to do so again on August 22. But that morning Sheriff McRae came into the IWW office and ordered them all to leave the county.

That night, however, Thompson, along with Rowan and twenty other men and women, came up from Seattle to test the sheriff's determination. For a while they mingled with the people gathered around the Salvation Army band at Hewitt and Wetmore, then they quietly measured off fifty feet and put up their stand. When the army had finished and moved away, Thompson's voice rang out across the street as he urged people to stay and hear the truth about American industry. He attacked the lumber barons, then aimed directly at Everett, declaring that the Industrial Workers of the World would support the shingle weavers in their conflict with the shingle industrialists. After Thompson had spoken for maybe twenty minutes, city police pushed through and seized him.

When Thompson had been dragged away, Rowan leaped to the platform and began to speak. Police quickly pulled him down. After Rowan, the other Wobblies took their turns to say a few words and then be arrested. But even when the last of the twenty from Seattle had been taken, the marathon continued. Mrs. Letelsia Fye of Everett, apparently well schooled in the subtler techniques, took the platform to recite from the Declaration of Independence. When police witlessly pulled her away, Jake Michel, the Trades Council representative, moved out from the crowd to protest, and he too was hauled off toward the city jail.

A boisterous and threatening crowd followed. Among them were Socialist and labor leaders, and they demanded to know what would happen to those who had been marched from the street. Jake Michel, who was released when he was recognized, talked to the police and then to the crowd, assuring them that the prisoners would not be mistreated. His calm may have averted a serious riot. The next morning, police put the free-

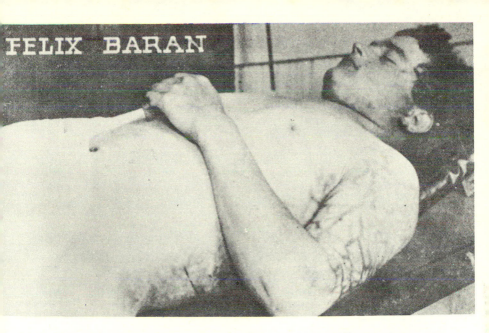

Massacre victim in IWW photograph, 1916 (Photo courtesy of Everett Community College Library)

Part of the IWW prisoners in Snohomish County Jail, December, 1916 (IWW photo courtesy of Everett Community College Library)

Port Gardner Bay in recent times (Photo courtesy of *Labor Journal*) speech fighters on a boat bound for Seattle, where they enthusiastically organized a free speech committee to raise funds and recruit volunteers for the class struggle in Everett.

When the Wobblies opened their Hewitt Avenue office again a few days later, they were amazed that no one arrested them. For a week they spoke on the streets without interference, and Thompson and others boasted of an easy victory. It is more likely that the police had been ordered not to harass Wobblies while a federal labor mediator was in the city, and the city council was no doubt reluctant to burden the forthcoming Labor Day festivities with any unnecessary evidence of the city's industrial distress.

Even before Labor Day, however, there was more violence. On August 29, Neil Jamison chose to parade his strikebreakers and their armed guards through the downtown streets to a theater for an evening's relaxation away from the mill. While they were inside, an angry group of men formed along the sidewalk. When the Jamison workers emerged from the theater, challenges and insults erupted into fist fights. One striker with a baseball bat stood just inside the alley near the theater door, and as strikebreakers ran around the corner and into the alley to escape, he laid them out with a vicious swing. When police arrived, they had to fire their guns to break up an ugly mob.

Though Jamison may have hoped for it, there was no evidence that the Wobblies had anything to do with this incident. Later that evening, in fact, Thompson spoke at Hewitt and Wetmore against the use of violence by strikers in any situation. The next day, the Trades Council took pains to disassociate the unions from responsibility for the brawling. In its concern, the council went so far as to propose to the city commissioners that a special labor force be authorized to keep the peace in Everett during the Labor Day weekend, but this offer was quickly refused.

It was refused probably because David Clough had already decided to link the violence with both the IWW and the shingle weaver's union. Even while the union men were making their proposal, several hundred members of the Commercial Club were formulating more plans for keeping Everett safe from unions. The IWW came to Everett to inspire the shingle weavers and to prolong the strike, Clough told them, and the IWW must go. He asked the city officials what they could do. The commissioners were at the moment mindful of Spokane's earlier tribulations, and they said that the police could not suppress a major free-speech fight—it would bankrupt the city.

Clough encouraged gentlemen with business interests to look toward the months ahead and to grasp the full implications of what the commissioners were saying. On the eve of a glorious prosperity, Everett could be permanently crippled by a foolish strike that was being directed by big-city radicals. And then the city could be invaded by hordes of impious and impudent logging-camp troublemakers and harvest bums who had no interest in Everett except to ruin it. They could destroy a city just for the pure satanic hell of it. They were in many cases not even Americans, and they might ruin Everett with nothing to gain for themselves but to satisfy their mad leaders and their own essential criminality. These were men—he might recite the old stories—who befouled their own bunks, defiled the flag, burned wheat fields, and sanded the bearings of expensive machinery. They should not be allowed to steal Everett's future.

Clough suggested that Sheriff McRae might be able to save the city, and McRae acknowledged that he could indeed keep strangers out of the county if he had enough volunteer deputies. Urged on by Clough, and probably by others who had explored the idea before the meeting, McRae agreed to deputize a force of several hundred club members. The volunteers were immediately forthcoming, and the captains placed them in companies of fifty men each and gave each company a specialized assignment. Some were to take Wobblies from the railroad cars before they entered the city. Some were to watch the boats at the city dock. Others were to patrol the interurban, while still others would handle any IWW's who might infiltrate the blockade and actually get to the city streets.

For reasons which the union leaders never did understand, Donald McRae took full command. His "citizen deputies" were soon studying tactics and conducting drills in the rooms of the Commercial Club almost every night of the week. As they did so, several ministers, attorneys, and businessmen, led by Robert Faussett, resigned in protest, and signs reading "We Are Not Members of the Commercial Club" began to appear in shop and store windows. These resignations served only to give Clough, Hartley, Jamison, Butler, and the other organizers a completely free hand. Without serious opposition, they used the organization to threaten businessmen who advertised in the *Labor Journal* or the *Washington Socialist*, to work boycotts against those business and professional men who had deserted them, and to appropriate money for leaded clubs, guns, ammunition, and spies.[3]

X

The Iron Hand

!!!

Amid rumors that the offenses of "citizen deputies" were more frightful than those of common criminals, Sheriff Donald McRae and the Commercial Club captains organized and trained their semiprivate army. While municipal agencies and daily newspapers seemed fixed in coordinated paralysis, the eyes of the city were closed to a tide of violence. "Armed patrols," Ernest Marsh later recorded, "were established as darkness fell each day. . . . Stories began to filter out of brutal beatings in the jail . . . of men being taken to the city limits, stripped and severely beaten. . . ."

During these weeks McRae did indeed seem ubiquitous. He led companies of deputies through the railroad yards and railroad water stations east and south of the city. Guided by intelligence phoned to him from the offices of the Great Northern, he and his men surrounded boxcars and flourished

guns and clubs while they searched every hobo for evidence
of IWW membership. On the docks, too, McRae was omni-
present, watching the passengers who stepped from each
boat and taking aside any who looked suspicious. McRae had
a remarkable memory for names and faces, and no Wobbly
who had been seen by him was ever safe thereafter. His deputies were quick to note the dress and personal appearance that
marked a wage earner and, after some experience, even the
bearing and demeanor that suggested IWW. When they found
a red card, a red lapel pin, a songbook, a newspaper, or a
pamphlet, they might rough up the apparent leaders of the
group and threaten them all with serious violence. They
held some of these men, at McRae's discretion, on vagrancy
charges, and these unfortunates undoubtedly suffered in the
county jail before they were sent south with suspended sentences. McRae threatened them with charges of theft or arson
and the consequent penitentiary sentences if they ever came
to Everett again.

Within a week after the blockade began, Wobblies knew
that they could no longer use the common carriers. This was
indication enough that McRae was serious, or desperate, and
it challenged some of the more venturesome free-speech soldiers to anticipate a winter of games with the sheriff and
the officials of Everett. Late in September, a group of twenty
Wobblies bought train tickets from Seattle to the town of
Mukilteo, just south of Everett, and from there took a small
boat, the *Wanderer*, which was owned by a friend. The boat
had room for only half of the party, and the other ten found
seats in a dory which was towed behind as the *Wanderer* set
out across Port Gardner Bay to Everett.

In the middle of the bay, a tugboat carrying about sixty
deputies intercepted the *Wanderer*. McRae fired across the
bow of the smaller boat, then into its muffler, bringing it to
a stop, and took the Wobblies aboard his tug. Shortly thereafter the skipper of the *Wanderer* told this story:

. . . they had made fast my stern line and as I bent over with the line McRae struck me with his revolver on the back of the head, and when I straightened up he struck me in here, a revolver about that long. I said something to him and then he ran the revolver right in here in my groin and he ruptured me at the same time. I told him, "It's a fine way of using a citizen." He says, "You're a hell of a citizen, bringing a bunch like that," he says, "to cause a riot in this town." I says, "Well, they are all union men anyway." He says, "You shut your damn head or I will knock it clean off." And I guess he would, because he had enough whiskey in him at the time to do it.

McRae later admitted this particular beating. The IWW claimed many more, and they claimed also that McRae held those from the *Wanderer* in the county jail for nine days without blankets or beds before sending them back to Seattle.

On the streets of Everett, the companies of deputies swung their clubs against any speaker who was not clearly from the Salvation Army, and night by night a terror began to rise. The violence lured crowds where there otherwise might have been none—at Hewitt and Wetmore, hundreds of curious or angry citizens came out each evening in hopes that some Wobblies would take courage and defy the deputies. The day after the *Wanderer* had been captured, the Seattle IWW found two more martyrs for the Everett streets, Harry Feinberg and William Roberts. They were guided through the blockade by Jake Michel, who had been appointed by the Trades Council to monitor Wobbly activity and who by this time had become deeply committed to the cause of free speech. Michel walked with the Wobblies to the corner, where Feinberg went up on a box before a sizable audience. Within a few minutes, three companies of deputies apppeared on Hewitt Avenue and began dispersing people with shouts and swinging clubs.

As Feinberg and Roberts were being dragged away, John Ovist, an Everett man who had joined the IWW only a week before, was spontaneously possessed with the spirit and leaped to the box. "Fellow Comrades, . . ." he shouted, but he could say no more. He was knocked to the street and beaten with the clubs specially made for the citizen deputies —tubes of rubber and leather filled with lead shot, so flexible that they did not usually break the skin on the back, the shoulders, the hips, or the groin.

Another local victim that night was a shingle weaver named Frank Henig, who was employed in one of the few operating mills. He later testified that he had come out with his wife and child to see a movie:

When we got to Wetmore there was a big crowd standing there. I had worked the night before and I had cedar asthma, so I said to my wife, "I would like to stay out in the fresh air." And she said, "All right, I will meet you at nine o'clock at Wetmore and Hewitt." There was quite a crowd and I got up pretty close in front so I could hear the speaker. I stood there a little while and finally the sheriff came along with a bunch of deputies, and the speaker said, "Here they come, but now people, I will tell you, don't start anything; let them start it."

Caught in the attack, Henig said, he was knocked unconscious by McRae and dragged to the jail. There he was recognized as a resident and allowed to escape by a back entrance. He returned to the corner, he said, his face still streaming with blood, to tell his story and to hear about the old men, the women, even the children who had been knocked down and injured.

A few days later, an editorial by Marsh in the *Labor Journal* insisted that the Trades Council "holds no brief for the I.W.W." and had no part in bringing them to Everett. The real agitators, he wrote, were not the IWW "who, foolishly or otherwise, persist in speaking on Wetmore Avenue, but the business and professional men who have allowed themselves to be buncoed into a private standing army." The editorial called for yet another mass meeting at which the citizens of Everett might discuss the facts and plan action: "An in-

tolerable situation exists in this city. . . . The beating up of
men and boys by citizens clothed with temporary authority
and armed with clubs, which is almost a nightly occurrence
. . . is a disgrace to a civilized community."

This meeting, on September 22, brought about fifteen thousand people to the park, most of them moved by terror, rumor,
or outrage. They heard union leaders, Socialists, and Wobblies, who had been escorted up from the dock by a group of
Socialists with a brass band. City officials answered some angry questions, then McRae himself faced a critical and threatening crowd to promise that he would not molest any groups
or individuals in Everett as long as they obeyed the laws.

The sheriff did not indicate that, only hours before, the
city commissioners had, in effect, given him full authority to
stop any future street meetings in areas where the Wobblies
might want to hold them. Mayor Merrill had signed and
published an ordinance which prohibited public speaking or
meeting "within one block either north or south of Hewitt
Avenue" and which, moreover, declared an emergency to
exist so that the new law could become effective that very
day. According to interpretations they had even earlier requested, the commissioners understood that a violation of
the new ordinance would constitute unlawful assembly, a
matter clearly within the jurisdiction of both the sheriff and
the city police.

But even though McRae was armed with new legal powers, he had no intention of allowing Wobblies to test the new
law. He amplified his blockade by keeping his companies
active at the far boundaries of the county, and however far
he had to go along the railroad tracks or into the forest, he
sprang quickly to investigate any report of Wobbly movements. The Mayor, himself a trooper in the blockade, later
estimated that during the month of October, McRae and his
deputies had turned back as many as five hundred Soldiers of
Discontent. And in doing so—according to his victims—

McRae was raising the level of bloody violence for which he was by then notorious.[1]

Donald McRae, in the eyes of both friend and foe, was performing a role of legendary proportions. Many Everett residents saw him as the one official in the state who possessed the strength of character and moral intelligence to lead the forces of law and order against a wave of chaos. Others cursed him as a depraved but willing tool of criminals who conspired to break the shingle-weavers' union even if in doing so they had to break the Constitution of the United States. One might see the lines of both legends in a remarkable photograph of McRae in 1912 published in the *Labor Journal*. He was then forty-six years old, a strikingly clean-cut and even handsome man whose hands, nose, and mouth suggest great physical strength. He was elegantly dressed. His large liquid eyes might indicate a capacity for soulful brooding.

The Wobbly writer Walker Smith, however, saw "swinish eyes set closely on either side of a pink-tinted, hawk-like nose that curved just above a hard, cruel, and excessively large mouth." Smith described a swaggering, foul-mouthed, brutal puppet of David Clough, a traitor to his class, a former worker who had learned to take his liquor in the Cascade Club with his odious new friends. Smith saw a drunken sadist, a mad bull of a man who derived a glow of pleasure from mashing a skull or cracking a bone.

If Donald McRae were in fact drunk on every occasion that Smith chronicles, he must have consumed enough whisky to flood the rooms of the Commercial Club during the months of September and October alone. One can dismiss this in part as IWW bias against drunkenness, widely regarded in radical circles as a threat to class-consciousness, and in part as pure propaganda for a nation turning prohibitionist. But one cannot entirely discount all of the stories of McRae's roaring through the streets and railyards swinging a club and his fists. If even some of these stories are true—and most of them seem to be —they detail the violent ragings of a drunken and perhaps demented man.

But the Donald McRae one sees in the early issues of the *Labor Journal* is almost impossible to imagine as Smith's bleary-eyed villain. The younger McRae was, like Ernest Marsh, a shingle weaver, among the first union men in Everett, for years the secretary-treasurer of the International Shingle Weavers' Union of America. The *Journal* celebrated McRae's running for sheriff in 1912 as a Progressive. After his election, McRae continued to pay his union dues, and he was a frequent visitor in the *Journal* office, where he spent many a long afternoon with Ernest Marsh. When he sought re-election in 1914, Marsh called him "the best sheriff Snohomish County ever had." McRae seemed to be a representative figure in the idealized Everett of Ernest Marsh's dream: he was a working-man who had promoted brotherhood and the union with loyal and competent service, a public servant who knew the reality of the mills and the camps, a politician who had risen from the ranks of wage earners, a married man, a homeowner.

It was thus a profound shock to most union men when McRae, in the spring of 1915, told the millowners that he could stop the trouble along the picket lines by taking a hundred special deputies and running the union troublemakers out of town. Why didn't he move against the hired trouble-makers brought in by the millowners? Still, the *Journal* had kind words for the sheriff later that year, and McRae donated an impressive twenty-five dollars to the strike fund in May, 1916. The Trades Council voted to return this money to him when he refused to protect the Jamison pickets in August. Thereafter the unions saw McRae as the enemy.

The only clue to his defection was the story—recalled years later by Joe Irving—that during that fateful night at the Commercial Club, Donald McRae had resisted the pressures being brought upon him. Finally, though, he had allowed

David Clough to convince him that the city government was
impotent and that someone had to save Everett. Even then,
the story was, McRae had made it clear that he would have
no part in bullying local union men. But he proved to Clough
and to the townspeople alike that he could be a terror to
strangers. McRae's conversion may have resulted from his
seeing the Wobblies as intruders, as carriers of a passion alien
to Ernest Marsh's dream of community. Donald McRae considered Everett to be *his* town; these were *his* people, and he
would not allow the outsiders, the boxcar revolutionaries, to
corrupt them. To many other westerners of middle-class circumstances in their new but yet unstable societies, the Wobbly was, in Robert Tyler's phrase, "the hobo in the garden,"
a threat to sacred values, the rogue of wanton criminality.
He was the foreigner, or he was the surly and delinquent
youth from unknown but evil cities. The people in Everett
who shared this fear could also share a hero.

Or it may have been that like others of his political faith,
McRae could be stimulated into a kind of hysterical apprehension over socialism or radicalism. There is no evidence, though,
that he had ever given serious attention to what was then
called "political economy" or that he ever listened with any
interest to the speeches he so rudely interrupted. In fact, by
1916 he had tired of politics, or of law enforcement, and was
not seeking re-election. It may have been—many thought so
—that he wanted a good job after the new year and that David
Clough or Roland Hartley or Joe Irving had promised him
one.

Or it may have been that IWW impudence and terrorism
lit in him an uncontrollable fury. He saw the "black cat" symbol—an ominous Wobbly warning—pasted on his windows.
He received threatening and abusive mail. He buried his two
highly prized dogs—poisoned in the dark of night. He knew
that anonymous phone calls were driving his wife toward
nervous collapse. But whatever silent grief or terror or demented longing inspired him, McRae became the champion

of those who would drive into the earth the Industrial Workers of the World.[2]

As he was about this task, a feverish recurrence of class-consciousness swept across the city. The promiscuous violence upon Wobblies and suspected Wobblies soon brought many people to realize that a man in working clothes, simply because of his appearance, was no longer safe on the streets. At the same time, men in business suits read the daily newspapers carefully for reports of alleged arson, riot, or sabotage that showed how workingmen, bitten by the bitch of Wobblyism or drunk on vandalism, had gone mad.

The *Labor Journal*, which had for years attacked the Wobblies as a hazard to the labor movement, moved more and more to their defense. The IWW, said the *Journal* repeatedly, had taken an interest in Everett only because of the "open shoppers." The "agitators for violence" in the city were in the Commercial Club, Ernest Marsh said, and he repeated many times his early conviction that, "think what you will of the I.W.W. and his doctrines, you cannot kill his beliefs with a club." Jake Michel became so aroused by the lies and rumors he heard downtown that he offered one hundred dollars to anyone who could prove that any act of violence had ever been committed in Everett by a Wobbly.

Michel kept his one hundred dollars. But the Commercial Club, convinced that the IWW would intensify the torment of the strike, was actually taking actions which would make its assumptions come true. The more vicious the acts of McRae's deputies, the more active and persuasive were the local IWW and Socialists who worked among the shingle weavers and longshoremen. Though Marsh always denied it, it does seem likely that in late September and October—when the mills were operating with fink labor and the picket lines stood lean and sullen in the cold rain—that Wobblies did reinforce the striking unions and that many strikers took red cards. As the days became wetter and drearier, Joe Irving, who took such pride in his rapport with the roughest logging and milling crews, scanned the picket lines for men he knew did not live in Everett. If he found one, Irving would call him aside and ask him to leave the city so that the local people could settle their problems in their own ways. Despite his bulk and strength, Irving's solicitude brought him only obscenities. Late in October, old David Clough himself, accompanied by Donald McRae, was confronting the pickets with imperious warnings that he would respect an Everett man's right to demonstrate but would not tolerate the intrusion of outsiders.

As he did so, there were rumors around the city that the weavers' strike was dying. Smoke rose regularly from the mills each day, and with the coming of winter the strikers were taking what jobs they could find. The sheriff's blockade was so painfully effective that it reduced the demonstrators to a thin line of only the most hardened sufferers. The longshoremen's strike had been broken in other ports, and the Everett union appeared to be doomed. Marsh and his AFL lieutenants again seemed impotent as they waited for nothing, as they met each day with tight faces to discuss matters they could not control while the unions collapsed around them.

After studying these symptoms, the IWW activists in Seattle could see that Everett needed a crisis and perhaps a climax. They decided to revive the free-speech fight with an open attack on the blockade and an open challenge to the restrictive street meeting law passed in September. The time was right, they reasoned, for they could call upon both the faithful older soldiers and the impetuous young men from the harvest crews who were beginning to come west from the grain fields and fruit orchards. These men customarily wintered on the Skid Road in Seattle, and they were usually brimming with ideological vigor and radical irreverence while they waited for the snow-shoveling jobs that came up later in December. On October 30, the Seattle office recruited a soldiery of forty-one men. Armed with boisterous songs, the Bill of Rights, and an exuberant capacity for mischief and suffering, these Wobblies left Seattle on a passenger ship for Everett and the corner of Hewitt and Wetmore—and, they assumed casually, for the Snohomish County jail.

As they embarked, the Commercial Club's Pinkerton informed the sheriff that a force twice the size of any previous one was moving against the blockade. He also reported that these forty-one were migrants from the orchards, perhaps the first wave of unwashed rabble that might be inspired to violate the city. As the call went out for deputies, the myth could seize the mind's eye: the intruder, the vagrant rapist, the arsonist, the vandal with a leer and a knife. This image moved the deputies to determine that they would meet this attack upon their homes with such ferocity that they would never be menaced again.

When the ship docked in the evening, Sheriff McRae stood ready to screen the passengers. Behind him were more than two hundred citizen deputies, all of them wearing handkerchiefs tied around their upper arms as identification. With his unerring eye and instinct, McRae singled out the forty-one, few of whom he had seen in Everett before. Nor had he ever seen so many Wobblies in one group. When he and Joe Irving questioned them, the young men defiantly admitted who they were, but they acknowledged no leader, and they refused to act like prisoners. They did indeed intend to go to Hewitt and Wetmore and hold a street meeting, just as soon as the sheriff and his hired tools of the lumber trust would recognize the rights of American citizens and get the hell out of the way.

McRae, with studied politeness, told them that they could not use Hewitt and Wetmore, but they could use Hewitt and Grand, a corner almost at bayside and fairly remote from the city center. The response was insolence and a spontaneous obscenity. Whatever the word, it touched a raw nerve in the sheriff, who impulsively whipped his sap across the face of the man who had spoken. The word also caused Joe Irving to catch fire, and he lunged into the group to grab himself a Wobbly. "The Wobbly leader," he said years later, "a dirty little runt of a fellow, got nasty, and I lost my temper." Irving shoved the first man he could touch against an automobile and split his scalp with the barrel of a Colt 45. In his blind fury Irving did not realize that his victim was John Schofield, an arm-banded deputy. Schofield later testified in court that he had been hospitalized after the blow and that both Irving and McRae were drunk at the time.

After the deputies had restrained Irving, they searched the Wobblies for weapons and herded them into automobiles. In the growing darkness and rain, they drove their captives to a remote area called Beverly Park, where, as Irving later recalled, "We took down their pants and beat them with Devil's Club—you know, the plant with the heavy stalk and poisonous thorns . . . and made them run the gauntlet."

The gauntlet quickly became a frenzy of automobile lights, rain, screams, curses, and blood lust. There were perhaps one hundred vigilantes on each side of a path that ended in the cruel blades of a cattle guard—two hundred men with saps, clubs, ax handles, rifles, fists, and boots. While those to the rear pushed or dragged the Wobblies down the path, the men on each side struck savagely at heads and backs, or kicked full-booted into gut and testicles. The glare of headlights caught fragments of a tableau of near-butchery: bloodied heads and trousers, broken teeth, split lips, dislocated bones. The wonder of Beverly Park is that the Wobblies lived at all. But the forty-one did survive, their screams alarming farmers a quarter of a mile away through the woods. Beyond the cattle guard, they struggled back to Seattle, some of them walking the full twenty-five miles.

When word of the beatings reached the streets of Everett the next morning, Ernest Marsh was already on the site—he, Jake Michel, Commissioner Clay, the Reverend Joseph Marlatt, the Reverend Elmer E. Flint, Robert Faussett, and the

Reverend Oscar McGill, an "industrial evangelist" holding services in Everett. These men, not unfamiliar with violence, were shocked and saddened by the evidence that even heavy rain could not wash away. "The tale of that struggle was plainly written," Marsh recorded. "The roadway was stained with blood." [3]

When he and the others returned to Everett, Ernest Marsh felt the surge of rumor and terror through the city. Some people feared a massive Wobbly retaliation; others feared that the vigilantes could not restrain their own brutality and that Everett had become a lawless wilderness. The newspapers printed nothing about Beverly Park, and this silence encouraged people to imagine the very worst. To bring some sense of fact and proportion to what was becoming a hysteria, Marsh and his group decided that they must call for still another mass meeting so that the community could learn what had actually happened and discuss what might reasonably be done to restore order and justice.

In advising the Seattle Wobblies of this meeting, Marsh's committee tried to be carefully considerate of Wobbly sensitivities and sorrows by proposing the Everett tabernacle as a suitable place and by asking the Wobblies themselves to suggest a time when it might be possible for at least a few of the Beverly Park victims to come to Everett again. The IWW leaders, who cared less about the maladies of Everett's spirit than about dramatizing the class struggle, seized this almost perfect opportunity to convert a public investigation and discussion into a grand protest and demonstration. Without consulting Marsh, they scheduled the meeting for the afternoon of Sunday, November 5, at the corner of Hewitt and Wetmore. Almost at once the Socialists in Everett were at work distributing thousands of handbills that announced the meeting and asked the citizens of Everett "to come and help maintain your and our constitutional right." The Seattle

IWW simultaneously requested the other state IWW locals to call up two thousand volunteers for what they said was an invitation from the people of Everett to protect free speech. Out of Marsh's polite proposal the Wobblies created the possibility of a monumental free-speech fight and a historic confrontation.

These moves were so quick and so skillful that they left Ernest Marsh and his committee of concerned citizens without power or control. His devices and techniques of reason had again produced no progress; they had, rather, rolled the hours on toward disaster. The committee had quieted no fears and exposed no rumors, for there were people all over town who could imagine two thousand leering maniacs coming to burn their homes to the ground, to loot, and to rape like the barbaric Hun.

At the Commercial Club, where Fred Baker kept the rooms open every night to enroll more citizen deputies, McRae's forces soon numbered over five hundred. While these club rooms became an armed command post, the industrialists who had built Everett seemed adamantly committed to a course of events that promised to destroy it. Although they seemed to share a contrived conviction that barbarians were indeed preparing to sack the city, at no time did any official ask the governor to provide the city with protection. On the contrary, Commercial Club leaders on November 3 introduced to the membership a guest speaker—the manager of the Employers' Association of Washington—who told the five hundred assembled deputies how a similar group of five hundred in Detroit had taken the law into their own hands to put down "the Wobbly menace." He urged his patriots to do the same, to show the whole world that "a city of red-blooded Americans . . . would not be bullied and cowed by a handful of men." His ringing conclusion was that "the only way to combat force is with force."

The next day, the companies of deputies met to take their orders for Sunday, when they intended to repel the invasion of what the *Tribune* called the "2000 foot-loose cats." And the "cats"—explained the editor, who had printed nothing about Beverly Park—were terrorists who were coming "to use the bludgeon or apply the torch." On Sunday, November 5, this newspaper bannered, "IWW Entitled To No Sympathy."

In Seattle, the editors of the *Industrial Worker* were no less resolute. Their message of November 4 was that "the entire history of the organization will be decided at Everett." With a masterful ambiguity, the writer made his point that "workers cannot expect any rights . . . except such as they have the power to enforce." But he was not, he said, advocating violence. It was "the sheriff and the viligantes" who were advocating violence. What, then, should a worker do? He should go to Everett, and if necessary, go to jail there: "Workers of America, if the boss-ruled gang of Everett is allowed to crush Free Speech and organization, then the Iron Hand will descend upon us all over the country. Will you allow this? It is for you to choose! Every workingman should help in every way to put an end to this infamous reign of terror. ACT NOW!!!"

To Wobbly theoreticians, the free-speech fight was a revolutionary act, an existential dynamics, an individual and collective commitment of moral courage and dedication. It was calculated to raise everywhere the level of class-consciousness and to provoke bourgeois society into a revelation of its decay and fraud. It was also a form of communion, vital to the truly enlightened, even if the price were sometimes bone and blood. Everett, in November 1916, gave the Wobblies the classic conditions. Arrogant industrialists were choking the legitimate requests of wage earners; they clearly planned to crush the hopes of labor unions everywhere. There was the urgent issue of civil liberty, which the enlightened in the cause of freedom would surely defend. The strike, the brutality, and the unrest generated enough bitterness, enough idealism, and enough manpower to kindle ancient grievances and fan the flames of discontent.

To Wobblies less impressed by theory, the free-speech fight was at least a sort of ritual in the fraternal order of wage slaves, at best a rousing hell-of-a-good-time, the substance of song and cherished memory. It was what should happen to Everett after the blood of Beverly Park had fixed the city forever in the cartography of class war.

By Sunday morning, the call for two thousand had brought forth about four hundred men and enough cash for perhaps three hundred tickets to Everett. After a final stump sermon in the IWW hall, the volunteers sang as they marched to the dock, where about half of them boarded the *Verona* and the others waited for a second steamer, the *Calista*. Walker Smith described the scene: "Laughter and jest were on the lips of the men who crowded the *Verona*, and songs of One Big Union rang out over the sparkling waters of Puget Sound. Loyal soldiers were these in the great class war, enlightened workers who were willing to give their all in the battle for bread, happiness, and liberty. . . ."

One can believe the laughter, the jest, and the song. These men were from the logging camps, from the hobo jungles, from the dreary monotony of grubby street corners and drafty rooming houses on the Skid Road. They carried a kind of tribal memory of Spokane—memories of how others had remembered it—and they talked of brotherhood, wage slavery, social revolution, and their obligations to their fellow workers in Everett. Some were cocky with confidence. It would be a great day, part picnic, part holy war. Probably only a few of them knew where Everett was, and even fewer knew what it looked like or what was really taking place there. One may doubt that any of them were prepared to "give their all," if by that phrase Walker Smith seriously meant life itself, or that they anticipated any really violent battle for bread or liberty. They were indeed prepared to disobey what they regarded as an unjust law, to resist passively, and to go to jail, even to be bloodied up a bit—a Wobbly could count on that sooner or later. But they counted also on their strength in numbers and on their public support this day to humble a sheriff and a clan of bosses who, their speakers assured them, so richly deserved humiliation.

But there were also some among the crowd on the *Verona* who could not laugh or jest. These were "enlightened workers" whose enlightenment had been the wrath of Donald McRae. These men carried memories in broken noses, missing teeth, and mashed genitals, and they were not prepared to sacrifice a second time in these painful ways. With pistols snuggled in a coat pocket or belted under overalls against the belly, they were grimly determined not to suffer Everett's kicks or clubs again.

Nor were all of the 250 or so really "loyal soldiers." At least two of them were Pinkerton spies and *agents provocateurs*, one of whom had been regularly suppressed by the free-speech leaders for urging violence. The other had loudly offered to buy phosphorus—a favorite tool of professional arsonists—before he left for Everett. These men may have telephoned to McRae an account of what was actually happening in Seattle, or they may have told their employers only what the Commercial Club wanted to hear. More probably, the Commercial Club generals announced only what they wanted the city to believe. In any event, the word as many heard it in Everett was that the *Verona* was loaded with armed anarchists intent upon burning the mills and the city in total revenge. For the rest of his life, Roland Hartley made this comment to any criticism of McRae's vigilantes: the IWW, he said, "came here to burn Everett and to burn the mills. The citizens had to arm to repel the invasion." Yet "the colonel" was curiously inconspicuous that afternoon, and neither he nor anyone else called Governor Ernest Lister to cry that the city was in peril.

When the sheriff called for the mill whistles to assemble the deputies at ten o'clock in the morning, about two hundred citizens responded. They spent the next few hours in the rooms of the Commercial Club, gathering arms for themselves and exchanging rumors. The commander of the United States Naval Militia in Everett, who was also a businessman and a deputy, later reported to his superior militia officers that during the morning he had heard that the Wobblies intended to raid the naval armory and seize arms and ammunition. "I therefore took the precaution to safe-guard same," he wrote tersely, "and had them removed to a room in the commercial club," where, he noted with apology, during his brief absence "the arms and ammunition were removed and taken to the dock."

When this small army left the rooms at half past one and drove to the waterfront, it was sustained at least in part by the courage of bootleg whisky, or by mob inertia, or by the assurance that it must save Everett from the satanic hosts. It included millowners, executives, sons who happened to be home from college, foremen, clerks, thugs, dentists, physicians, lawyers, merchants. Hartley, who had been sworn in as a deputy, had been campaigning that week and later claimed that he was out of the city that day. Clough, McChesney, Butler, and some of the older men probably stayed behind, in the manner of staff generals, aloof from the rush of events which they had set in motion.

Probably all that McRae and his citizen-deputies had really decided to do was to meet the *Verona* as she docked and prevent the Wobblies from landing. They no doubt assumed that their presence as armed men in such numbers would be sufficient threat to turn the Wobblies back. Irving and McRae, who were giving the field orders, planned simply to augment the usual blockade. But their augmentation quickly became one of almost unmanageable proportions.

The dock was a scene of vast confusion. Because unpre-

dictable crowds of curious citizens began to grow everywhere, McRae drew a rope across the wharf to keep people
away and assigned men to guard the rope and control the
crowd. For reasons perhaps more of confusion than of pre-
meditation, he concealed many of the deputies in a warehouse,
advising them to march out when he signaled them to make
a show of force. Other deputies stayed on the dock, while
others took their guns to positions in wharf offices and on
tugboats. Soon the pier where the *Verona* would land was
nearly surrounded by armed men. Certainly McRae made no
intelligent military deployment. He did not anticipate possible
lines of fire, and he gave no thought to the problems of fire
discipline that would become calamitous should the men
with guns suddenly be moved to use them. Nor, apparently,
did he plan what he would do if the men aboard the ship
refused to retreat.

On the hillside above the waterfront, sunshine played across
an audience of thousands who had come out into the salt air
of a clear afternoon to watch. The union leaders were there,
tense and anguished, and the strikers, and some millowners,
some businessmen, lawyers, executives, physicians, many
women, even some young children. Like the chorus in a
Greek amphitheater, they sat and stood along the tracks of the
Great Northern awaiting the next developmental crescendo
in the somber drama on the stage below them. Their hostility
to the citizen deputies was open and vigorous, for many of the
spectators cheered when the *Verona* steamed into Port Gardner Bay. Cheers came in turn from the decks of the ship.
As the engines slowed, people ashore could make out words
of the Wobbly hymn which the free-speech soldiers sang
with increasing ardor: "We meet today in freedom's cause
and raise our banners high!" The final verse was for one long
moment not yet ominous: "We'll join our hands in union
strong, to battle, win, or die!"

Armed with two pistols, the sheriff gave his signal and

moved briskly toward the landing. Behind him more than a hundred armed men filed out of the warehouse and formed in ranks, while Joe Irving and regular sheriff's deputies Charles Curtis and Jefferson Beard came forward to stand at McRae's side. They saw the bowline curl out from the ship into the hands of the wharfinger, who secured it to a piling. The decks of the ship were densely packed. Some Wobblies were still singing; others ventilated their spirits with hoots and yells. As those nearest the shore struggled to lower the gangplank, men behind them shoved shoulder to shoulder toward the dock. But before anyone could secure the gangplank, McRae stepped to the edge of the dock and shouted to be heard: "Boys," he called, "who's your leader?"

With laughter and jeers, a voice came back: "We're all leaders!"

McRae—according to the Wobblies—pulled a pistol and held it up to the gangplank. He said he was the sheriff, that he was enforcing the law, and he shouted very clearly, "You can't land here!"

The noise subsided almost to silence, but suddenly a Wobbly near the front ranks pushed forward and yelled, "The hell we can't!"

Before McRae could speak again, a gunshot exploded somewhere on his right. While thousands gasped, another shot rang out, then another, probably from a revolver held by one man who fired deliberately three times before anyone could react with movement. Then men were screaming and running around the pier and firing guns at the *Verona*, and this ignited a barrage that shook the wharf and the ship.

McRae and Irving fell, shot in the legs, then Curtis and Beard crumbled beside them. Just as they went down, a man who had climbed the ship's mast to wave at the crowd ashore slipped from his grip and crashed dead on the deck. Facing a hundred guns, Wobblies rushed in contagious terror to the other side of the ship, shifting so much weight that the decks tilted and spilled some of the living and some of the dead over the side.

Many deputies ran for the warehouse, but others crouched and fired, then staggered back as they received bullets from the *Verona* and from the tugboats where their fellow deputies were raking the deck of the ship with murderous crossfire. After perhaps two minutes, a burst of power from the engines broke the ship's lines, and the *Verona* churned out toward the open bay.

Gunmen ran forward to shoot repeatedly at the fleeing ship and at the men in the water below. As the firing slowed and the deputies began to see clearly again, they found that Charles Curtis was dead and that Jefferson Beard, who had been dragged into the shelter of the warehouse, lay dying with a hole in his chest. Twenty others were bleeding, and they were loaded into automobiles and rushed toward the hospital.

This caravan was slowed almost to a halt by the crowd that had come down from the railroad tracks to jeer, threaten, and curse defiantly at each carload of the wounded. To McRae, these jeers were more painful than the bullet in his knee, and the threats caused him more fear than he had known at the dock. Worried that the local IWW's might be reinforced from any direction and might rip through the town with an insane fury while he lay crippled, he asked the Everett officers to call out the naval militia while he telegraphed the governor: "Terrible riot in Everett. At least 25 citizens shot. Some dead and others mortally wounded. Send militia at once without fail and plenty of them."

This message was also signed by David Clough and John T. McChesney. Ernest Marsh had already phoned the governor with a similar request, for he saw, he wrote later, "half a thousand citizens under arms enraged at the Industrial Workers of the World and deadly determined to stamp out that organization . . . thousands of the working people of Everett were just as enraged toward members of the Commercial Club who participated in the gun battle."

Even while these messages were being worded, the local Wobblies, incredibly pursuing the martyrdom they had escaped at the dock, went up on the box at Hewitt and Wetmore to begin the scheduled meeting. Citizen deputies, roaming mindlessly through the streets, dragged them off to McRae's jail.

Governor Lister responded by sending National Guard units to Everett and Seattle. The commander of the two guard companies sent to Everett found the situation there "very grave." Commercial Club leaders were demanding from the adjutant general "that troops be immediately placed on duty" in the streets because they saw "the greatest danger of serious rioting and incendiary fires." The general inspected the streets for himself and then talked with McRae, who had recovered enough of his senses to advise that troops in the streets would "tend to create trouble that might otherwise be avoided." The troops remained in the city, but they stayed in the armories and out of sight.

Meanwhile, the *Verona* had returned to Seattle. Officials there planned to jail the passengers, and they feared more violence. But it was a quiet group that left the ship, for the men realized, as Walker Smith wrote, that "the class struggle was not all jokes and songs." On the ship, four were dead, one was dying, and twenty-seven were wounded, many of them critically. The number that fell from the decks to be swept under the sea—it could have been six or twelve—can never be fixed with certainty, for no one had imagined that a precise count of the *Verona*'s paid and unpaid passengers would ever be so dreadfully important.

The dead and bleeding were for the most part young men. Some were very young, and their ages illuminate the most strikingly morbid statistics of the tragedy: Hugo Gerlot, shot down from the mast, was no more than twenty; Abraham Rabinowitz, whose brains were shot out just as the ship tipped, had graduated from college only a few months before. Of the wounded, thirteen were under twenty-six, four were under twenty-one, and two were only eighteen. On the dock, the wounded included young Edwin Stuchell and a friend home from the university for the week end, but McRae, Irving, Curtis, Beard, and the others were all middle-aged men.

The bitterness drawn across Everett during that afternoon would linger for at least a full generation. Among the survivors and partisans even today, there are many who see the events of November 5 as the result of a necessary, if tragic, police action that revolutionaries had forced upon the sheriff and other loyal citizens who accepted the responsibility for keeping law and order in a terrified city. Others with equal sincerity reject any challenge to Walker Smith's phrase, now fixed in regional history, "The Everett Massacre." Smith's phrase implicitly answers a primary question that is also a basic assumption upon which any interpretation rests: Who fired the first shot? And this remains a question to which the historical method yields no confident answer.

If a historian searches for truth in the manner of Thucydides, as indeed he should, and examines critically the firsthand accounts of participants, he can stack such accounts into impressive heaps of mutually contradictory evidence. Personal accounts of the climactic moments, recorded yesterday or half a century ago, often conceal or distort more than they reveal, and the historian gains from them only another melancholy insight into the ways men remember what they want to remember. Thus Donald McRae, under oath before the court that tried the Wobblies for murder three months after he had been shot at the dock, again told what had happened immediately after he had shouted to the *Verona* that the men could not leave the ship: "I turned around to say something to the deputies behind me and that instant I was shot through the left heel. . . . I began to fire back. . . . There were no shots from the dock until I fired."

Joe Irving, who had been standing at the same spot, recalled the moment for an interviewer in 1951:

We went down to the wharf to meet them. Curtis, McRae and I stood on the dock and the rest got back in the warehouse. We wanted no violence. They took a rope ashore and made it fast to a pile. McRae stepped out, showed his badge and said they couldn't land here, that they must go back. Then he asked who their leader was, and a big fellow up on the bow said they were all leaders. Then they started firing. McRae was hit in the knee, and instead of doing anything, he kept saying, "I'm hit, I'm hit." Curtis was hit, and I was hit in the foot. I looked down and here was blood spurting from my foot, and I said, "They have shot *me!*" . . . We were on the dock firing any old way, just pointing our guns, but Rashaway [one of Irving's employees] took aim and got his man each time, got eleven. . . . When the Wobs all ran to the other side of the boat, all that kept it from capsizing was the rope on the dock. We could have cut that and she would have turned over and gone down, but I am glad we didn't. It was bad enough as it was. . . .

And Scott Rainey, the deputy who was also commander of the naval militia, wrote in his official report of November 8, 1916:

Upon approaching the dock these agitators on the boat began singing and hooting. When they came alongside, the sheriff and the deputies marched out from a warehouse on the dock; the sheriff approaching within thirty feet of the boat threw his hands up and asked who the leader of the organization was. The reply from the mob was that they were all leaders. Thereupon the sheriff told them that they were not allowed in Everett and that they could not come up town. During all of this there was no display of arms. As soon as the sheriff had finished his speech someone in the cabin or the lower part of the boat shot some firearm three or four times. Immediately after this one of the I.W.W. members on the forward deck of the Verona whipped out a revolver and commenced firing. As I was within five feet of the sheriff at the time . . . and not having any firearm on my person I got under shelter, during which time Lieutenant Curtis was shot. Immediately after the second shot came from the boat the deputies began firing. . . .

One man there had anticipated nothing at all out of the ordinary that day. He was Oscar Carlson, an innocent passenger on the *Verona* who wanted only to go about his business in Everett. Just as the gunfire started, Carlson was attempting to leave the ship. Lying in a hospital a week later, he tried to remember what had occurred before he lost consciousness: "I tell you as it comes to me now, it seems one shot came from the dock, then three or four from the other side, then all sides at once."

Ernest Marsh wrote his report to the Washington State Federation of labor before the year was out:

I hope I never live to see such an occurrence again. The passions loosed in the breasts of men and women, the lust for revenge, the curses and reviling heard on every hand, were more sickening and heartbreaking than could be the sight of any number of dead men. . . . A great deal seems to hinge in a legal sense upon establishing whether the first shot was fired from the boat or from the dock. . . . I am convinced in my own mind that these men had not the slightest intention of coming to Everett to attack life or property . . . they calculated to come in force, march up the streets in broad daylight, and figured that the sympathy of the larger proportion of the city's population would prevent physical attack upon their forces such as they had hitherto experienced.

Standing near Marsh on the hill that afternoon was Donald M. Rigby, a logging camp foreman who knew many of the Wobblies by their first names. Rigby had pointedly refused to become a deputy, and he told this story in 1951: ". . . several [deputies] were shot in the rump, one of them was furious about it—said he was facing the ship. . . . One man behind the smokestack on the boat had sworn to shoot McRae's balls off, and he was firing at him there but just missed his target. . . ."

Mayor Hiram Gill of Seattle was not at the dock, but he felt so strongly that he made a public statement to the Seattle newspapers: "In the final analysis it will be found that these cowards in Everett, who, without right or justification, shot into the crowd on the boat, were murderers and not the I.W.W.'s. . . . If I were one of the party of forty I.W.W.'s who was almost beaten to death by 300 citizens of Everett without being able to defend myself, I probably would have armed myself if I intended to visit Everett again. . . ."

George Vanderveer of Seattle, defense attorney for the Wobblies who faced murder charges following the death of Deputy Jefferson Beard, raised the question in his final remarks to the jury:

The court has told you that in this case it is not a question of who shot first, not a question of which side shot first, it is a question of who was the aggressor, who made the first aggressive movement, who did the first hostile thing. The man who did a thing to excite fear was the aggressor, and that man was McRae when he pulled his gun. McRae clearly did that before there was any shooting.

In determining who the aggressor was, you are entitled—not only entitled but must take into account—the past behavior of all parties. And what does that show you? Was it the I.W.W.'s who had never offered violence, who had never done an act of violence, as members of their audiences told you, and advised caution against it? Or was it McRae and his deputies?

And H. D. Cooley, the prosecution's counter to Vanderveer, made in part this summation:

There are a few uncontested and undisputed facts in connection with the occurrence at the dock. Jefferson Beard was killed on that dock. No doubt about that! The defendant was on that boat. No question about that! There is no question that the conversation between McRae and the people on the boat occurred substantially in the language that you have heard repeated here by witnesses for the State and for the defense, all agreeing that the conversation preceded the shooting. There is no dispute that McRae turned partially away from the boat and that one of the first three shots fired hit McRae while he was turning. The burden of the whole argument of the defense was that when somebody on the boat saw McRae put his hand on his gun he was justified in shooting.

The jury's verdict, rendered five months after the event, was that the Wobblies could not be found guilty. Their decision was based on the probability that Beard and Curtis were killed by rifle bullets from their fellow deputies. After November 5, almost everybody in Everett knew that Jefferson Beard's wife never forgave McRae, and that she kept as her own evidence the jacket her husband had worn that day. This jacket had a bullet hole in the back but none in the front. The prosecutor, of course, knew this, but his view was that a pistol bullet had hit Beard's chest, missing his open coat, then had passed downward and out his back. He had built this contention upon the report of an autopsy performed by three physicians, all of whom were members of the Commercial Club and two of whom were at the dock with guns in their hands when Beard was shot.

The facts, then, do not rise easily from the inductive method. Unhappily, the deductive approach is only slightly more rewarding. What does seem clear is that the deputies, in view of their sloppy deployment, did not plan a massacre, though it is obvious that they may have precipitated one. This may also be true of the *Verona* passengers, more than a few of whom, surely, were armed. But would these men have conceivably fired first? Their purpose that day was not to shed blood; it was, rather, to goad McRae toward the grotesque extreme of his determined course and make him prove to all the world that the lumber barons of Everett, and the capitalism they represented, were thoroughly depraved. As a revolutionary act, the free-speech fight could gain no advantage from murder. Maybe the Wobblies shot nobody at all.

To make the assumption that each Wobbly acted soberly and rationally or avoided any act that might denigrate the group would, however, be artlessly uncritical. The Wobblies were, in their own words, "all leaders," and as leaders they were more creative than they were disciplined. In their excitement or terror of confrontation, it is unlikely that each individual romantic found the inner strength to control an explosive impulse—or an existential opportunity—for martyrdom or blind revenge. From the scattered fragments of misty recollections there emerges this image: a young harvest worker from Illinois or Montana responds to Wobbly fellowship but not to the sacrament of passive resistance. He comes to Everett with his friends, just for the hell of it, and survives a terrible beating and humiliation at Beverly Park. He swears a deep and private revenge—more passionate than any thought of his own or the union's future—and lays plans to take this vengeance on November 5. With studied care, he finds a position at the bow of the ship. Though he is no accomplished marksman, at the crucial moment he draws a pistol from under a heavy coat, then aims deliberately to shoot the balls off McRae.

And it may have been, finally, that no one really wanted to shoot anyone, and that whatever happened, it seemed at the moment to the men on the boat and to the men on the dock that the first fire came from the enemy. The possibilities of such moments are crystallized in an account of a remarkably similar incident—one even potentially more tragic than the event in Everett—that occurred when the *Verona* docked in Seattle, where a company of National Guard with loaded rifles had already assembled to assist the police in maintaining order. As the men left the ship, they were received by their sad and angry comrades who might easily have raised their wrath to violence against the police and troops. A sergeant's report of this incident is clearly relevant to any judgment about police actions or massacres:

There was a large crowd in front and on each side who seemed to be unfriendly, as they hooted, shouted, and jeered. There were many people on the bridge leading from the Coleman Dock who shouted encouragement. After we proceeded about 30 paces, a shot was fired. This did not stop our men in any way . . . at the time the shot was fired I was not able to tell whether some enlisted man's gun had accidentally fired, or whether the shot had come from the crowd. I decided it was the former and was very much relieved.

Who fired the first shot in Everett is probably something we can never know with certainty. But surely it is not the most significant question about November 5. The answer, then or now, would reveal no ultimate social truth or wickedness. The better questions to ask about Everett are why such antagonisms were possible and what social turmoils propelled events toward and beyond that tragic day.[4]

XI

Kings for a Day

THROUGH long hours of darkness, Mayor Dennis Merrill struggled with his fear that night would cool no passions and day could break in another flash of gunshot and murder. There were soldiers standing ready in the armories, but Merrill's distress was so deep that he took his own rifle and stood off from the sullen pickets who marched again at Clough-Hartley and Jamison. He warned the men that snipers on the bluff might shoot them, but he, the mayor—no longer making fine distinctions between city and county lines—would defend with his own life their right to demonstrate peacefully.

At the same time, Ernest P. Marsh was calling together a group of state and federal officials to meet with him and other community leaders who feared revolution. This committee, Marsh wrote later, prevailed for a day upon him and J. G. Brown, arguing that "as a first step toward industrial

sanity, the Shingle Weavers' strike must be ended." Marsh
and Brown replied that they could not betray the men who
had "braved danger, gone hungry, deprived their little ones
of the necessities of life for long and weary months," and
they requested that the committee work with equal zeal to
persuade the millowners to "make some concession in the interests of the city's welfare."

The committee did send three local clergymen—Elmer
Flint from Congregational, Joseph Marlatt from First Methodist, and Edgar M. Rogers from Trinity Episcopal—to approach David Clough and a small group of his fellow industrialists. Though these ministers carried their own solemn
prayer for peace as well as urgent pleas from the mayor,
from state officials, and from federal authorities, the employers would concede nothing. Clough himself ended the interview with an abrupt observation that nothing had changed
since the week before and that "the price of logs is common
knowledge." Marsh and the committee marveled to learn that
men like David Clough and Roland Hartley could "lay claim
to every civic virtue, boast loudly of their patriotism, wrap
the flag of their country about them" and declare that they
were fighting for the principles of freedom and independence.

Though Marsh and Brown refused to ask the men to end
the strike, they did invite the committee to a general meeting
of shingle weavers the next day. From Wednesday afternoon
until midnight, the ministers and government representatives
pleaded for peace, and they finally won a promise from the
strikers to call off the pickets for an indefinite period while
the committee left "no stone unturned" in its continuing
efforts to win some significant concession from Clough. During the weeks following, pickets did not march, but no union
weaver entered a nonunion mill, and no committee turned
David Clough and his associates from their determined course.

If anything changed, it was that both sides drew the lines
of conflict more sharply than they had done before November 5, and that both forces found more unity. The Com-

mercial Club continued its patrols across the city. While the
ministers talked, Roland Hartley and a group of friends "arrested" a man who had openly threatened "to get" him and
David Clough. Though he was an eager deputy, Hartley
could not possibly have arrested everyone who had a similar
plan in mind. The Trades Council, fearing that too many
people were trying "to get" too many others, asked the
governor to disarm the citizen deputies. They received no
response at all from the state capital, where officials were
studying a confidential report from John McChesney, who
apparently believed—and so warned the governor—that
IWW members all over the state were planning to invade
the city and free the Wobbly prisoners who were locked up
in Everett.[1]

The seventy-four prisoners, all identified by Pinkertons as
"leaders" aboard the *Verona*, remained in the Snohomish
County jail through November. The number was important,
one prisoner named Jack Leonard later recalled, only because
it was the number that McRae's jail could hold. Leonard also
remembered a lively crowd: "Not many days afterwards we
were charged . . . by the prosecutor of Snohomish County
with first degree murder. Now as I mentioned before, we
were of all temperaments, and as the information was read
. . . one fainted. Some were sarcastic enough to tell the
prosecutor that they thought the charge might be something
serious, some jeered, some were indignant, but before the
prosecutor could leave we were all singing the 'Red Flag' or
'Solidarity Forever.' " As soon as they had been moved from
Seattle to Everett, they began to complain that McRae was
giving them no heat, no bedding, no decent food, no night-
time toilet. With almost effortless efficiency, they formed a
protest committee, which led a terrifying series of hunger
strikes and jail riots. Day by day they sprang the new steel
doors, jammed the locks, dismantled the plumbing, and
threatened to take the building apart brick by brick if they
were not treated properly. All the while, another committee

prepared lectures on the class struggle, and another composed new songs ("Don McRae, You've Had Your Day"), which the people of Everett might at any hour hear shouted across the center of the city.

Fearing perhaps that the public might learn the wrong IWW songs, the editors of the Everett *Daily Herald* selected several verses from the Wobblies' hymn against World War I, called "Christians at War," and printed them with the clear implication that all Wobblies were anti-Christian fiends:

Onward Christian soldiers
Eat and drink your fill
Rob with bloody fingers
Christ O.K.'s the bill.

But the Wobblies probably found more friends than the *Herald*. Their movement to expose capitalist degradation had found its real martyrs on the bloody decks of the *Verona*. What happens—their leaders could now ask in every mill town—what happens in the lumber industry when workers attempt peacefully to protest and to demonstrate their grievances? The rhetorical answer seemed beyond challenge: they get their asses shot off; they get killed. In Seattle, Wobbly leaders had carefully photographed the bodies laid out on cold marble for all the world to see. And what happens to millowners who shoot workers? Nothing; absolutely nothing. No legal action was ever taken against any member of the Commercial Club for events of November 5.

These answers, dramatically overpowering and utilized with considerable skill, brought the IWW to the moment of its greatest public support in the Pacific Northwest. In Everett, one man lost his job for saying on the streets that Clough, Hartley, and Jamison should be in jail, not the Wobblies, but everybody could read the same sentiment in any issue of the Socialist paper. Week by week into the new year, Socialists printed the ghastly morgue photographs of the dead free-speech soldiers. In a parallel column, under the caption "We Never Forget," they listed the names of the men who on

November 5 had been members of the Everett Commercial Club.

Late in November, in a move boldly calculated to inflame feelings on both sides, the IWW again opened an office in Everett. Led by a millowner, deputies quickly raided the office at night, burned all the literature, and planted an American flag in the pile of ashes. "The true commercial club spirit," the Socialist editor wrote, was reflected in such acts and in an anonymous letter to all Wobblies which, he said, had just reached his desk: "I wish they had a machine gun and killed all of you sons of ———— and threw your bodies in the bay. I hope the president sends out a bunch of soldiers to hang every one of you to a tree and fills you with bullets. . . ."

While such raw irritants to public wounds became more and more frequent, the Reverend Elmer Flint prayed each Sunday at the Congregational Church, where he probably faced more citizen deputies than did any other minister. Flint had resigned from the Commercial Club during the early protest movement before the massacre. By this personal action he had dramatized and validated his social gospel, but in doing so he had alienated himself from a significant following. Clutching for the leadership he had enjoyed for a decade as a progressive minister for a business-minded congregation, he spoke of peace and restraint, moderation and compromise. But as a man who in the recent past had stood out among Everett's moralists, he seemed curiously insensitive to the violation of almost sacred community values which, to many people, the massacre represented. Flint hoped, he said, that newspaper stories about violence would be suppressed. He hoped and prayed that the shingle weavers were capable of some magnificently Christian response to honest pleas for peace and safety. The millowners, he knew, had honorable hearts. "I want you to know," he said in a sermon printed without comment in the *Labor Journal*, "what true men, what noble men [there are] on both sides."

Such moderation, in December, 1916, was to most wage earners the flatulence of a fink mind. In the months that followed, both the Congregational and the First Methodist—where the Reverend Marlatt during the depression had expressed his "fullest sympathy for the toiling classes"—lost their liberal character. Their "reform committees," like their progressive rhetoric, faded quickly from memory. Flint and Marlatt left Everett early in 1917. Their colleague at Trinity, Father Rogers, stayed on, but there is no indication that he ever participated in industrial affairs following his unsuccessful approach to the millowners in November, 1916. And in the minutes of the county Ministerial Association of 1916 and after, there is no suggestion that Everett had ever known bloodshed or hatred, or that preachers had ever sympathized with wage slaves, or that tattered radicals had ever hooted at the city's masters.

Early in December, while Flint was speaking of nobility, David Clough announced that the industrialists had suddenly found it possible to raise wages by one cent a thousand shingles for sawyers and a half cent a thousand for packers. To union leaders, this was a cynical and insulting gesture, for they knew that shingle prices had risen fifty cents a thousand since the strike began, and Clough's generosity amounted to average wage increases of seven and a half cents a day. During the union meeting that followed Clough's announcement, the shingle weavers voted again to send out the pickets.

Each day thereafter, bands of over one hundred embittered men came forth to march in front of Clough-Hartley. The picket lines were stronger than they had been at any time since May 1. This resurgence so alarmed members of the Commercial Club that they hired gunmen to reinforce McRae's men who escorted the strikebreakers through the lines each morning. And each morning larger groups of citizen deputies, armed with rifles, appeared on the bluff overlooking the mills.

At the next meeting of the Everett Trades Council, no

one argued that the industrialists were not manipulating events toward another explosion of violence, or that Commercial Club deputies were not aiming their guns at the citizens of the city. In a mood that marked the end of patience and caution, the council informed the governor that it had voted to purchase five hundred rifles.[2]

At that stark moment there was nothing in the style or mood of the city to suggest that only a few years earlier Everett had demonstrated so many progressive achievements. Nor was there any indication that these achievements had been the work of men and women who for a decade had been confident that in the clash of machine upon the wilderness they could shape a truly humane environment. The social-gospel churches, for example, which had been so boldly relevant since the 1890s, had by 1917 lost the pulse of their social vitality. They would not easily recover it. Another vigorous measure of community before 1914 had been the movement toward municipal ownership, whose leaders had won the battle for public water and had crippled Stone and Webster. But after 1916 the leaders themselves were severely crippled by the mood and style of their supporters. By 1920, because nobody seemed to care but John McChesney of the Everett Improvement Company, they had lost their battle for public power. Direct legislation, the tool of a people's democracy with which optimistic reformers had encouraged so many social aspirations, had in practice apparently convinced many people that democracy in this form served them less than it served the selfish interests it was designed to circumvent. Leaders of the Washington State Federation of Labor had gathered thousands of signatures in Everett for their initiative campaigns in 1914, but soliciting among the same people for similar measures in 1916 yielded less than two hundred. In partisan politics, businessmen defeated labor candidates, and the political freedom of women seemed

strangely to have elevated more than a few politicians like
Roland Hartley. Events during the years since 1912 had denied the sense of community that many people had once
believed possible. In 1916 there was instead a feeling of hard
and relentless class-consciousness driving two classes of citizens toward civil war.

In this social polarity, Everett's experience was extraordinary only in the intensity of its drama. It belongs to the
chronicle of years when the tools of industrialization, riding
the newly laid rails, stripped the natural resources of the
western frontier, and when the owners of those tools shaped
an industrial environment that often erupted in violence. In
the 1880s, Jim Hill's railroad had brought machinery for the
deep mines of the mountains. The miners in Butte rioted in
1891, in the Coeur d'Alenes in 1892. In 1899 a thousand men,
joined in a desperate brotherhood, burned the town of Ward-
ner, Idaho, and used forty-five hundred pounds of dynamite
to blow up the mine that was to them the symbol of the
iron law. In Colorado, Nevada, San Diego, and Butte, as in
Spokane, Aberdeen, Seattle, and Everett, within twenty years
after the machines first began to extract the treasures of the
West, furious men were tearing at the throats of other
furious men whom they could identify by business suits or
overalls.

Within twenty years, laboring men lost their early faith
that reasoning could ever produce the possibilities for a decent human life. Some, like the IWW, urged the workers
to sneer at the reasoning and act directly in their own interests. They angrily predicted the downfall of government
itself in an imminent general strike. And in what may have
been a more representative statement than Americans cared
to realize, a timber industrialist told the United States Commission on Industrial Relations, meeting in Seattle in 1914,

that all unions were "an absolute abomination," and that his industry would fight them to the death. "We will fight . . . we have a right to," he exclaimed. "It is coming to civil war, gentlemen, and we will fight." Such men—and their opponents—were quite willing to use the tactics of war. With a steel-like obduracy, wage earners and industrialists raised their fists and rushed toward doom as if locked into an almost Newtonian determinism—as if social movements must remain in motion until acted upon by some outside force.

The men on the picket lines in Everett early in 1917 seemed to share a sense of hopelessness over the prospects of any outside force intervening; they seemed to be sullenly resigned to the currents of hatred that would inevitably convulse the city in still another massacre.[3]

It may be that the World War prevented civil war in Everett. In April, 1917, men found for a moment a deep sense of relief from the critical anxieties that had so long held them in confusion and pain. Ernest Marsh wrote for the state federation, saying that while he did not welcome the country's going into the war, he did believe that American participation would advance the cause of democracy. When the city planned a patriotic parade for April 25, Marsh enthusiastically urged the full cooperation of organized labor.

But it was yet too early for patriotism to burn away all traces of class-consciousness. In defiance to Marsh, the Trades Council in Everett focused instead on May Day, and, with the Socialists, sponsored a red-flag festivity and antiwar demonstration which it hoped would counter the smugness of April 25. Their afternoon was filled with Wobbly oratory and defiant condemnations of the war as an imperialist-manufacturers'-capitalist war in which the workingman had nothing to gain. In response, the millowners lit their own May Day fires by hiring more guards and by sweeping their searchlights across the night—a harsh reminder to friend and foe of the city's affliction and a cold symbol of baronial intransigeance.

But the defiance and the intransigeance soon seemed ludicrous and irrelevant. Even before the end of May, the Shingle Weavers' Union could not find enough sawyers and packers to operate the mills which had broken from Clough's discipline and were paying union scale. Clough-Hartley and Jamison held out, presenting themselves as rocks of integrity against an unprincipled world, but their principles soon left them immobile in the passage of their greatest opportunity. Prices went higher and higher, and in early summer, with an irony delicious to the Trades Council, Clough-Hartley faced a strike by their carefully selected strikebreakers. Only then did David Clough discover that he could pay union wages, and only then did Marsh announce that the long, bitter, and tragic strike was ended.

Again the sky over the city was heavy with the smoke of prosperity. There had never been more glorious days for prices and wages, and the industrialists worked long hours to capture another fortune. Ernest Marsh and his state federation assistants used the fat days to revive the old Timber Workers Union, enlisting thousands of workers in the lumber mills and logging camps. When in the summer of 1917 Marsh and J. G. Brown called the shingle weavers to convention, they knew that full employment and the urgencies of war had brought to the union an unprecedented sense of common purpose, and they intended to use this immediately.

On the convention floor Marsh had no difficulty in winning endorsements for the series of resolutions that were central to his plans. Delegates gave their allegiance to the American Federation of Labor, to its canon of trade agreements, and to its full support for the country's role in the war. They denounced the IWW as a threat to union ideology and as a contemptibly unpatriotic obstacle to the war effort. To demonstrate their own loyalty, delegates resolved to expel any weaver who carried an IWW card.

Speaking to these commitments, Marsh urged the weavers to step confidently toward the historic goals he had so long promised them. If Americans were advancing the cause of humanity on the battlefields of Europe, then the industrial army at home must press on in its battle for social progress. Clough and Hartley, he noted, had demonstrated their patriotism by "raising prices to the skies." The shingle weavers, he demanded, should now raise again the banner of the eight-hour day.

At this moment, Marsh was suddenly the fiery militant. He would not be delayed or distracted. When the industrialists ignored him, he applied a degree of power that millowners had never thought possible: all across the state, the shingle weavers walked out, leaving 95 percent of the shingle mills idle, then the timber workers closed down about 65 percent of the lumber mills. Working all the while for even more unity, Marsh had within three weeks organized about fifteen thousand workers in the nonunion mills and convinced them to leave their machines. As he was doing this, the IWW quickly voted to participate in what appeared to be the grandest of all lumber strikes, and their walkouts stopped most work in the woods. In less than a month, the unions had paralyzed the entire industry. For the only time in his life—and it must have been sweet—Marsh had reduced the millowners to apoplectic spasms of rage.

Yet they were unbending. Marsh offered them eight hours' work at eight hours' pay, but they refused to bargain. He offered to authorize ten-hour shifts on lumber orders from the government, but they would not listen. Marsh then coordinated a series of attacks upon the industrialists that in its virtuosity seemed for a moment to be irresistible. The governor announced to the lumbermen "that peace . . . cannot come to the industrial life of the State of Washington until the principle of the eight-hour day is established," and that with this principle he was in "full accord." United States Senator Miles Poindexter made known his promise to introduce a bill in the Senate that would bring a mandatory eight-hour day to all American lumber mills. The state's other United States Senator, Wesley Jones, was working on a bill to prohibit the interstate shipment of ten-hour lumber. The secretary of war addressed the Lumbermen's Protective League, which millowners had formed to fight the eight-hour day, and pleaded with them to accept the twentieth century and get on with the production of lumber which the country's war effort so urgently needed. Some Puget Sound shipbuilders, booming with war industry, even refused to work ten-hour wood.

After the mills had stood silent for a full month, Marsh spoke out to the public and to the government that the real conflict was between the "archaic paternalism" of the industrialists and wage earners who had been "liberated" by war prosperity. "Lumber barons," he said, "kings for a day, will . . . find themselves swept aside by a rising tide of democracy." Or, he warned, if they resisted the democratic movement toward trade agreements, they would surely face the total war on capitalism which the IWW was so eager to bring upon them.

But Marsh marveled again that the baronial mind had such impregnable defenses against feeling or reason. The Lumbermen's Protective League maintained its adamant position against the union, the government, and the public, holding its members in their sternest test of character. And if Marsh marveled, he might also have wept, for the lumbermen were winning. To the unions, it was not so much a test of character as one of food and clothing against a coming winter, and after three months without pay, thousands of men were talking of liberating themselves from the strike and the union. Local leaders began tacitly to encourage the men to go back to their jobs, and as the word passed quietly, Everett was again a city of smoke and cinders, of full lunch pails and the ten-hour day. When the mills cried for timber, the IWW could not hold its men away from steady work and high wages. By the middle of September the industry was in full production, and, although Marsh had not formally ended the strike, the industrialists could boast of an unqualified victory.

And this time, more than ever before, it seemed that for the union there would be no resurgence, no recovery. Marsh's mournful predictions across a decade about the IWW were to him a dire reality. The men were grumbling that they had been humbled too often by AFL incompetence and baronial brutality, and they began streaming toward the Industrial Workers of the World. A federal commission later reported that 75 percent of the workers in the lumber industry joined the IWW during 1917 and 1918. What most distressed the government was that this number of radicals found a balm for their spiritual wounds in fanning the flames of discontent.

As the older Wobblies shuffled back to the camps and mills in September, they did so without any deep or enduring grief. Defeat, to them, was the climax of most experience, and they took it with a proud if surly grace that prepared them again to enter the whirlpool. In September, 1917, however, they learned with infinite delight that they did not have to return to the job in humiliation. The war markets had created an acute shortage of labor, and this kindled the arrogance and impishness that burned in the depths of the radical soul. With fires brightly burning, their numbers increased so rapidly that the power to conquer was suddenly thrust upon them.

Wobbly theorists revealed that, like the AFL, the IWW had not really called off the strike. They had, instead, retreated to the mills and camps, there to wage a kind of guerrilla warfare called "taking the strike to the job" which ultimately could bring the industry to its knees. Workers found it simple enough to stretch eight hours of work across a ten-hour shift and in so doing to achieve a revisionist version of the eight-hour day. It was also an easy and sometimes exhilarating experience for them to feign stupidity or ignorance, since the bosses expected them to be stupid and ignorant, and to follow orders with a literal-mindedness that not only infuriated foremen and managers but threatened the essential efficiency of every mill. In these techniques of sabotage, moreover, there were exciting conceptual sophistications: men could have the eight-hour day without losing wages, and no one had to march in picket lines, get beaten up, or go to jail. The union no longer required strike funds, nor did it have to wrestle with scabs. Clearly there was more than one way to bring the capitalist system down. The doomsday of general strike might be consistent with high wages and full employment.

With a deviousness that they constantly refined as they spread it among the new recruits in the camps and mills, woodworkers learned such stupidity, incompetence, and ineptitude that they choked the industrialists with a terrible frustration. The millowners' fortunes gleamed like mirages which they could never quite grasp, and they soon despaired of ever meeting any production schedule. William Butler found his investments in such morbid disorder that he could not make his usual escape from Everett during the winter of 1917–18. All around him, the detached and broken parts of the industry staggered like trees in a gale.

That winter, finally, the federal government could no longer tolerate this industrial debauchery and intervened to bring order to a sick environment. Using the Espionage Act, the federal courts convicted dozens of the most articulate IWW leaders and sent them, along with the Socialist leaders, to jail. The government deported the editor of the *Northwest Worker*. In the mills and camps, federal officers organized a uniquely official company union which they named the Loyal

Legion of Loggers and Lumbermen. In order to work thereafter, a wage earner had to swear to give his "best efforts
. . . to the production of logs and lumber for the construction of Army airplanes and ships to be used against our common enemies." Almost all the woodworkers—one hundred
thousand in the Pacific Northwest—abandoned the IWW
and the AFL and joined the Loyal Legion. With it, at least,
they found their way toward better wages, and they found
an opportunity in ritual and allegiance to demonstrate their
patriotism, which seemed very important in 1918. They also
found shelter from the strife and deprivation that for a decade had so disrupted their lives. The government thus assured the millowners of an obedient labor force, but it also
demanded that the mills accept the eight-hour day. While the
war chewed up lumber at a fantastic pace, the industry found
a rough sort of harmony.[4]

After the armistice, the rejuvenated peacetime market demanded fir and cedar, and the Panama Canal finally opened
this market as wide as the world. Into 1920, the mills ran
three eight-hour shifts across days of unequaled prosperity.
There seemed to be no barrier to the upward swing of prices.
David Clough had his third fortune, and this enriched the
faithful members of his extended family. For the larger circle
of "the Butler interests"—for those who gambled in land and
logs—there were even larger rewards. Butler himself probably
increased by three times his holdings in cash, land, mills, logs,
and securities.

Roland Hartley, who had been deeply hurt by the army's
rejection of his offer to lead troops against the Germans,
drew upon Butler's resources in 1917 and with a cousin outbid the Rucker Brothers for the logging rights of the Tulalip
Indian Reservation. What appeared to be a high risk
became a fabulous enterprise as log prices rose again and
again, and by 1920 Hartley had taken a million dollars from
Tulalip alone. There was the story—perhaps apocryphal, but
repeated by Hartley himself—that he then presented himself

before his father-in-law, slapped down the evidence of his
million in front of the old man, and shouted in triumph,
"There, you old son-of-a-bitch, I told you I could do it!"
But a more graphic and trustworthy evidence of this harvest
of new fortune is in the recorded Weyerhaeuser sales: eleven
million dollars in 1918; eighteen million dollars in 1919;
twenty-four million dollars in 1920. As William Butler had
known, the war did make kings.

During the protracted struggle of 1917-18, the Everett
Commercial Club had disbanded. A new Chamber of Commerce elected Albert Brodeck its president and sent him to
appear before the Trades Council, where he declared himself
a friend of labor and a defender of the closed shop. He invited the working class to join with businessmen in guiding
the city toward postwar prosperity. After the war, however,
AFL leaders learned to their sorrow that the Loyal Legion
had captured both the flag and the industry. Millowners were
recognizing the legion locals and encouraging them to stay
organized for peace. The *Labor Journal* noted in 1920 that
the mills in Everett were employing mostly "4 L's and aliens"
and that the traditional unions were dying from starvation.

They were indeed. As membership did not return after the
war, the *Journal* itself took on the appearance of a neighborhood scatter-sheet rather than of a vigorous voice of community. By May, 1920, it could list only ten AFL locals as
members of the new Central Labor Council, though there
were probably other locals around the city in various stages
of life and death, unable to pay their Labor Council dues.
By 1921, there was no significant labor movement in Everett
at all.

But for years thereafter the life or death of any particular
labor union was of little significance. That winter the crash
came with the dramatic suddenness that had always marked
developments in timber: Weyerhaeuser sales dropped 50 percent, and the Weyerhaeuser books showed a negative figure
for income in 1921. Log prices went out with the tide, im-

poverishing many a millowner who had stocked a probable
fortune in logs on the mud flats beside his mill. While leaders
of the Loyal Legion begged employers to cut wages so that
there could be at least some work, the mills closed everywhere. In December, 1921, mass meetings were again held in
Everett, but there were no questions of unions or militancy,
of villains or moderation, of peace or conflict. With quiet
voices men talked of how they might feed hungry children
as the face of winter grew dark and cold.[5]

XII

Epilogue: Sing It to the Wage Slave

FEEDING hungry children was a primary concern in Everett throughout the winter of 1921–22. This fact alone is a sad indication that the city's labor unions had failed to do what their leaders had most wanted to do: they had not led wage earners toward the conventional securities of middle-class American life. To look back over twenty years is to see the failure as even more strikingly complete. In 1901, wages in the Everett mills averaged $3.71 a day. By 1920, the average wage had risen to $5.80 a day, but because the cost of living had roughly doubled during the two decades, the rise was meaningless. Twenty years of compromise and reason, militancy and conflict, suffering and violence had not brought the progressive dream of liberation. It had not relieved wage earners of the class-consciousness which, as they took their ominous step into the industry, the iron law had so harshly imposed upon them.

These are stark facts and rueful conclusions that tend to diminish the significance of moderates like Ernest P. Marsh and to underscore the integrity of the radical critique. Industrial conditions during this period were marked by a sometimes nefariously cutthroat competition, which encouraged plunder. And a system based on competitive plunder was constantly at war with rationality and order. As the Wobblies so vividly explained and sang, it pressed an indomitable brutality upon the workers caught behind the machines. Industrial reality was that wages did remain at barely tolerable levels. Human reality was that even the most eloquent reasoning could not persuade capitalists to share what they had gained at such high risks.

Yet what the Wobblies never learned was the futility of threatening men like David Clough, for simple force applied to individuals such as he could never carry the workers into the promised land. A really effective strike at Clough-Hartley, rather than softening the family with fear for their profits and trembling for their security, would probably have closed the mill forever. The Cloughs and the Hartleys simply would not produce for fewer gains. And had the workers ever transcended the drudgery of a strike and been able to possess the machinery of production and keep for themselves the wealth that they themselves produced, the wage slaves at Clough-Hartley would in twenty years have been richer by maybe three million dollars. If this estimate—a reasoned guess by the next Clough generation—is correct, then for each worker the annual average gain would have been about $375. This would have been a significant improvement but surely not enough to advance him into the ranks of the truly liberated. Moreover, this dividend would have been possible only if the workers had also been able to hire and retain the cunning and industrial intelligence of a David Clough,

and to do this might have cost them as much as a million
dollars. The sad truth, which the timber-worker radicals did
not seek and which Clough would never submit to exami-
nation, was that the timber industry as they knew it, in a
competitive society at that level of industrialization, was not
and could not be a humane system. There were too many
mills, too many logs, too many workers, too many inefficient
machines. Only if there could be revolutionary changes in
these factors could the mills provide workers with the way
of life that both Marsh and the radicals demanded.

At that level of industrialization, in fact, not even the con-
vulsions of war could abate class conflict for more than
a moment. The following flood tides of patriotism may well
have intensified it. On the anniversary of the armistice, 1919,
in the lumber town of Centralia, Washington, the IWW
played out a sordid climax in its celebration of defiance.
There, at the high point of a patriotic parade, uniformed
patriots of the American Legion attacked a small band of
Wobblies who had been watching from a rented hall. To
protect themselves from what they knew was coming, the
Wobblies opened fire with rifles, and in so doing they drew
upon themselves a horrible vengeance: some were beaten and
tortured; one went mad; one was hanged; the survivors were
summarily tried, convicted of murder, and sent to prison for
twenty years. As it had been in Everett, the businessmen of
the Centralia Chamber of Commerce provided the men who
would tear the flesh and serve as executioners. But the
Centralia Riot in 1919 was a particularly grotesque ritual, a
phantasmagoria of fanatics mobbing a group of leaderless,
confused, and perhaps thoughtless young men. It had less to
do with the realities of the timber industry—though they
were an excuse—than with the passions of a nation made sick
by war. The Centralia Chamber of Commerce in 1919 had
no local grievance that demanded blood, for no one then

could regard the IWW as a serious menace to wages or profits. And the Wobblies, on the other hand, were surely not committed to win or die for the union, which was already a ghostly derelict from another age. Only a fool would shoot a Legionnaire on Armistice Day, and only a moral idiot would murder a Wobbly. Centralia saw the final and probably least meaningful struggles of a historic industrial conflict heated to an especially vicious madness by a passing national pathology.[2]

As the madness passed, it seemed that the industrial conflict itself had lost its tension and momentum. The class struggle, however, did not end because of the war. Nor did it end because industrialists learned benevolence or because labor leaders learned moderation. It began to recede when a new technology made individual workmanship more efficient and productive and when the capitalizations for these new machines in money and intelligence forced all but a few mills from the competition. In this regard, the depression of 1921–22 was more than a crisis: it was an end and a beginning.

By 1920 the old steam-operated machinery was obsolete. Even if it did turn an odd dollar now and then, the mills probably burned down before the owners could bank a profit. Mills that could not afford to make major investments in electrical machinery sputtered for a season or two, then died. These included most of the shingle mills, for the time when a semiliterate could compete profitably with the manufacturers of composition shingles was rapidly passing. Among the first to recognize a new era were the leaders of the Pope and Talbot enterprises, and after the armistice they sold out the mills, the townsites, the logs, and the timberlands of the Puget Mill Company which since 1858 had yielded so handsome a return. The Weyerhaeuser Company, with its vast resources for innovation, would thrive on the misfortunes of its competitors.

In 1923, Weyerhaeuser opened its Mill C at Everett, a

marvel of new machines where electricity and compressed air made possible an unprecedented efficiency. At about the same time, the Walton Mill Company established a veneer plant on the waterfront, introducing an all-electric technology which marked a revolution in the use of logs and the production of lumber. And all across the region, the Crown Zellerbach Corporation and the Scott Paper Company were making the manufacture of pulp and paper the most attractive sources of employment for a new generation.

These new plants had managers with engineering degrees from universities, and their employees were more technicians than laborers. They had boards of directors who spoke smoothly of tree farms, "sustained yield," market control, and a "rationalized" industry, and they had no place for the language of David Clough or Roland Hartley.[3]

The class struggle also receded as the public schools accepted an obligation to prepare a new generation to use the new language and the new machines. In a quiet way, the Progressive Era had taught the people of Everett that education was an easier route toward middle-class securities than union militancy or class war. If, indeed, to be radical was to open new avenues of class mobility, then the school system developed as the most radical of the community's institutions. In 1905, the people voted to provide students with free textbooks. By 1912, the barrier of a rigid college-preparatory curriculum had crumbled before a radical attack, and the high school added a series of "commercial," "domestic science," and "manual training" courses structured to open options, raise ambitions, and hold students in school for two or even three years beyond the age when most working-class boys had fashioned a lunch bucket and followed their fathers to the mills.

This radical expansion of opportunity was largely the personal achievement of Alexander C. Roberts, principal of the high school during the most vigorously progressive years.

Roberts doubled the enrollment of the high school between 1910 and 1915. In the fall of 1915, and working with Professor Frederick E. Bolton of the University of Washington, he opened the first of the state's "junior colleges" which would radically challenge the conventional educational barriers to class mobility. The Everett college offered students still another year of education without tuition, and it invited them to attempt college-level work without the ordeal of the tradition-bound—and consequently class-discriminatory—entrance requirements of the established colleges, and without the expense of leaving home. Even in 1915 Roberts could convince the progressive board of education that it should find the money to hire teachers with master's degrees to protect the integrity of his college.[4]

The photographs of Hewitt Avenue taken in 1925 record no subtle traces of a sense of community that had once crystallized and then shattered. They show no shadows of wide-eyed immigrants or ambitious carpenters or sullen wage slaves or imperious capitalists; they betray no scars of industrial war. Rather, the new masonry buildings, composition roofing, and steel railroad cars reveal the absence of an industrial environment that had once been the core of a city. In the new buildings, the moving-picture theaters, the automobiles, the traffic-control lights, and the paved streets, they record a new life style, and a new energy that would find its own issues and its own heroes.

When John T. McChesney died in September, 1922, the mayor of Everett ordered flags lowered to half-mast as he proclaimed a period of mourning. For five minutes, all industries stood silent in tribute to a man to whom, said the mayor, the city was so deeply indebted. But the new generation honored few such debts, and John McChesney was even then nearly forgotten. The Everett Improvement Company, which was his work and his identity, had since the

war lost most of its holdings in utilities, docks, and land—
the instruments of profit and baronial control so favored by
James J. Hill, the Empire Builder. Soon only a few people
would know that the Everett Improvement Company had
ever meant anything at all.

Everett is a city without statues. It has streets named to
honor Hewitt, Colby, and Rockefeller, but it has never taken
a mature view of its more significant origins or made any
effort to identify the more meaningful symbols of its past.
David Clough, for one, has never received any enduring tribute, yet his death in 1924 was surely an event that marked the
passing of an age dominated by extraordinary men. Then
seventy-eight years old, he had been the stern governor of a
state, the shrewd builder of an industry, the firm master of a
city. He had mastered also a style of life, becoming in his
own day a legend, a monster to working-class children, a
marble god of strength and integrity to his own grandchildren
and to the children of his neighbors and friends. A representative of an age which his lifetime so appropriately spanned, he
made the most of it. If there can ever be an appreciation of
heroic capitalism, David Marston Clough might well be its
model, for whenever the circumstances of his life were within
his control, he bent them to his personality and character.

In the year of Clough's death, Roland Hartley was elected
governor of the state of Washington. He went on to win the
office again in 1928, and he did not return to active life in the
timber industry or in Everett. Though he was never widely
admired in his own city, Hartley's political career is itself a
significant indication of a public mood during the years of his
triumph. He fought unions and taxes. He promised to give
the state the same tight-fisted management he had given to his
logging camps and mills. Yet his administrations were not
happy for him or for the people who elected him. Because he

never understood the differences between government and primitive capitalism, he never accepted a society that was learning to protect those least able to survive in an industrial wilderness. He was censured by the legislature for his language and his dictatorial manner. He was attacked and subjected to an unsuccessful but embarrassing recall movement by the leading newspapers because many sincere people thought he was wrecking the educational system of the state. And in his last years, when even the Great Depression could not choke off the endless clichés, he was ridiculed almost everywhere as a helpless and irrelevant voice of the past who held absurdly to the values of David Clough while the world seemed to crumble. But few men represented these values so well.

The shifting foundations of the timber industry had opened fascinating opportunities for William C. Butler. He had maneuvered so skillfully through the wreckage of 1921 and 1929 that each disaster had brought him a more solid increment of money and power. During the 1930s in Everett, as always, it was William C. Butler who made most of the decisions about land and capital that spelled survival or failure. But in the early winter of 1944, he closed the secret books of his long and secret career. Then seventy-eight years old, he was at the hour of his death the president of two banks, the director of two hospitals, the silent controller of unknown fates and fortunes. His wife Eleanor died in the early spring of the same year. Both were honored in the quiet dignity of private services in their quiet and private home high on the bluff over bayside, where they had looked west to the forests and to the sea.

By 1925, Ernest P. Marsh had left the city whose history was the substance of his personal development. For Marsh, almost every street and building in Everett marked a memory of feeling or crisis that had shaped his talents and character. During the war, though, he left Everett to become a labor mediator for the federal government. There is a fine symbolism in his leaving when he did, for when Everett's problems were no longer regional, Ernest Marsh was no longer bound to the region. During the next twenty-five years he built a second career out of his encyclopedic knowledge of the men and forces that generated industrial conflict. Highly esteemed for his ability to analyze these forces and to bring men together in reason, Marsh was a prominent figure in moderating the new militancy of the 1930s and in humanizing the forces of automation in the forties and fifties. When he retired from government service after the Second World War, he built a third career as an adviser to the Crown Zellerbach Corporation. In his handsomely appointed office in San Francisco, there was little to remind him of the grim years in Everett, and Everett did not notice his death in 1958.

There were those less fortunate than Marsh who survived the changes of the first war and of the 1920s without adapting to them. Among these men, the most pitiful was Donald McRae. After 1916 the former labor leader and sheriff took a farm across the river and soon became—according to some who saw him—a haunted man, afraid of the shadows, afraid of the light, oppressed by the thought that he could not escape some terrible retribution for some terrible violence. Unseen snipers shot his animals and sometimes fired into his house at night. One day his wife took a rifle from the wall and put a bullet through her head. Shattered and alone in 1925, McRae went to Olympia with Roland Hartley, where the governor found him a menial position that carried him into retirement. The hero-for-a-day of a cause and an ideal—and justly so—McRae may have been remembered by those who hated him and those who admired him, but today one cannot find so much as a newspaper notice of his death.

After Clough had died and Hartley had moved to the state-house, it fell upon Hartley's older son, Edward, to assume the management of the family mills. In his grandfather's office, where a photograph of the old man hung on the wall behind him, Edward Hartley made an appraisal of his own estate. He learned that his father, during Clough's last years, had taken only a casual interest in the mills and actually had known little about them. The colonel's pleasure had been in the talk and the style of entrepreneurship, not in the hard practice or mastery. Edward Hartley also found that his grandfather, as he extracted every dollar of profit the system would yield, had worked the machines beyond obsolescence and to the brink of ruin. Clough had maintained the mills only from day to day, and only for a maximum day-to-day profit. In 1925, these days were clearly numbered. It was Edward Hartley's dreary obligation in the family continuum to sit with the mills until they became utterly worthless.

Shortly after he had gained these melancholy understandings, he was approached by representatives of the Central Labor Council—the new name for a new generation of labor leaders. These young men had lost the eight-hour day when the government left the industry, and in the crush of events they had lost most of the older unions. They were, in 1925, politely stressing peace and cooperation with business and industry. Edward Hartley, who suffered few of his father's prejudices and even fewer of his ambitions, astounded these men by opening his books to show them production costs and profits and to explain why it was of no importance to him whether his mills were union or nonunion. What was clear in 1925 was that there was no possibility of improving wages, hours, or working conditions at Clough-Hartley.

Edward Hartley was a genial manager and a careful steward of the family interests, but there was nothing he could do after 1929 to stop the disintegration of the mills into rusting heaps of useless machinery, into sagging and decaying build-ings, into dry pools of family sentiment. He then dutifully supervised the junking of the saws, belts, and engines that had once kept the skies dark with smoke and cinders, and he sold the land to the Scott Paper Company, which soon commanded the waterfront with the largest sulphite pulp mill in the world. Closing out the past, Edward Hartley turned away from what was done and finished to find a new and uncertain future.[5]

Notes

I. Prologue: A Banquet Hall Deserted

1. The early years are covered at length but still superficially in William Whitfield's subscription history, *History of Snohomish County, Washington* (2 vols., Chicago: Pioneer Historical Co., 1926). There are also a number of pamphlets published in Everett which are valuable for their factual content: Everett Land Company, *Everett: The New Manufacturing and Commercial City at the End of the Great Northern Railroad on Puget Sound* (1892), and by the same authors, *City of Smokestacks, Everett, Washington* (1893); Everett Commercial Club, *Everett, Washington: A City of Industries* (1897); and George Martin, *Early Everett: The Story of How a City Began* (1952). The best sources, however, are the early newspapers: the Port Gardner *News* (1891–92), the Everett *News* (1892), the Everett *Times* (1891–96), and the Everett *Daily Herald* (1893——).

2. The Hill banquet was reported by the Everett *News*, Feb. 19, 1892, and by the Everett *Times*, Feb. 25, 1892.

3. A biography of Emory C. Ferguson unfolds between the lines of unpublished materials: Ferguson's own "Early History of Snohomish River and Vicinity" (typed MS in the Washington State Library, Olympia); Eldridge Morse, "Notes of the History and Resources of Washington" (MSS in the Bancroft Library, Berkeley). The Washington Writers' Project in the 1930s produced the unpublished "Snohomish County Interviews" (MSS in the Washington State Library, Olympia), which refer frequently to Ferguson. The William Whitfield Papers (MSS in the Washington State Historical Society Library, Tacoma) contain a note about Ferguson's being arrested for selling whisky to the Indians.

Ferg's land deals are clarified in part by an article in the Everett *Times*, Oct. 11, 1893, which shows that the land he sold to Hewitt was actually the estate of Ezra Hatch, a Mexican War veteran who bought a Tulalip girl for blankets and whisky in 1873, then filed a homestead claim for the land that became Everett. The best subscription biography of Ferguson is in *An Illustrated History of Skagit and Snohomish Counties* (Chicago: Interstate Publishing Co., 1906). Background for this fascinating period is given vividly by Richard Berner, "The Port Blakely Mill Company, 1876–89," *Pacific Northwest Quarterly*, 57 (October, 1966), 158–71, and by Edwin T. Coman, Jr., and Helen Gibbs, *Time, Tide, and Timber: A Century of Pope and Talbot* (Stanford, Calif.: Stanford University Press, 1949), and by Edward H. Hartley, "Report of the Grand Historian to the Most Worshipful Grand Lodge of Free and Accepted Masons of Washington" (typed MS, 1956).

II. The Wreck of Misspent Fortunes

1. For HENRY HEWITT: Everett *News* and Everett *Times*, *passim;* William Whitfield, *History of Snohomish County; An Illustrated History;* Ralph W. Hidy et al., *Timber and Men: The Weyerhaeuser Story* (New York: Macmillan, 1963) covers the background for Hewitt's enterprises, and Allan Nevins, *John D. Rockefeller: The Heroic Age of American Enterprise* (2 vols., New York: Scribner's, 1940) reveals some of Hewitt's triumphs and misfortunes.

2. For the Everett Land Company, see note 1 of this chapter.

3. For Gates, see Nevins, *Rockefeller;* Everett *Times;* Everett *News.*

4. The impact of the depression is reflected in the Lenfest Papers and the Thomas Burke Papers (MSS in the University of Washington Library), in the Washington Writers' Project, "Snohomish County Interviews," in Whitfield, *History of Snohomish County,* in Nevins, *Rockefeller,* and in the newspapers.

5. This discussion of values rests largely on my reading of the newspapers, 1891–1900.

III. A Radical Response

1. For FRAME: *An Illustrated History of Skagit and Snohomish Counties;* C. M. Barton, *Legislative Handbook and Manual* (Olympia: State Printing and Publishing Co., 1891); Frame's stories and editorials in the Everett *Democrat* (1895–96); stories about Frame and the Populists in the Everett *Times* (1895–96). For John Rogers' agrarian populism, see Gordon B. Ridgeway, "Populism in Washington," *Pacific Northwest Quarterly,* 39 (December, 1948), 284–311; Russell Blankenship, "The Political Thought of John Rogers," *Pacific Northwest Quarterly,* 37 (January, 1946), 3–13; and David B. Griffiths, "Far-western Populist Thought: A Comparative Study of John R. Rogers and Davis H. Waite," *Pacific Northwest Quarterly,* 60 (October, 1969), 183–92.

2. APA: Donald L. Kinzer, *An Episode in Anti-Catholicism: The American Protective Association* (Seattle: University of Washington Press, 1964), and the Everett *Democrat* (1895–96).

3. 1896: Everett *Democrat;* Everett *Times;* Whitfield, *History of Snohomish County.*

IV. The Sawdust Baronage

1. For MCCHESNEY: There are a few minor items in the Thomas Burke Papers, but most of the facts are in *An Illustrated History of Skagit and Snohomish Counties* and in Whitfield, *History of Snohomish County.* For WEYERHAEUSER: Hidy, *Timber and Men.*

2. CLOUGH, HARTLEY, IRVING, STUCHELL, BAKER: James H. Baker, *Lives of the Governors of Minnesota* (St. Paul: Minnesota

Historical Society, 1908); *An Illustrated History of Skagit and Snohomish Counties;* Whitfield, *History of Snohomish County;* Albert Gunns, "Roland Hill Hartley and the Politics of Washington State" (Master's thesis, University of Washington, 1963); Edwin Parker, "Everett Interviews" (typed MSS in the Everett Public Library); Peter Kraby scrapbooks (news clippings, 1901–15, Everett City Hall); Everett *Tribune* and Everett *Daily Herald, passim;* and my interviews with David Hartley (Everett, 1963), Edward Hartley (Everett, 1967–70), and Herbert Clough (La Jolla, Calif., 1966). For BUTLER: Nicholas Murray Butler Papers (MSS in the Butler Library, Columbia University), and my interview with Charles Westrom (Everett, 1966).

3. LUMBER, SHINGLE, AND LOGGING INDUSTRIES: Hidy, *Timber and Men;* Coman and Gibbs, *Time, Tide, and Timber;* John H. Cox, "Trade Associations in the Lumber Industry of the Pacific Northwest, 1899–1914," *Pacific Northwest Quarterly,* 41 (October, 1950), 285–312; Puget Mill Company Papers (MSS in the University of Washington Library); newspapers, *passim,* and my Hartley interviews. For SHINGLES, see also W. A. Spencer, "The Cooperative Shingle Mills of Western Washington" (Master's thesis, University of Washington, 1922), and Harold B. Watt, "Stabilization of the Shingle Market" (Master's thesis, University of Washington, 1924).

V. A Search for Community

1. From William Appleman Williams's New Foreword to his *The Contours of American History* (Chicago: Quadrangle paperback edition, 1966), I have found this definition particularly useful: "Our true goal should be an American community. Now community is a process as well as an achievement, and the process is more important. Community as process is the ever-deepening understanding of our nature and potential as human beings, and the sustained creation of ways of living together that are appropriate to that nature and potential." "Community as process" can be seen most clearly in the newspapers, 1900–1910. Essential data are also in the *Everett City Directory* (Seattle: R. L. Polk Co., 1900——), the Everett Commercial Club's pamphlet, *The City of Smokestacks* (1910), and in the *Thirteenth Census of the United States Taken in the Year 1910; Supplement for Washington* (Washington, D. C.: Government Printing Office, 1913). See also Francis W.

Anderson, "The Urban Geography of Everett, Washington" (Master's thesis, University of Washington, 1951), and Mary Carrass, "Everett, Washington: A Demographic and Ecological Analysis" (Master's thesis, University of Washington, 1954).

2. Max Miller, *The Beginning of a Mortal* (New York: E. P. Dutton, 1933), *No Matter What Happens* (New York: E. P. Dutton, 1949), and *Shinny on Your Own Side* (Garden City, N.Y.: Doubleday, 1958).

3. SCHOOLS: newspapers, *passim;* Clarence Horensky, "A Historical Study of Elementary and Secondary Public School Education in Everett, Washington" (Master's thesis, University of Washington, 1958); Alexander C. Roberts, "A Study of Scholarship Records in the Everett High School" (Master's thesis, University of Washington, 1917).

4. HANS SOLIE: interview with Hans and Olga Solie (Everett, 1967), and Olga B. Solie, *Deep Roots* (n.p., n.d.).

5. CHURCHES: newspapers, *passim;* Snohomish County Ministerial Association, records; Trinity Episcopal Church, Everett, records; First Congregational Church, Everett, records; First Methodist Church, Everett, records. *Journal of the Puget Sound Conference of the Methodist Episcopal Church* (Bellingham, Wash.: Union Printing and Binding Co., 1914–18). "Chronik der Gemeinde" (MS "Kirchenbuch der Deutschen Evangelischen Zions Gemeinde zu Everett, Washington, 1900–1915"). Marion Clark, "History of the First Congregational Church of Everett (typed MS, n.d.). Arvid Johnson (ed.), *Minneskrift över Svenska Evangeliska Missionsförsamlingen, Everett, Washington* (Tacoma, Wash.: Puget Sound Posten, 1928). Louis Tucker, *Clerical Errors* (New York: Harper and Bros., 1943).

6. UNIONS: *Labor Journal* (1909–10), and the serial documents titled "Report of the Bureau of Labor" and "Report of the Health Commissioner," *Washington State Public Documents* (Olympia: State Printer, 1889———).

VI. Radicals of the New Order

1. BILLY SUNDAY: newspapers, summer, 1910.

2. SALOONS: newspapers and Kraby scrapbooks. There are six of these books—newspaper clippings, dated, but without other identity—kept by Captain Kraby and dated 1900–1915. They are presently in the office of the Commissioner for Finance, Everett

City Hall. See also Norman Clark, *The Dry Years: Prohibition and Social Change in Washington* (Seattle: University of Washington Press, 1965); Clarence Darrow, *The Story of My Life* (New York: Scribner's, 1932); and the George Cotterill Papers (MSS in the University of Washington Library).

3. LABOR PROBLEMS: the *Labor Journal*. FINANCIAL PROBLEMS: W. D. Hulbert, "Experiences of a Dry Town," *Outlook*, 98 (July 15, 1911), 594–95, and Vanderveer Curtis, "Case of Voluntary Subscriptions Toward Municipal Expenses," *Quarterly Journal of Economics*, 26 (November, 1911), 164–69. CHURCH PROBLEMS: see the list of records in note 5 of Chapter V. The loss of community is clear also in my interviews with Hans and Olga Solie. Hartley's career during this period is in the newspapers and in Gunns, "Roland Hill Hartley."

4. The richest sources for the Socialists are the newspapers, especially their own *The Commonwealth* (1911–14), published in Everett for the county and state. The Kraby scrapbooks help here, and my interview with Hans Solie was rewarding. For the beginnings in the state there is Charles LeWarne, "Equality Colony: The Plan to Socialize Washington," *Pacific Northwest Quarterly*, 59 (July, 1968), 137–46, and Paul B. Bushue, "Dr. Herman F. Titus and Socialism in Washington State, 1900–1909" (Master's thesis, University of Washington, 1967). The following books are also useful: Chester McArthur Destler, *American Radicalism, 1865–1901* (New London: Connecticut College, 1946); Philip Foner, *The Industrial Workers of the World, 1905–1917* (New York: International Publishers, 1965); Ray Ginger, *Eugene V. Debs* (New Brunswick, N.J.: Rutgers University Press, 1949); Harvey O'Connor, *Revolution in Seattle* (New York: Monthly Review Press, 1964); Howard H. Quint, *The Forging of American Socialism* (Columbia: University of South Carolina Press, 1953); David Shannon, *The Socialist Party in America* (New York: Macmillan, 1955); James Weinstein, *The Decline of Socialism in America, 1912–1925* (New York: Monthly Review Press, 1967).

5. PROGRESSIVES: Everett *Herald*, Everett *Tribune*, *Labor Journal*, *The Commonwealth*; Kraby scrapbooks; and the newspaper *Shingle Weaver* published in Seattle, 1912. See also Samuel P. Hayes, *The Response to Industrialism, 1885–1914* (Chicago: University of Chicago Press, 1957), and Robert Wiebe, *The Search for Order, 1877–1920* (New York: Hill and Wang, 1967).

VII. The Raised Fist

1. BUSINESS CONDITIONS, 1913–15: newspapers, *passim; Proceedings of the Annual Sessions of the Washington State Federation of Labor* (Olympia: 1911———); "Report of the Bureau of Labor," (1912–15); Watt, "Stabilization of the Shingle Market," Coman and Gibbs, *Time, Tide, and Timber;* Hidy, *Timber and Men;* Foner, *IWW*, Ray Ginger, *Age of Excess; The United States from 1877 to 1914* (New York: Macmillan, 1965); Robert Wiebe, *The Search for Order.*

2. OPEN CITY: Kraby scrapbooks, Everett *Herald,* Everett *Tribune.* Faussett's career is seen in the newspapers and in his reports to the governor in the Lister Papers (MSS in the Washington State Archives, Olympia). The phrase "white slave panic" is in Henry May, *The End of American Innocence* (New York: Alfred A. Knopf, 1959). CRIME, RECALL, IWW, BRODECK: Kraby scrapbooks.

3. SOCIALISTS: the Everett *Daily Herald,* Everett *Tribune, Labor Journal,* and the Socialist papers—*The Commonwealth, Washington Socialist,* and *Northwest Worker.* Also *Shingle Weaver* of Seattle, 1912, and *The Timber Worker,* Seattle, 1914–15. Also Ernest P. Marsh's presidential reports in *Proceedings of the Annual Conventions of the Washington State Federation of Labor* for these years. MAYNARD SHIPLEY's career is the subject of Mariam A. DeFord's biography, *Up-Hill All the Way* (Yellow Springs, Ohio: Antioch Press, 1956).

4. TIMBER WORKERS AND THE 1915 STRIKE: all newspapers in note 3 above; Bureau of Labor reports; State Federation of Labor proceedings. Most vital are Ernest P. Marsh's "Report on the Timber Industry" in the *Labor Journal,* March 6, 1914, and his report of 1916, with supplement, in the *Proceedings of the Sixteenth Annual Convention of the Washington State Federation of Labor.* Ernest Marsh is clearly the key figure, not only of this chapter, but of this entire study. His writings in the union papers are the most perceptive and most complete primary sources of information about this period. There are, unhappily, no Marsh papers that I have been able to locate. Despite a long and significant career, Marsh died in obscurity, and I have been unable to find anyone who knows the circumstances of his death.

For several insights into Marsh's work I am indebted to Mr. Otto Hartwig of Portland, his friend who was president of the Oregon State Federation of Labor during these years. Clough's remarks in 1915 are in the Everett *Daily Herald* of April 28, 1915.

VIII. Phlebas, the Phoenician

1. BUTLER: His correspondence (note 2, Chapter IV) with his brother contains the only archival evidence of Butler's work and mind. But this material is very lean, and there is enough of it for only the most hazy portrait. This chapter is based in part on that correspondence and in part on my interviews with the late Charles Westrom of Everett, who was Butler's private secretary after 1920 and closer perhaps than any other man to Butler's methods and goals. Westrom was a most gracious and valuable source of information about the principals of this book. The Butler will is in the Everett Trust and Savings Bank, Everett. I have, in addition, my interviews with Herbert Clough, Edward Hartley, and David Hartley, and Parker, "Everett Interviews." In the 1950s Edwin Parker interviewed dozens of people who remembered the events of 1915–17, including some of the principals. He was then writing "They Cleaned Up The Woods" (typed MS in the University of Washington Library) and his novel, *Timber* (New York: Exposition Press, 1963). These interviews are an invaluable primary source. My chapter title is from Part IV of T. S. Eliot's *The Waste Land* (1922).

IX. The Iron Law

1. DEFEAT OF SALTER: daily papers, the *Washington Socialist*, and the *Northwest Worker*.

2. REORGANIZATION OF THE COMMERCIAL CLUB: newspapers, *passim*. NEW SHINGLE WEAVERS' UNION: *Labor Journal*, and *Working Card and Constitution of the International Shingleweavers' Union of America* (Seattle, Wash., 1916).

3. 1916 STRIKE: These events have been covered most recently by Foner, *IWW*, by Robert Tyler, *Rebels of Woods: The I. W. W. in the Pacific Northwest* (Eugene: University of Oregon Books, 1967), and in Melvyn Dubofsky's *We Shall Be*

All: A History of the I. W. W. (Chicago: Quadrangle Books, 1969). The last of these is a superb study, and all of these works contain excellent notes. The earliest version is Walker Smith, *The Everett Massacre: A History of the Class Struggle in the Lumber Industry* (Chicago: I. W. W. Publishing Bureau, 1918). Smith's work, while solidly prejudiced, is also solidly based on primary sources and cannot be dismissed as an IWW tract. An interesting piece of early scholarship—largely a careful summary of Everett and Seattle newspaper stories—is Robert Hull, "I.W.W. Activity in Everett, Washington, From May, 1916, to June, 1917" (Master's thesis, Washington State University, 1938). Hull's uncle was a citizen deputy, and Hull was one of the last to interview Roland Hartley. I have, of course, used all these works, but rather than tell the same story again, I have tried to integrate existing scholarship with the primary sources which have as yet been unused: Marsh's writings in the *Labor Journal* and in the *Proceedings of the Annual Conventions of the Washington State Federation of Labor* and Edwin Parker's "Everett Interviews." JAMISON VIOLENCE: "Account of R. H. Mills" in *Labor Journal*, August 25, 1916.

X. The Iron Hand

1. This chapter reflects again the sources noted above for Chapter IX. The first quotation is from Marsh, "Everett's Industrial Warfare," a special supplement to "Report of President Ernest P. Marsh" published in the *Proceedings of the Sixteenth Annual Convention of the Washington State Federation of Labor*. THE *Wanderer* EPISODE: Smith, *Everett Massacre*, and Hull, "I.W.W. Activity in Everett." SEPTEMBER 22 AND THE STREET ORDINANCE: Hull, "I.W.W. Activity in Everett," and *Labor Journal*.

2. MCRAE: *Labor Journal*; Smith, *Everett Massacre*; Parker, "Everett Interviews." There are also a number of miscellaneous newspaper clippings in the Everett file of the Labadie Collection of Labor and Radical Materials in the University of Michigan Library. The "Wobbly as intruder" is an important theme of Robert Tyler's *Rebels of the Woods*.

3. BEVERLY PARK: This event has been described in great detail in Smith, *Everett Massacre*, Tyler, *Rebels of the Woods*, and Foner, *IWW*. My account relies heavily on Parker's "Everett Interviews," of which the Irving and Michel pages are the most

revealing. See also *Labor Journal,* and Marsh, "Everett's Industrial Warfare."

4. EVERETT MASSACRE: Heretofore unused primary sources are the papers and Correspondence of Governor Ernest Lister (MSS in the Washington State Archives, Olympia), which contain the National Guard reports, the naval militia reports, and Lister's correspondence from Everett; Parker, "Everett Interviews," especially the Irving and Rigby pages; my interviews with David Hartley, Edward Hartley, and Herbert Clough. See also the accounts in the Everett *Daily Herald,* the Everett *Tribune,* the Everett *Labor Journal,* the Seattle daily papers, the Everett *Northwest Worker* (Socialist), the Seattle *Industrial Worker* (IWW), and the Everett *Cooperative News* (Socialist), and miscellaneous clippings of the Everett file in the Labadie Collection. See also Gunns, "Roland Hill Hartley," Foner, *IWW,* Tyler, *Rebels of the Woods,* and Dubofsky, *We Shall Be All.* Donald M. Barnes, "The Ideology of the Industrial Workers of the World, 1905–1921" (Ph.D. thesis, Washington State University, 1962), has insights into the Free Speech Fight. BEARD'S DEATH: Smith, *Everett Massacre; Northwest Worker;* Charles Asleigh in the *Labor Journal,* Jan. 12, 1917, and my interview with Beard's granddaughter, Mrs. Nancy Smith of Everett. There are excellent reports of the murder trial testimony in the Everett *Herald* and the Everett *Tribune,* January–April, 1917.

XI. Kings for a Day

1. MAYOR MERRILL, THE PEACE COMMITTEE, AND THE UNION RESPONSE: Marsh and Brown signed a long letter to "Officers and Members of Local Unions," dated Nov. 9, 1916, that explained why the pickets had been called in. A copy of this letter, along with other correspondence to the governor from Everett, is in the Lister Papers. Marsh also wrote to Merrill, explaining why the pickets marched again (*Labor Journal,* Dec. 8, 1916). He covered these events also in "Everett's Industrial Warfare."

2. THE WOBBLY IN JAIL: Jack Leonard, "Jails Didn't Make Them Weaken," which first appeared in the *Industrial Worker* and is reprinted in Joyce Kornbluh (ed.), *Rebel Voices: An I. W. W. Anthology* (Ann Arbor: University of Michigan Press, 1964). "WE NEVER FORGET": *Northwest Worker.* FLINT: Parker, "Everett Interviews," and *Labor Journal,* Dec. 1, 1916.

MARLATT AND ROGERS: church records. Renewal of the strike: *Labor Journal*, Dec. 1, 8, and 15, 1916.

3. AMERICAN INDUSTRIAL VIOLENCE: Graham Adams, Jr., *Age of Industrial Violence, 1910–1915* (New York: Columbia University Press, 1966); Foner, *IWW;* Tyler, *Rebels of the Woods;* Robert Smith, *The Coeur d'Alene Mining War of 1892: A Case Study of an Industrial Dispute* (Corvallis: Oregon State University Press, 1961).

4. THE WAR YEARS: *Labor Journal*, Everett *Herald*, Everett *Tribune;* Tyler, *Rebels of the Woods;* Dubofsky, *We Shall Be All;* Harold M. Hyman, *Soldiers and Spruce: Origins of the Loyal Legion of Loggers and Lumbermen* (Los Angeles: UCLA Press, 1963); William Preston, Jr., *Aliens and Dissenters: Federal Suppression of Radicals, 1903–1933* (Cambridge: Harvard University Press, 1963).

5. POST-WAR: newspapers; Hidy, *Timber and Men;* Coman and Gibbs, *Time, Tide, and Timber;* "Report of the Bureau of Labor," *Washington State Public Documents* (1918–22); Cloice R. Howd, *Industrial Relations in the West Coast Lumber Industry* (United States Department of Labor, Bureau of Labor Statistics, Bulletin No. 349; Washington, D.C.: Government Printing Office, 1924).

XII. Epilog: Sing It to the Wage Slave

1. WAGES AND COST OF LIVING: *Labor Journal*, May 3, 1918, and "Report of the Bureau of Labor" (1902——). CLOUGH'S PROFITS: there is no solid literary evidence. Interviews with Herbert Clough, Edward Hartley.

2. The best account of the CENTRALIA RIOT is John M. McClelland, Jr., "Terror on Tower Avenue," *Pacific Northwest Quarterly*, 57 (April, 1966), 65–72.

3. END OF STEAM CAPITALISM: Hidy, *Timber and Men;* Coman and Gibbs, *Time, Tide, and Timber*. See also Peter Drucker, "A Warning to the Rich White World," *Harper's Magazine*, 237 (December, 1968), 67–75: "We did not, during the late nineteenth and early twentieth centuries, overcome class war by philanthropy. What overcame class war was, first, new technology, particularly electric power. This new technology created new, more productive, and therefore better-paid jobs. Secondly, the class war was overcome by education."

4. EDUCATION: Roberts' own Master's thesis, "A Study of Schol-

arship Records in the Everett High School" (University of Washington, 1917), was a subtle attack upon the traditional curriculum. Roberts' relationship with Bolton is in John Rulifson, "Frederick Elmer Bolton: American Educator in the Pacific Northwest" (Ph.D. thesis, University of Washington, 1967).

5. Interview with Edward Hartley.

ACKNOWLEDGMENTS

Some people with whom I have discussed parts of this study have expressed fears that present-day "interests" in Everett would deny me the sources of information which could make this study possible. With a few exceptions that I do not now regard as significant, this has not been the case. On the contrary, I have found the "interests" in banks, churches, public offices, and libraries to be in every way cooperative and as eager as I am to assemble facts without distortion.

It has been my good fortune to find Mr. Edward Hartley and Mr. Herbert Clough more genial, patient, and generous than I could have imagined. Mrs. Mildred Simpson led me to the Kraby scrapbooks, which she has so fortunately preserved, and to the archives of the city of Everett. My work was then accelerated by a grant from the American Philosophical Society, which allowed me to visit the Labadie Collection of

Labor Materials at the University of Michigan, and by a stipend from the National Endowment for the Humanities, which gave me a full summer for research in the Pacific Northwest.

I have enjoyed the cordial assistance of a host of my friends and colleagues. John Broussard has, from the very beginning of my inquiry, helped me clarify many ideas and facts that are important to this book. Truth Henderson, Ward Henderson, Floyd Sage, and Tod Burnam have given me the benefit of their sympathetic and careful reading. In uncovering primary sources, Robert M. Humphrey and Marilyn Buckridge have offered me valuable suggestions. Edward Gilliland's craftsmanship has made possible the illustrations. Marilyn Carleton's skill has converted my pages into legible typescript. Edwin Parker, author of the novel Timber, *has generously given me the manuscripts of his Everett interviews and a copy of his own unpublished historical study. For all of this I am very grateful.*

Del Caryl and John Dwyer have made the Everett Community College Library perform the services of a much larger institution. I have been extended unusual courtesies by the staffs of other libraries: the Everett Public Library, the Washington State Library, the University of Michigan Library, the New York City Public Library, the Suzzallo Library at the University of Washington, the Butler Library at Columbia University, and the Bancroft Library at Berkeley. In my search for primary sources I have been further indebted to Richard Berner of the Suzzallo Library, Sidney McAlpin of the Washington State Archives, and Lamont Ingram, editor of the Everett Labor Journal.

I feel an especially deep appreciation for Robert E. Burke of the University of Washington, who has constantly favored me with the vitality of his critical perceptions and the warmth of his friendship.

I want to thank Karen Clark and Kenneth Clark for the good will with which they have helped me in innumerable ways.

My incalculable debts, finally, are to Kathy Clark, who in good times and bad times has encouraged me and assisted me —graciously, selflessly, confidently—in every part of this work.

                                        N. C.

Everett, Washington
April, 1970

Index